Essay Index

D0773205

THE FACTS OF FICTION

THE FACTS OF FICTION

by

NORMAN COLLINS

Essay Index Reprint Series

BOOKS FOR LIBRARIES PRESS
FREEPORT, NEW YORK

First Published 1932

Reprinted 1970 by arrangement with
Norman Collins and his literary agents, A. D. Peters & Co.

STANDARD BOOK NUMBER:
8369-1599-2

LIBRARY OF CONGRESS CATALOG CARD NUMBER:
70-111821

PRINTED IN THE UNITED STATES OF AMERICA

To S.H.C.

CONTENTS

INTRODUCTION

Such a volume as this might seem to call, if not for an apology, at least for an explanation. Studies of English fiction have already appeared from the pens of writers of such catholic and unobtrusive culture as Professor Walter Raleigh (*The English Novel*), of such minute and exact scholarship as Dr. Baker (*The History of the English Novel*, 4 volumes), and of such delicate and delicious discursiveness as Mr. Percy Lubbock (*The Craft of Fiction*) and Mr. E. M. Forster (*Aspects of the Novel*).

Mr. J. B. Priestley with conspicuous clarity has put the whole matter into one of Benn's sixpenny nutshells (*The English Novel*). Mr. Gerald Gould, whose victorious weekly battles with novels have made him the greatest hero of contemporary fiction, has acted as Registrar-General in a Census of novelists writing in the Post-War world (*The English Novel To-day*).

Why then, the reader may ask, give us more? And the answer must be that histories like those of Professor Raleigh and Dr. Baker start too early to interest any but the scholar and end too early to satisfy that voracious, protean creature, the general reader. Mr. Lubbock and Mr. Forster have both been content that their lovely luminous minds should dart about like king-fishers from side to side of their subject, and not cover the whole course like a homing pigeon. Mr. Priestley was bound to reject most of the amusing inessentials that make for the fun of the thing. And Mr. Gould is all finely drawn, finely detailed for ground—of 1924. The only complete study of the subject is by a Frenchman, M. Abel

Chevalley (*Le Roman Anglais de Notre Temps*) and is dis-
qualified by reason of its language before it even com-
petes.

There does therefore seem to be room enough and reason enough for a volume in which those English men of
letters who chose the form of fiction are to be seen in
something like their essential originality if not in their
entirety ; a volume in which, when the critic collapses,
he may temporarily turn biographer, and when biography proves bald he may turn commentator again.

I realise that starting this historical romance of fiction
at Richardson, and not at Defoe, or at Swift, or at Bunyan,
or at Mrs. Aphra Benn, or at Lyly, or at Deloney, may
seem rather like starting the Grand National on the easy
side of Becher's Brook, and romping home unfairly
ahead of the winner. I have deliberately overlooked the
claims of everyone up to Defoe, just as the historian of
horse-racing must overlook the claims of the primitive
three-toed horse.

True, Defoe could do most of the things that a modern
novelist can do, and do them as well. But he does not
happen to have been interested in those things that have
become the main topics of modern fiction. His mind in
fiction remained the busy mind of a brilliant boy. The
mental age of *Robinson Crusoe* is, I suppose, somewhere
between 10 and 15. The intelligence, it is perfectly true,
is fully developed : which is why it remains so strangely
satisfying to the adult mind. But the imagination is fertile
and unforced with the feverish and natural fertility of
youth. And the subject owes some of its perpetual youthfulness quite simply to its author's own youthfulness of mind.

Robinson Crusoe is as much a piece of everyone's boyhood
as a rubber ball ; something that we can take a whack
at so long as there is any strength left in us.

I do not know exactly how I can explain to anyone who does not see it at once how *Robinson Crusoe* remains such famous fiction, yet never quite becomes a novel as we understand the term to-day. But perhaps I can hint at my meaning by suggesting what a colossal blunder—in a modern novelist's eyes—the creation of Man Friday really was. It would have needed the arrival of Woman Wednesday in place of Man Friday to make a modern novel of that nursery romance.

Now is not the moment to take the plunge and inspect the salt-mill of sex that is ceaselessly turning and giving the whole sea of fiction its savour. Some later novelists have turned their backs on sex. But they have been like men deliberately looking away from it and not like a boy looking through it without seeing it.

Moll Flanders, it might be objected, is not unrelated to the subject of sex. It might be argued that it deals with sex not only as a man, but as a bad man—that is one who is too much of a man—sees it. But really there is more of the bad boy than of the bad man about it. Moll Flanders sins so artlessly that it is not sin at all, but a commercial contract of a particular kind that she so conscientiously, good-humouredly and frequently fulfils. Her simplicity of demeanour or more particularly of misdemeanour is very different from the tormented emotions of Richardson's heroines.

For Richardson had seen at least one of the centres of complexity in the female heart—the ideal of chastity. And Defoe saw woman simply as a brave, buxom, jolly body that could be beaten and bought. Much modern fiction, incidentally, is based on the same idea ; though the beating has descended to a gentle social pressure and the buying is no more than marrying.

No one, I think, minds the omission of writers like

Malory, or Nashe or Dekker or Deloney, together with the writers of idyllic romance, and Bunyan, or even Swift, from a volume that pretends to give no more than the scantiest outline of the novel.

Swift, it is perfectly true, wrote a sharper, more pointed prose than any writer who succeeded him. But to call such a work as *Gulliver's Travels*, or more particularly *The Battle of the Books*, a piece of fiction, as is sometimes done, is either to forget the allegory or to return to the nursery in the demands we are to make upon the novel.

As narrative *Gulliver's Travels* may be better than, say, *Sense and Sensibility*. As a curious, ingenious invention it may be preferred. But granted the narrative capacity, the work of writing it stopped at the moment when the thought came to Swift. A-little-man-among-big-men, and a-big-man-among-little-men was the extent of the creation : which is what Johnson said in one of those moments when he is often quite wrongly imagined to have come a critical cropper.

Sense and Sensibility on the other hand—and, indeed, any true novel—continues in energetic succession of creation from sentence to sentence, and from the first chapter to the last. The charm of both *Gulliver's Travels* and *Robinson Crusoe* lay in the idea and not in the application of it. Richardson, on the other hand, is to be met assiduously applying the very principles that are the foundations of modern psychological fiction.

There is one other apology or explanation of this book required. And that is because it is not based upon any new or startling philosophy of fiction that rejects all the favourites and fixes on the freaks. It does not promote Henry Kingsley above his brother Charles, or Mortimer Collins above Wilkie, or Frances Trollope (not that *she*

was a freak) above Anthony, or make any quixotic attempt to fling a great load of praise or blame into the
scales of literary justice that Time has patiently been
levelling.

The object of this volume is merely to show the authors
of the past in as much detail as we know those of the
present : to show the long romantic spectacle of these
men at work as well as of the works of these men.

THE FIRST PSYCHOLOGICAL NOVELIST

Art for art's sake has never been one of the popular national slogans. The English, indeed, have always rejected, with perfect composure and little sense of loss, the metaphysical delights of æsthetics for the more practical pleasures and displeasures of ethics. And to this Samuel Richardson owes the thick nimbus that surrounded his head from his fifty-first year onwards.

He did not pretend that he had invented a new prose form : which he had done, and which could have interested only a few. But he claimed to have discovered a new way of teaching morals : which, of course, he had not done, but which naturally interested everyone. And his novel *Pamela* came into the world with a title page as well devised, as nicely directed, and as long-winded as any in the language :

PAMELA
or
VIRTUE REWARDED.

*In a Series of Familiar Letters
from a Beautiful Young Damsel
to her Parents.*

Now First Published

*In order to cultivate the Principles of Virtue and Religion
in the minds of the Youth of both sexes. A narrative which
has its foundation in Truth and Nature ; and at the same time*

that it agreeably entertains, by a Variety of curious and affecting Incidents, is entirely divested of all those Images which in too many Pieces calculated for amusement only, tend to inflame the minds they should instruct.

The success of the work was unspeakable. No doubt it owed some of its success to the fact that those who plunged about in its somewhat scabrous recesses (it was all founded on fact) felt that they always had the title page to excuse their suspiciously deep interest. Indeed, so far as the cultivation of virtue and religion go, Richardson's novel seems to us very little better than almost any other novel of the time, sewn between the two boards of a devotional work. Pope said of it that it would "do more good than many volumes of sermons," but though he said it in an age of sermons it is not as a judge of them that Pope is remembered.

In the vivid and economical language of our day we should probably express the affecting story of *Pamela* thus :

PRETTY SERVANT GIRL'S AMAZING ALLEGATIONS
AGAINST WEALTHY EMPLOYER.
ASTOUNDING LETTERS HOME PUBLISHED.

These two terse and accurate headlines serve a doubly useful purpose. They tell the entire story of the novel in a dozen words, and they show the extreme modernity—or, in its essentials, agelessness—of the plot. They show also the unsavoury and sensational, as well as the subjective and sentimental nature of the story. For Richardson was interested in the darts and arrows of the world only as they lodged in the breast of mankind. He was the reporter of the human heart ; and more especially of the human heart in perplexity or distress.

The plot of his second novel, *Clarissa*, transcribed into modern headline English would come out to nothing less than :

INNOCENT GIRL RAPED IN HOUSE OF ILL FAME.
VICTIM'S DEATH UNNERVES SEDUCER:
MORE LETTERS.

It would be possible to expatiate endlessly on the change in educated taste since Richardson's day. Pamela, the handsome housemaid, who brings off the *coup* of marrying her dissolute master, seems to us in the twentieth century a model of the adventuress rather than a model of virtue. Richardson saw this too late ; Scott saw it later still. At this date we can hardly forget it.

But, at the time, Richardson's novels were considered by all but a few to be models of decorous entertainment. Despite the lurid luxury of their plots they were devoured by women. This, perhaps, is not so surprising as it may seem. Women always adore stories about womanly women and male men ; the luscious landscape of love where every prospect pleases and only man is vile satisfies feminine curiosity and vanity simultaneously. And Richardson was essentially a feminine author. Adapting Austin Dobson's phrase, we might say that Richardson was the first important woman novelist in the language. His thoughts all moved in skirts. His novels are the apotheosis of vapours and virtue. He wrote as women write ; only a little better. He describes his pleasant girlhood in these words :

As a bashful and forward young boy, I was an early favourite with all the young women of taste and reading in the neighbourhood. Half a dozen of them, when
Bf

they met to work with their needles, used, when they got a book they liked, and thought I should, to borrow me to read to them, their mothers sometimes with them ; and both mothers and daughters used to be pleased with the observations they put me upon making. I was not more than thirteen when three of these young women, unknown to each other, having a high opinion of my taciturnity, revealed to me their love secrets, in order to induce me to give them copies to write after, or correct for answer to their lovers' letters ; nor did any one of them ever know that I was secretary to the others. I have been directed to chide and even to repulse when an offence was either taken or given, at the very time when the heart of the chider or repulser was open before me, overflowing with esteem and affection ; and the fair repulser, dreading to be taken at her word, directing this word, or that expression, to be softened or exchanged.

There is something hauntingly repellent about the notion of this priggish and clammy infant assiduously " correcting " and " chiding " and " repulsing." There is, at least, when the scene is viewed in the light of ordinarily decent human conduct. But to the literary historian the scene is one of life's more nearly golden moments. The first English psychological novelist is actually to be seen gathering his material.

It would be inopportune at this point in the book to consider at length what we mean by a psychological novelist. But it might be well to clear up one or two of the current misconceptions on the subject. In the first place it is merely the word " psychological " and not the thing that it describes, that is young. The word entered the language in force about 1870, and from that moment it has been used incessantly and often incorrectly by writers who have meant anything in fiction that has attempted to catch the will-o'-the-wisp of the human mind, by those who have meant something that satisfied their own theories of thought in relation to life, and by those who have meant nothing at all but " profound " or " penetrating."

Richardson's claim to be considered not only as the father of fiction but as the father of psychological fiction (for of course there is a difference, largely dependent on the proportion of action to attitude and so on) is considerable. In the first place he was minutely interested in sex— which has come to be an almost indisputable claim to psychological celebrity. In the second place, though he describes in vivid and sufficient detail such hair-bleaching events as befel the formidably virtuous Clarissa, he really was not interested in them at all, and was concerned only with educating the reader's mind into the necessary state of horror, remorse, penitence and good resolve. Johnson, with his uncanny gift of saying absolutely the right thing in utterly the right way, once remarked : " If you were to read Richardson for the story, your impatience would be so much fretted that you would hang yourself. But you must read him for the sentiment, and consider the story only as giving occasion to the sentiment."

There is nevertheless something curiously misleading about this remark. With so many hungry minds all gaping for a story, it has certainly had the effect of driving readers away. And that is a pity. For Richardson's novels are not all spells to raise the spirit of sentiment. The only way to prove this is to read them. They will be found to contain innumerable passages of vivid, economical description, unmarred by manner or moral ; exactly the kind of thing, indeed, that the story-reader wants.

Such a chapter as the death of the bawdy-house keeper in *Clarissa* contains writing as energetic and disgusting as the best that was done by those two writers Fielding and Smollett, whose fame has overshadowed his. The unfortunate woman spent some days in dying, thus giving Richardson ample time to say the worst of her :

> Behold her, then, spreading the whole troubled bed with her huge quaggy carcass : her mill-pot arms held up, her broad hands clenched with violence : her big eyes goggling and flaming red as we may suppose those of a salamander ; her matted grisly hair made irreverent by her nakedness (her clouted head-dress being half off) ; her livid lips parched, and working violently ; her broad chin in convulsive motion ; her wide mouth by reason of the contraction of her forehead (which seemed to be half lost in its own frightful furrows) splitting her face, as it were, into two parts : and her huge tongue lolling hideously in it ; heaving, puffing as if for breath ; her bellow-shaped and various coloured breasts ascending by turns to her chin and descending out of sight, with the violence of her gaspings.

He had, however, reserved an ample store of abuse for the others :

> . . . seven (there were eight of her " cursed daughters " in all) seemed to have been but just up, arisen perhaps from their customers in the forehouse, and their noctural orgies, with faces, three or four of them, that had run, the paint lying in streaky seams not half blowzed off, discovering coarse wrinkled skins, the hair of some of them in diverse colours, obliged to the

black-lead comb where black was affected, the artificial jet, however, yielding apace to the natural
brindle, those of the others plastered with oil and
powder ; the oil predominating ; but everyone's hanging about her ears and neck in broken curls or ragged
ends, and each at my entrance taken with one motion,
stroking their matted locks with both hands under their
coifs, curls or pinners, every one of which was awry.
They were all slip-shod, some stockingless, only under-
petticoated all ; their gowns made to cover straddling
hoops, hanging trollopy, and daggling about their
heels ; but hastily wrappt round them as soon as I
came upstairs. And half of them (unpadded, shoulder-
bent, pallid-lipt, limber-jointed wretches) appearing
from a blooming nineteen or twenty perhaps over
night haggard well-worn strumpets of thirty-eight or
forty.

Richardson, indeed, in these transports of Com-
stockian delight goes so far as to describe the creatures as
being as revolting as the aerially incontinent harpies
whose unhygienic habits above the Trojan lines provided
Virgil with one of his few passages that remain in the
mind of every schoolboy.

If Richardson had written in this vein throughout, he
would have been popular as none but a few writers have
been. But instead of allowing his mind to work like the
good camera it was, he was constantly rattling it like a
church poor-box to remind his hearers of another and a
higher life. Thus in the letter describing the melancholy
demise of Mrs. Sinclair, the wanton but still reclaimable
Mr. Belford suddenly exlaims in one of those bathwaste
gurgles of penitence that established Richardson's respect-
ability beyond all reasonable doubt :

Oh, Lovelace, what lives do most of us rakes and libertines lead ! What company we do keep ! . . . What woman, nice in her person, and of purity in her mind and manners, did she know what miry wallowers the generality of men of our class are in themselves, but would detest thoughts of associating with such filthy sensualists, whose favourite taste causes them to mingle with dregs and stews, brothels and common sewers.

And six pages further on we reach this passage, which suggests that either a sudden attack of delicacy, or merely a gradual decline in his stock of ideas on the subject of the unfortunate lady's deficiencies, had affected the author.

To have done with so shocking a subject at once, we shall take notice that Mr. Belford in a future letter writes that the miserable woman to the surprise of the operators themselves [all this fuss was because she had broken a leg] (through hourly increasing torture of body and mind) held out so long as to Thursday, Sept. 21 and then died in such agonies as terrified into a transitory penitence all the wretches about her.

There is a great deal in these six dreadful but uplifting pages. And there is more even than there seems at first. It would be impossible to deny that Richardson appears to have enjoyed writing them. He enjoyed writing about a lot of things that seem pretty cheap goods at the present day. He was half-way to Shakespeare in some of his jokes, as for instance in the " whimsical scheme " in *Pamela* when the disgruntled sister-in-law endeavours to discover whether the newly married pair are still in bed together at nine in the morning.

In the mechanical expression that is now current we should probably say that Richardson was obsessed by sex. We might with more justice say that he was obsessed by virtue. Certainly in his efforts to show what a hardy plant it was he never spared the pains of raking ; or even of muck-raking. Richardson was a moralist with an almost botanical respect for the Fair Lily view of women ; and a most unbotanical aversion from the Virgin Lily. Both *Pamela* and *Clarissa* are races between the Ring and the Rape, and in the better novel it is the rape that wins.

It would, however, be a mischievous view of Richardson to conclude that he enjoyed writing of the deflowering of women, except to show the perfection of the whole flower. If there had been so much as a single smear of real salacity in him it would have been detected at the time. It would be hard to imagine any man in the whole history of English letters harder to dupe on such a matter than Johnson ; and Johnson was perfectly satisfied with Richardson's deepest moral credentials. It was such later critics as Coleridge, who said, " His mind is so very vile a mind, so oozy, so hypocritical, praise-mad, canting, envious, concupiscent——" who had any serious doubts.

But what did not satisfy Johnson was the genuineness of the small change of Richardson's character. Boswell reports the Doctor to have said that :

His perpetual study was to ward off petty inconveniences, and to procure petty pleasures ; that his love of continual superiority was such, that he took care always to be surrounded by women, who listened to him implicitly, and did not venture to contradict his opinions ; and that his desire of distinction was so great that he used to give large vails to Speaker Onslow's servants, that they might treat him with respect.

Certainly so pitiable an action as tipping a porter to get a salute could only be the product of a tiny mind. To get satisfaction from the resulting bow would seem almost incredible. Vanity of this kind is a kind of self-deceit. And this dishonesty of his towards himself may give us a hint as to why his male characters, unlike his female—a most rare and remarkable thing—are such flabby failures. Writing of women, he had only to look about him to find his Pamelas and Clarissas and Miss Byrons in full bloom on every hedgerow. And he had a very good eye for them. But when he came to write of men he would naturally turn his eyes inwards, look into his heart, and find it all moral maxims and the manners of Tunbridge Wells ; a Grandison deprived of most of his grandeur.

Fielding said that the discovery of hypocrisy and the exposure of vanity are the true source of the ridiculous, the raw material of comedy. Probably it is for some such reason that Richardson appears to us such an absurd old buffer. He was more like a character sketch of his sort of man than any man should be. And he was not only like a character but like a caricature. He stands out from history with the pompous and unprepossessing dignity of a humane employer seen against a perpetual background of testimonials from his sober, industrious and grateful staff.

Richardson's trade was that of printer, and it is said that he used to hide half-crowns among his types to encourage the early-bird type of workman. History, in recording this brief but illuminating fact, has omitted to tell us whether the ruse was successful (it may have been, for Richardson certainly was) or whether it merely resulted in a frantic and upsetting treasure-hunt every morning. No matter which ; the picture of the solemn old donkey furtively popping his florins and sixpences into his type-case is sufficient.

One thing is certain : had young Samuel in his own apprentice days been fortunate enough to find so subtle and generous a master, he would have carried off the half-crown every time, just as he carried off his master's daughter and so succeeded to the business.

All through life, his diligence, his youthful assiduity, his perseverance and overwhelming honesty were a constant source of inspiration and reward to him. He once confessed rather gloriously :

I served a diligent seven years to . . . a master who grudged every hour to me that tended not to his profit, even of those times of leisure and diversion which the refractoriness of my fellow servants obliged him to allow them, and were usually allowed by other masters to their apprentices. I stole from the hours of rest and relaxation my reading times for the improvement of my mind, and being engaged in correspondence with a gentleman, greatly my superior in degree, and of ample fortune, who, had he lived, intended high things for me, those were all the opportunities I had in my apprenticeship to carry on. But this little incident I may mention ; I took care that even my candle was of my own purchasing, that I might not, in the most trifling instance, make my master a sufferer (and who used to call me the pillar of the house) and not to disable myself by watching or sitting up, to perform my duty to him in the daytime.

There is no record of what the " high things " were that the superior gentleman had in store for young Samuel. But since, despite his ample fortune, the gentleman died in the middle of a correspondence with a writer of such formidable verbosity, it is perhaps not surprising that Richardson glosses over the incident : he may even have had the superior gentleman's death on his conscience.

Even in those early days Richardson was already at his chosen task of letter-writing. Probably he was a man who could say a great many things in writing that he would not have had the spirit to say in the flesh : a great many feminine-minded men have this peculiarity. He only really became a man when he had a pen between his fingers. And then he became more than an ordinary man ; rich in invention, painful in his sincerity and as untiring as a ledger-clerk.

Indeed Richardson himself is the best answer to the objection that is commonly made to his epistolary novels : that no one could have found time to write the letters. The answer is that Richardson *did*. He wrote them himself without amanuensis or mechanical aid, and still found time to manage one of the great printing houses of his day. If Pamela had been half the girl her creator was she could have tossed off those three-thousand word documents of hers and still have earned her keep helping the grimy Mrs. Jewkes. Pamela herself excused her genius by saying with a charming gesture of depreciation : " I have such a knack of writing that when I am by myself I cannot sit without a pen in my hand."

It was probably the awkwardness and infrequency of the mails that assisted Richardson in the composition of his letters. It is practice in letter writing as in other things that makes imperfect. Richardson lived in an age of extended leisure and sought to fill it. As a letter-writer, with similar encouragements he might easily have become a serious rival in length to Walpole himself. His longest epistolary novel, *Clarissa*, is a million words in length. (The average length of a modern novel is about 80,000.) He certainly wrote as though the post were not going out until the day after to-morrow week and Time himself were the carrier.

Thus he allowed himself one of the strangest, most leisured and most decorous flirtations of which we have record in all the history of literature—first under an assumed name and then under his own—with a Lady Bradshaigh. She, poor rural dame, was a lady of culture weary of her husband's pigs. She saw salvation for her starving and thwarted soul in correspondence with a professional author. It is an eighteenth-century vignette of the country striving for the town. And Lady Bradshaigh began an interchange of letters with Richardson which steadily grew less purely literary and ideological, and more capricious and kittenish, until she provoked this portrait-of-the-artist-by-himself :

I will go through the park [wrote Richardson] once or twice a week to my little retirement, but I will, for a week together, be in it every day three or four hours, at your command, till you tell me you have seen a person who answers to this description, namely, short, rather plump than emaciated, notwithstanding his complaints about five foot five inches ; fair wig ; lightish cloth coat, all black besides ; one hand generally in his bosom, the other a cane in it, which he leans upon under the skirts of his coat usually, that it may imperceptibly serve him as a support when attacked by sudden tremors or startings or dizziness, which too frequently attack him, but thank God, not so often as formerly ; looking directly fore-right, as passers by would imagine, but observing all that stirs on either hand of him without moving his short neck ; hardly ever turning back ; of a light brown complexion ; teeth not yet failing him ; smoothish-faced and ruddy-cheeked ; at sometimes looking to be about sixty-five, at other times much younger ; a regular even pace, stealing away ground, rather than seeming to rid it : a grey eye, too often overclouded by mistiness from the head ; by chance lively ; very likely it will be if he has hopes of seeing a lady whom he loves and honours ; his eye always on the ladies ; if they have very large hoops he looks down and supercilious, and, as if he would be thought wise, but perhaps the sillier for that as he approaches a lady his eye is never raised first upon her face, but upon her feet, and thence he raises it up, pretty quickly for a dull eye ; and one would think (if we thought him at all worth an observation) that from her air and (the last beheld) her face, he sets her down in his mind as so and so, and then passes on to the next object he meets ; only then looking back, if he greatly likes or dislikes, as if he would see the lady appear to be all of a piece, in the one light or in the other.

It has become the custom to regard this letter as the supreme example of Richardson's vanity. I am not sure that it would not be better to regard it as the supreme example of Richardson's surpassing skill in describing the outward man—a great, and nowadays neglected, talent of the novelist. Personal vanity was, doubtless, at the bottom of it. But Richardson's ego explained in terms of Narcissism is an exercise that we may leave to our children.

Richardson as a realist, indeed, was as capable as any of his time. Neither Fielding nor Smollett brought a closer inspection to more solidly imagined characters. Richardson certainly could describe the appearance of his people with a gusto that comes as startlingly as a hearty handshake from an anæmic man. His portrait of Mrs. Jewkes in *Pamela* (she got into *Clarissa* under the alias of Mrs. Sinclair, and even possibly started her bawdy life as the nurse in *Romeo and Juliet*) is a piece of work that in its powerful simplicity is guaranteed to go smack at the human eye :

Now I will give you a picture of this wretch. She is a broad, squat, pursy, fat thing, quite ugly, if anything human can be so called, about forty years old. She has a huge hand, and an arm as thick as my waist, I believe. Her nose is fat and crooked and her brows grow down over her eyes ; a dead spiteful, grey, goggling eye, to be sure, she has. And her face is fat and broad ; and as to colour, looks like as if it had been pickled a month in saltpetre : I daresay she drinks. She has a hoarse, man-like voice, and is as thick as she is long, and yet looks so deadly strong that I am afraid she would dash me at her foot in an instant, if I was to vex her—so that with a heart more ugly than her face, she frightens me sadly ; and I am undone to be sure if God does not protect me ; for she is very, very wicked—indeed she is.

The qualities that are lacking, qualities that Fielding, and to a lesser degree Smollett, and to a greater degree Sterne, possessed—are detachment and even the first flickers of humour. Richardson, however, made up for his paucity of humorous detachment in his richness of purpose. But purpose, especially religious purpose, has a peculiarly destructive effect upon a novelist's talents.

Richardson, for instance, hated his villains and loved his heroines (he had no heroes to speak of) with a greater intensity of emotion than a novelist can safely allow himself. The reader is apt to feel a trifle self-conscious before Richardson's obvious anxiety over Pamela's virtue and Clarissa's entirety. The body of the spotless Pamela is simply a white target waved about in front of Fate. It is there to have mud slung at it. One hit and the game would be over.

By the time he came to write *Clarissa*, Richardson had made the supreme discovery that it is the mind and not the body that is virgin or debauched. Clarissa is one of those natural virgins, so much more sinned against than sinning that to appreciate their fate fully the reader must accept the difficult but essential Doctrine of the Immaculate Seduction.

When Richardson had finished *Clarissa* he felt that precisely two-thirds of the pattern he was trying to impress on life was finished. He wrote a preface to his last work, *Sir Charles Grandison*, that is rather like the prospectus of a solemn and sincere quack who offers to cure the sins of society in three bottles. He said :

> *Pamela* exhibited the beauty and superiority of virtue in an innocent and unpolished mind, with the reward which often, even in this life, a protecting Providence bestows on virtue. A young woman of low degree, relating to her honest parents the severe trials she met with from a master who ought to have been the protector not the assailer, of her honour, shows the character of a libertine in its truly contemptible light.

And he went on to explain that :

> *Clarissa* displayed a more melancholy scene. A young lady of higher future, and born to happier hopes, is seen involved in such variety of deep distresses, as

lead her to an untimely death. . . . The heroine, however, as a truly Christian heroine, proves superior to her trials, and her heart always excellent, refined, and exalted by every one of them, rejoices in the approach of a happy eternity. Her cruel destroyer appears wretched and disappointed, even in the boasted success of his vile machinations. But still (buoyed up by self deceit and vain presumption) he goes on, after a very short fit of imperfect, yet terrifying conviction, hardening himself more and more, till unreclaimed by the most affecting warnings and repeated admonitions he perishes miserably in the bloom of life, and sinks into the grave oppressed by guilt, remorse and horror.

Richardson always regarded the wages of sin as payable on this side. And he took considerable pleasure in acting as deputy cashier. But in his new book he chose to set a good example, and not a bad one, before his readers. The only trouble was that the example he set was too good. It was rather like setting up a photograph of Mount Everest as an inspiration for a suburban hiking club.

Richardson presented to the public in the person of Sir Charles Grandison " the example of a man acting uniformly well through a variety of trying scenes, because all his actions are regulated by one steady principle : a man of religion and virtue, of liveliness and spirit ; accomplished and agreeable ; happy in himself and a blessing to others."

And with conspicuous courage Richardson stood by his original intention of creating such a freak of virtue even when the loyal and lamblike critics turned against him. He admitted that it has been objected that Grandison " approaches too near the faultless character that critics censure as above nature." " Yet it ought to be observed," Richardson continued in defence, " that he performs no one action that is not in the power of any man in his situation to perform : and that he checks and restrains himself in no one instance in which it is not the duty of a prudent and good man to restrain himself." The real trouble with Richardson as a novelist is apparent in that passage : he never could quite throw off a manner rather like that of a Headmaster in Holy Orders talking to a new batch of prefects.

Richardson always used the prefaces to later editions as a sparring ground for fights with the casual critics of earlier editions. And, of course, he always won, because he could have the first and the last word every time. The prefaces, in consequence of these disputations, form a valuable family photograph-album of eighteenth century fiction, showing both sides of the family—the reader as well as the writer.

Thus we come upon the objection of an " anonymous gentleman " who suggests that " as soon as Pamela knows the Gentleman's love is honourable " the style of the whole story " ought to be a little raised " ; and the same anonymous gentleman makes this entirely salutary objection :

> That females are too apt to be struck with Images of Beauty ; and that the Passage where the Gentleman is said to span the Waist of Pamela with his hands is enough to ruin a Nation of Women by Tight-Lacing.

Poor Richardson ! No wonder he never grew out of being a novelist-with-a-moral-purpose. The public simply would not let him. As soon as he allowed his imagination the least rein one reader or another would creep up behind

and mutter " Judgment Day " in his ear. Thus though his
footsteps strayed always in a conspicuously straight and
narrow path there were always some who accused him
of trespassing.

Of course a man can stand a lot of criticism smilingly
when he has been compared with Homer by anyone of
the stature of Diderot. But Richardson found criticism
where he can least have expected it. Even his apparently
unexceptionable *Sir Charles Grandison*—his original title
The Good Man, shows how abysmally innocent it was—
stabbed the soul of Lady Bradshaigh. The plot of the
piece seems to us as innocuous as that of Meredith's
Egoist. Scott describes it in these words :

> The only dilemma to which he (Sir Charles) is ex-
> posed in seven volumes is the doubt which of the two
> beautiful and accomplished women, excellent in dis-
> position and high in rank, sister excellences as it were,
> both being devotedly attached to him, he shall be
> pleased to select for his bride ; and this with so small a
> shade of partiality towards either, that we cannot
> conceive his happiness to be endangered wherever his
> lot may fall, except by a generous compassion for her
> whom he must necessarily relinquish.

But the eighteenth century had its standards even though
they were not always our own. Lady Bradshaigh, immediately upon reading *Sir Charles Grandison*, wrote to
Richardson as follows :

> You have made me bounce off my chair that two
> good girls were in love with your hero, and that he was
> fond of both, I have such despicable notions of a divided
> love that I cannot have an idea how a worthy object
> can entertain such a thought.

C F

I have quoted Lady Bradshaigh's opinion, not so much for the amusing trifle it is as because in such a piece of criticism the chief difficulties and perils of a novel-with-a-purpose may be seen. Art, in such works, walks hand-cuffed and the policeman that is the public has its eye on Life itself. If the novelist ruthlessly carries out his purpose the result is certain not to please any readers of fiction, except those who belong to the same group as the author. And if the novel, for one moment, steps out on its own, using its own imaginative muscles, the moralists at once begin to beat the author over the head with his Preface.

Richardson as a novelist was always a little embarrassed by his exertions as a moralist. That he made *Clarissa* a tragedy of classical bleakness and insisted on its remaining so despite such hysterical appeals as that from Colley Cibber and Letitia Pilkington : " Spare her virgin purity, dear sir, spare it. Consider if this wounds Cibber and me (who neither of us set up for immaculate chastity) what must it be to those who possess that inestimable treasure?" is the most convincing proof that Richardson could prac-tise as a novelist as well as preach as a saint. And Richard-son, to whom such appeals were common, must often have felt rather as the Creator would have felt had he received a petition on the seventh day asking for the removal from the Garden of Eden of the Tree of Good and Evil, with attendant Serpent. Both were appeals which the Creator was bound, in the interests of intelli-gent creation, to ignore.

The true defects of *Sir Charles Grandison* are that it was so slow, so trivial, so proper and so Italian (Italy was far more genteel than France at the time) that had a petition been got up on behalf of Miss Byron or Miss Selby, or even for Sir Charles himself on the eve of his duel with Sir

Hargreave Pollexfen, no one would have put himself to the trouble of signing it.

Sir Charles Grandison was a failure (it can hardly be said to have failed) not so much because it was too Italian—Macaulay ingeniously suggested that shorn of its Italianate appendages it would make an excellent novel—as because its propriety was so uniformly of the order that led Johnson to remark that " Richardson taught the passions to move at the command of virtue."

For some reason, virtue, at least the kind of virtue that leads its possessors to be called good, is tolerable only in a woman. Virtue of that sort is usually the last resort of an idle feminine mind. In a man it can be a positive vice. And that monster of rectitude, Sir Charles Grandison, comes down to us as virtuous merely because the aggregate of his qualities amounts to nothing higher than his not being vicious.

Another reason why *Sir Charles Grandison* is a poorish novel is that Richardson in reaching above his height in society was also stepping out of his depth in experience. That is, however, more a reason why people should have affected to laugh at the book in its own day than now.

A reader has to be a formidable historian to be disturbed by errors in the differences of manners between one social structure and another two centuries distant. And though Lady Mary Wortley Montagu in her *Letters* remarks that Richardson " has no idea of the manners of high life," and adds that his virtuous young ladies " romp like wenches round a maypole," I doubt if many readers would be aware of such solecisms to-day if they had been left to find them out for themselves.

It is a habit, and almost an unavoidable one, in writing of Richardson, to enumerate all his weaknesses, faults and deficiencies, and conclude by saying what a great writer he is. He certainly does appear, when one comes to compare his books with his biography, to have given as an author more than he had as a man to give.

He is all but unread to-day, not because of any obvious defects in his work but because time is harder to come by than it was in his day. And to go to Richardson without time is like going to Homer without Greek. *Clarissa* is a full week's work. To get from it what it has to offer—a really amazing upheaval of the emotions—it has to be read as though it were being gone through for an examination.

Richardson's contribution to thought, Dr. Baker remarks, is "a loftier ideal of personality." He might have added that Richardson was the first novelist to raise women to the full dignity of literary responsibility. For he began a process that it was left for Meredith to complete.

Richardson's novels may seem antiquated to despair in their scenes and diction, but they are forerunners of a popular school of fiction in which someone, and it is usually a woman, is desperately eager to express himself or herself, without ever knowing quite why, what or how ; novels of suppressed individuality we should call them to-day.

There is, indeed, about the ceaseless striving of Richardson's characters the frantic, unearthly persistence of the actors in a dream. For Richardson in his simplicity believed that bad men spent the entire twenty-four hours of every day in being bad, and that good women (like Sir Charles Grandison) passed the entire twenty-four hours in indecently shaming the Devil.

Hazlitt said that Richardson " seemed to spin his materials entirely out of his own brain, as if there had been nothing existing in the world beyond that little room in which he sat writing." And when the outside world did flow into that little room, it was only women, as pure as ice and as anxious about rape as the most nervous, elderly memsahib at an Indian hill-station, that it brought in on its flood.

HENRY FIELDING

History has given us the portrait of Fielding as the archetype of eighteenth century genius ; a handsome decaying face and sprawling figure, with canary vest claret-stained, seen above a palisade of bottles, orange-wenches and dunning tradesmen. It is a picturesque contrast ; young Fielding, the man of the world, indolently loitering between Ranelagh and Vauxhall, and old Richardson, the man of letters industriously hurrying between Hammersmith and Salisbury Court.

It does not, however, require a literary critic to detect that something is wrong with this historic conception. Fielding was forty-eight when he died, Richardson was over fifty before he had started *Pamela*. And playing mad Kit cannot be all beer and skittles if one is to be remembered as a Marlowe at the end of it.

There is, indeed, no more fallacious view of Fielding's most popular achievement, *Tom Jones*, than that it is a work of unrelieved inspiration : that Fielding throughout the whole tumultuous stream of it was cox and not stroke.

Tom Jones, on the contrary, bears almost every mark of evidence that we should expect in a production of painstaking intelligence and conscientious application of intellect. It is the high spirits that disguise the hard thinking. And it is the richness of incident that conceals the author's recurrent poverty of something better. For it has to be admitted that the characters that are introduced on to the turntable of Fielding's wit, like so many gramophone records all waiting for their creator to flick the needle on to them and set them speaking, denote a creator of greater fertility than profundity. Not that we need object, as is often done, to the discursive episodes—and "The Man on the Hill" is not the worst—on the score of their interrupting the story. To attempt to interrupt *Tom Jones* would be like putting a mouse-trap in the way of a Chinese cracker. The telling of the story of a life was Fielding's especial talent ; and more particularly to-day, when the story has died beneath a load of motive, we may be grateful to a writer who gives us half-a-dozen stories in place of one.

There is perhaps in the whole history of English Letters no author more violently debated than Fielding. Richardson is now merely ignored ; which is a simple, if unsatisfactory, end to all controversy. Fielding, however, is neither forgotten nor forgiven.

It is possible to praise him extravagantly in the society of Hazlitt, Coleridge, Leigh Hunt, Gibbon, Jane Austen, Macaulay and Meredith, or to disparage him fiercely beside Johnson, Cobbett, De Quincey, Charlotte Brontë, Carlyle, Tennyson, Browning and Stevenson. On either side the society is so extremely good, that it makes the division more thoroughly bad.

It would be easy to say that it is all a matter of morals, to decide whether a reader can tolerate Fielding's heroes, who change their bed-fellows as other men change their bed-linen. But it is difficult to construct a world in which Carlyle, all frowns and blushes, recedes shocked from what is merely amusing to Jane Austen.

And pursuing this theory we should very soon see that Fielding's reputation hangs not upon the slender thread of a reader's sense of honour, but upon that infinitely more slender thread, the reader's sense of humour.

Thus, though there were perfectly adequate reasons why Fielding's ferocious Whiggism and his habit of draining

the cup of life dry and continually roaring for more
before payment, should have alienated Dr. Johnson in *his*
day, that is no adequate reason why Browning and
Tennyson and Stevenson should have been alienated a
century later. Fielding's humour, indeed, raises the question of every laugh in literature. To say that the fun in
Joseph Andrews is crude would be to consume prematurely
the words we shall be needing later to describe the innocent amusement in the *Pickwick Papers*. If Dickens is
crude, Fielding is barbaric.

It would be possible to have quite a good, working
sense of humour and still fail to be amused by Parson
Trulliber's pigsty. There *are* many funnier things in literature. But there are none told as though the author thought
they were funnier. And it is this huge and heroic convivi-
ality that leaves us until the cold walk home alone to
wonder why we laughed so loud a few short hours
ago.

Fielding's entry into the literature for which he is remembered has about it as much of the *gamin* as the man
of genius. The new laws of dramatic censorship had stop-
pered the chief outlet of his impudence. Lord Chesterfield
had seen what it meant when he wrote: "Wit, my lords,
is a sort of property ; it is the property of those that have
it, and too often the only property."

In those days to have the stage closed to a wit was as
ruinous as it would be for an author to-day to be forbidden
the craft of novel writing. It was a blow in the face for
Fielding. Penniless as he was, there was nothing for him
to do but to turn the other cheek—and the coolest and
most colossal cheek it was.

Richardson's *Pamela*, published in 1740, was everywhere being recommended in the parlour and pulpit, and
snatched from the maid to be devoured by the mistress.

Fielding sickened at the reiterated name of the popular and prosperous author ; or as Scott reasonably suggests, merely saw which way literary profits then lay. For whatever the reason, he perpetrated one of the memorable outrages of letters by publishing *Joseph Andrews*, a parody of *Pamela*, in which Pamela's virtuous young brother is assailed by all the assaults upon his innocence that his sister had suffered ; and finally sails into the haven of honourable marriage, the flag of chastity still flying, though the hull is riddled with the small shot of temptation—just as his sister had sailed in before him.

The fact that *Joseph Andrews* is ten times the book that *Pamela* is—indeed it is probably the best that Fielding ever wrote : which was the author's opinion of it—cannot have made things any the sweeter for Richardson. Had *Joseph Andrews* been grinned over and forgotten in a fortnight, as a previous parody, *Shamela*, also probably by Fielding, had been, Richardson could have been spared our sympathy. But it was not. It was grinned over and remembered.

Nowadays we are apt to be faintly amused at Richardson's loathing of Fielding and to attribute it to Richardson's Puritanic upbringing and commercial environment. In this it is Time that has betrayed us. Translate the affair into the present day and anyone can see at a glance the enormity of the offence. Imagine that a modern writer—and it would need to be a modern writer of Mr. Somerset Maugham's supreme audacity of talent—were to take a good and rightly-popular novel, say *The Forsyte Saga*, and parody it under the title of *The Forsytes Gaga*. No one would expect Mr. Galsworthy to forgive Mr. Maugham. They would merely enjoy the audacity and wait for the injunction ! Thackeray, with complete misunderstanding of values, endeavoured to reconstruct

the Richardson–Fielding affair in a passage which cul-
minates thus :

> Fielding couldn't do otherwise than laugh at the
> puny cockney bookseller, pouring out endless volumes
> of sentimental twaddle, and hold him up to scorn as a
> moll-coddle and a milksop. His genius had been nursed
> on sack posset, and not on dishes of tea. His muse had
> sung the loudest in tavern choruses, and had seen the
> daylight streaming in over thousands of empty bowls,
> and reeled home to chambers on the shoulders of the
> watchman. Richardson's goddess was attended by old
> maids and dowagers, and fed on muffins and bohea !
> " Milksop ! " roars Harry Fielding, clattering at the
> timid shop shutters. " Wretch ! Monster ! Mohock ! "
> shrieks the sentimental author of *Pamela* ; and all the
> ladies of his court cackle out an affrighted chorus.

From *Joseph Andrews* the incautious social historian
might deduce that the life of every gentleman of the
eighteenth century was an exhausting succession of
whores, bawds and orange-wenches ; play-houses, coffee
houses and the Temple ; singing, shouting, holloaing,
wrangling, drinking, toasting, " sp-wing " and " smoak-
ing " ; with Newgate Prison looming large and grinning
invitingly in the background. And this impression is
scarcely dispelled by Fielding's other novels.

Life as he saw it might have been designed for the
Hammersmith stage. No one, I suppose, imagines that
Fielding, in his best fiction, saw life as it really was—even
as Smollett saw it—and when life fell short of a sort of
Nigel Playfair–Lovat Fraser pageant, Fielding in his early
novels ceased to look at it.

His Preface to *Joseph Andrews* is better known than the

novel it introduces. His definition of his book as "a comic epic poem in prose" earns its living in quotation, as do his remarks about Affectations and Hypocrisies being the true source of the ridiculous. But there is one paragraph that is often overlooked by those who wish to defend Fielding from moralists with minds like magistrates, who attack him for his bawdiness.

Perhaps it may be objected to me, that I have against my own rules introduced vices, and of a very black kind, into the work. To which I shall answer : first, that it is very difficult to pursue a series of human actions, and keep clear from them. Secondly, that the vices to be found here are rather the accidental consequences of some frailty or foible, than causes habitually existing in the mind. Thirdly, that they are never set forth as the objects of ridicule, but detestation. Fourthly, that they are never the principal figure at that time on the scene ; and, lastly, they never produce the intended evil.

It was a good answer. But it fell at the fourth ditch. For in his next novel *Tom Jones*, Tom, the yokel Don Juan, *is* the principal character in scenes where evil occurs as often as he intends it.

It is well at this point for the reader to settle whether or no he is roused to disgust or to laughter by Fielding. A test case is to decide whether the notion of an aged hag ogling a fresh boy remains disgusting despite Fielding's hilarious treatment of it.

As when a hungry tigress, who has long traversed the woods in fruitless search, sees within reach of her claws a lamb, she prepares to leap on her prey ; or as a

voracious pike, of immense size, surveys through the
liquid element a roach or gudgeon, which cannot
escape her jaws, opens them wide to swallow the little
fish ; so did Mrs. Slipslop prepare to lay her violent
amorous hands on the poor Joseph, when luckily her
mistress's bell rung, and delivered the intended martyr
from her clutches.

And once through that test there is a stiffer one as to
whether this amuses or nauseates.

Lo ! a pan of hog's blood, which unluckily stood on
the dresser presented itself first to her hands. She
seized it in her fury, and without reflection, discharged
it into the parson's face ; and with so good an aim, that
the much greater part first saluted his countenance, and
trickled thence in so large a current down to his beard,
and over his garments, that a more horrible spectacle
was hardly to be seen, or even imagined.

Such scenes are common in Fielding. But it is doubtful
whether the blood in the latter would react to a modern
police test for blood stains. For the truth is that it is no
more blood than the red stuff that slops about everywhere
in *Treasure Island*. And the bruises, breakages, and injuries
mend themselves at far more than the normal clinical
speed. There is, indeed, throughout all Fielding something of that atmosphere of magic healing that hung over
Valhalla, where the warriors fought all day to amuse the
gods, and were restored every night to amuse themselves.

The innumerable booby-traps into which the adorable
old Parson Adams—a paternal great-grandfather of Mr.
Pickwick—falls must inevitably have prematurely ended

the blundering career of such a man in the inferior and less generous progress of life.

There are so many passages in Fielding which describe the ways in which the author looked at actual life—and he saw more than just the life on the Bath Road— that one is sometimes left wondering whether any novelist before or since has seen it quite full face. Such expressions as the " vast authentic doomsday-book of nature," from which he tells us he learned his material, announce, in a world that was still cluttered with Clelias and Astræas and other polite and pretty riff-raff of formal romance, a new method of literary craftsmanship.

The method was the new and revolutionary one of using a sitter for every portrait, even though this entailed rather obviously posing the sitter. It was poles apart from the old romantic method of turning one's back on life, to limn features of unearthly pallor and more than human loveliness.

But Fielding's was a deceptive method. It led him to believe that he was a realist. The truth is that nothing but Fielding's flow of high spirits has concealed for so long the fact that he was a hopeless romantic. The later breed of romantics has so rarely been high-spirited, that one is to be forgiven for not having immediately recognised Fielding as one of their company. But try to fit his glowing Sophia Western, or ill-treated but victorious Adams, or Fanny waiting at the altar clad in a white dimity nightgown, into the world of reality, and we can see at once that they stand out like a bunch of bright toy-balloons. Fielding's characters, by giving false details of their parents—though the author was honest enough about his debt to *Don Quixote* : which despite the general opinion to the contrary has done more to preserve the romantic tradition in the popular mind than to destroy it—have succeeded in getting through the frontiers of realism on the passports of romance. If Henry Fielding had been a character in fiction we should say that he had been conceived by a mind more anxious about art than about humanity. After his first success he described the downward drooping curve of tragedy. To compare the Fielding of youth who made those vulgar, purple splashes of ostentation that most truly vivacious young men make in trying to squeeze from life more than life is ordinarily prepared to give, with the Fielding of middle age—which is as far as we can follow him—trying to make three hundred pounds per annum do the work of five, and feeling life slipping through his sick fingers, not rendering even its natural dues, is to compare Success with Failure.

The biographer of Fielding is fortunate if he has preceded and not succeeded good Miss Godden. Her patient and laborious researches have stuck up the stock stories that concern Fielding like so many vermin on a wire. The best stories come from his first biographer, Murphy, who did not know what a lynx higher criticism was to be. But many of the apocryphal stories even if they do not bear the stamp of truth at least contain the spirit of it. And we may reassure ourselves that there is no man of genius who left no letters, of whom we know more and have a fairer general impression.

It is no part of our work to give a complete and concise biography of Fielding. It will serve our purpose far better merely to plot a few points on the ascending curve. We catch the first, vivid, unmistakable glimpse of Fielding almost in schoolboyhood, a rakish Etonian abducting an heiress " on a Sunday, when she was on her way to church," and assaulting her guardian so that the aid of the Law had to be invoked ; then we see him living the life in town, the poor but successful, practising dramatist

of twenty-one, declaring that he must be " hackney
writer or hackney coachman " ; a man who could write
eighteen plays in nine years, and those so casually that
when Garrick begged him to revise a scene he refused, and
remarked when the crowd hissed the frantic Garrick, who
had the misfortune to be acting in the piece, " Oh, damn
'em. They have found it out, have they ? "

During all this time, like the unfortunate young man
in *Joseph Andrews*, he

> met with smart fellows who drank with lords they did
> not know, and intrigued with women they never saw.
> Covent Garden was now the farthest stretch of my am-
> bition ; where I shone forth in the balconies of the play-
> houses, visited whores, made love to orange-wenches,
> and damned plays.

Next we see Fielding married to an heiress of most
modest fortune, setting up a showy equipage in extravagant yellow, and running through his wife's fortune in
three years. After that he is to be seen more in the Temple
than in Covent Garden—first obvious pathetic sign of a
man of moods trying to become a man of substance—
leading a lawyer's life, and writing plays that were suppressed by the censor.

Then in 1742 came *Joseph Andrews* and in the words of
his first biographer : " Fielding's genius broke forth at
once in an effulgence superior to all the rays of light it
had before emitted like the sun in his morning glory,"
which is to say that he found himself.

There are few writers who have tasted success more
frequently, yet have ended their lives so near to failure, as
Fielding. At the very moment when his genius was breaking forth Fielding himself was living in the valley of the

shadow of death, or in that worse darkness, the thick
shadow of the sick-room. His wife was wasting away, and
Fielding discovered how much of his vitality she was
carrying with her. He could not write; though his need
was greater than before. The hackney writer who had
been able to toss off two acts of a play in a morning writing on the paper his tobacco had been wrapped in, now
had to apologise to a public that was being kept waiting
for his miscellanies.

And when these did appear it seemed as though the em-
bittered blood of the harassed anxious husband had been
transfused into the. veins of the mischievous, mercurial
writer. Where in *Joseph Andrews* he had hit and left no
bruise, in *Jonathan Wild* he carefully broke the skin, and
not only the thin skin, of his readers every time. This
polite, satirical eulogy of a cut-throat highwayman stung
like a wasp ; or like Swift. And the sting hurt because
there was poison behind it. Then came *The Journey from
This World to the Next*, which fairly reeks of sick-rooms and
which offered yet more release for a whole load of hatreds
that he was carrying ; hatred of misers, cruel men, hypo-
crites, ungrateful men and traitors. And all the while his
wife was growing sicker and more wasted on her thin diet
of Bath Waters, and Fielding more racked by anguish in
the mind, and gout in the body. This, indeed, is one of
the moments in his life when it must have appeared to him
as though the hounds of a malicious Fate were on the
point of closing round him.

In 1744 his wife died. And three years later he married
her maid. Here there is a conspiracy of Fate to distort the
truth. Any normally imaginative reader will reconstruct
the marriage as a sordid affair, simply a righting of the
wrong side of the sheet. But Lady Wortley Montagu's
granddaughter, speaking from family hearsay, where she

would have picked up the worst, had there been any, assures us that the second Mrs. Fielding was " an excellent creature devotedly attached to her mistress and almost broken-hearted by her loss."

It is hard to imagine what Henry Fielding, descendant of the Earls of Denbigh, found to talk about with a housemaid ; probably the first Mrs. Fielding was the topic of their conversation. And with all her deficiencies the second Mrs. Fielding must have been a good wife. She soothed her husband's mind out of satire into sympathy, and gave the world *Tom Jones* and *Amelia* in place of more *Jonathan Wild*.

And since *Tom Jones* is our objective we will press on to it across hot acres of Jacobite politics. In February 1749 it appeared. By May of the same year Walpole had written, " Millar the bookseller has done very generously by him (Fielding). Finding *Tom Jones*, for which he had given him six hundred pounds, sell so greatly he has since given him another hundred."

Just a year later, Fielding was begging the Duke of Bedford to arrange easy terms for him to rent one hundred pounds' worth of property that was needed to qualify for a magistrateship. And Dukes were Dukes then : patronage had not yet been killed by a democratic budget. The Duke arranged for Fielding to have his property. Fielding got on to the Bench and London got her best magistrate. But Fielding seems to have been designed by nature to repel money as well as need it. For by living honestly in a wicked world he straightway contrived to halve the income he had striven so hard for. He dolefully records :

> I will confess that my private affairs, at the beginning of the winter, had but a gloomy aspect ; for I had not plundered the public, or the poor, of those sums which

DF

men, who are always ready to plunder both as much as
they can, have been pleased to suspect me of taking ;
on the contrary by composing, instead of inflaming, the
quarrels of porters and beggars (which, I blush when
I say, hath not been universally practised) and by refusing to take a shilling from a man who most un-
doubtedly would not have had another left, I had reduced an income of about five hundred a year of the
dirtiest money upon earth, to little more than three
hundred, considerable portion of which remained with
my clerk.

At this period there strays upon the scene a cad with
a camera, Walpole, who leaves us with this snapshot of
the magistrate's ménage. He was banqueting, writes
Walpole, with a " blind man and three Irishmen on some
cold mutton and a bone of ham, both in one dish, and the
dirtiest cloth." It is a falsifying photograph : Fielding's
company may have been poor, and his food bad, and his
cloth dirty. But his mind was rich, his intentions good,
and his official life immaculate. Indeed, in the fine vigour
and human comprehension of his magistrature we can
detect the first advertisement of those qualities that made
Fielding a novelist of more than common energy and more
than common compassion.

He made London a place where a man might walk
along the Strand without molestation from footpads ;
and gangs were then almost as destructive to human life
as traffic in the same locality is to-day. Fielding, indeed,
ranks with Peel and Lord Byng as one of the great reformers of the corps of public safety. He found a watch
that was, he says, " chosen out of those poor old
decrepit People who are from their want and bodily
Strength rendered incapable of getting a livelihood."

" These men armed only with a pole which some of them are scarce able to lift " were his troops for a punitive expedition against the massed rogues and vagabonds of London. For Fielding came of hot-headed and military stock. He had Hapsburg blood in his veins, or thought he had. And Mr. Justice Fielding, with spectacular indiscretion, led the army of the watch himself. And won. Such an action is a piece of the whole man.

Six years after the publication of *Tom Jones* came *Amelia*. And here the pot-house roaring of the former had died down to a melancholy domestic plaint. The object of *Amelia* was to " Promote the cause of virtue "—words that won the immediate attention and respect of Johnson for the whole work—" and to expose some of the glaring evils as well public as private which at present infest the country."

In short, it was the production of a moralist rather than of a novelist ; it elevated rather than excited. And the publisher, with that unflattering estimate of human nature that is the safeguard of his kind, knew that the public would not like it, and that the booksellers would not buy. He had paid a thousand pounds for it, and with more than common cunning he withheld his usual trade discount from *Amelia*. The trade was first angry, then interested, then completely deceived. And finally bought the whole impression to show that they knew a bargain.

After the publication of *Amelia* Fielding showed the first alarming signs that he was feeling the pace. His body sagged in dropsy. His mind still lively was now denied life. He grew spiteful like a hornet. He antagonised everyone, including Smollett, who was always ready to come forward when two were wanted to make a quarrel. He drank the Bath Waters and grew worse. He was tapped by surgeons and grew desperate in health. When finally he took a trip to Lisbon his emaciated face and swollen body drew jeers from a quayside crowd.

Once on board the ship he dicovered that the sea can be a most uncomfortable element for a sick man. His temper was always on the point of discharge. He abused a custom's house officer for not removing his hat in the presence of Mrs. Fielding, the risen lady's maid, cursed the captain because he was deaf, and later threatened to prosecute him because he was a thief.

Four months after Fielding arrived in Lisbon he was dead.

Lady Mary Wortley Montagu wrote the best short memorial account of him :

> I am sorry for Henry Fielding's death, not only as I shall read no more of his writings, but because I believe he lost more than others, as no man enjoyed life more than he did ; though few had less occasion to do so, the highest of his preferment being the raking in the lowest sinks of vice and misery. I should think it a nobler and less nauseous employment to be one of the staff officers that conduct the nocturnal weddings. His happy constitution (even when he had, with great pains, half demolished it) made him forget every evil when he was before a venison pasty, or over a flask of champagne ; and I am persuaded he has known more happy moments than any prince upon earth. His natural spirits gave him rapture with his cookmaid, and cheerfulness when he was starving in a garret. There was a great similitude between his character and that of Sir Richard Steele. He had the advantage both in learning and, in my opinion, genius ; they both agreed in wanting money in spite of all their friends, and would have wanted it, if their hereditary lands had been as

extensive as their imagination ; yet each of them was so formed for happiness, it is a pity he was not immortal.

In our present age when we have almost forgotten how life should be enjoyed, the loud laughs and huge gusto of Fielding make him loom out strange and gigantic like a man seen in a mist. Indeed, in spirit, Richardson, the analyst of the emotions, the man with his eye for ever on the sensitive, shrinking, human mind, comes far nearer to the modern novelist than Fielding. It is only in the irresistible ease of his method that Fielding steps so easily across the century and three-quarters that divide him from us.

Thackeray, in the midst of misgivings, once almost exploded with affection for Fielding.

What a genius ! What a vigour ! What a bright-eyed intelligence and observation ! What a wholesome hatred for meanness and knavery ! What a vast sympathy ! What a cheerfulness ! What a manly relish of life ! What a love of human kind ! What a poet is here —watching, meditating, brooding, creating ! . . .

That is all very well. But it has been quoted so often that a reader unacquainted with the novelist himself might not realise that there were faults besides. Fielding could not, for instance, with the single lovely exception of Amelia, draw a woman. Sophia Western is no more than a dutiful daughter with a naughty temper ; and Fanny is merely healthy. Richardson's Pamela and Clarissa are both developed women—it is obvious that he spent more time in thinking about his characters than ever Fielding did—beside them.

Thackeray was right when he said that the wit of

Fielding " is wonderfully wise and detective ; it flashes
upon a rogue and lightens up a rascal like a policeman's
lantern." And he was skilful in keeping women altogether
out of the range of illumination. For Fielding had a jovial
habit of making his women like men ; and blackguardly
men at that. His Jenny Jones and Molly Seagrim and
Mrs. Slipslop, Mrs. Townsend and Mrs. Waters are
eighteenth century characters in the accepted dissolute
male tradition. Fielding's women sin as artlessly as Moll
Flanders ; and in *Tom Jones* they sin almost as tediously.
And that unfortunate sentence in *Tom Jones* : " though
Sophia came head foremost to the ground, she happily
received not the least damage " may possibly explain
their failure.

And not on all the men who cheated and reeled and
swore their way across his pages did Fielding leave the
signature of creation. His Blifil, for example, whose
author loathed him with imperfectly explained hatred,
serves no purpose but to be so morally jet black that the
dark shadows of Tom are forgotten. And Squire All-
worthy, " a human being replete with benevolence,
meditating in which manner he might render himself
most acceptable to his Creator by doing most good to his
creatures," would be more nearly tolerable as a parody
of Grandison than as an original character earning his
own living in fiction.

When Fielding used his wit as a bat to beat his characters over the head he produced the immortal army of
caricatures, Adams, Trulliber, Western, and the rest. A
caricaturist is perhaps the only artist who is honoured in
his own country more than abroad ; and Fielding's talent
for putting Hogarth into words explains Scott's remark
that " of all the works of imagination to which English
has given origin the writings of Henry Fielding are perhaps

most decidedly and exclusively her own." The caricatures are perfect of their kind ; human enough to be horrible, and brutish enough to be our brothers.

Johnson made the remark that there is as much difference between Fielding and Richardson as " between a man who knew how a watch was made and one who could tell the hour by looking at the dial plate." There is ; and there are more people who need to know the time than want to set up as watch-makers. And in his best characters, even if he did not know much about their inner intricacies, Fielding at least wrote as though he did.

Anyone who cannot enjoy Fielding will probably have a thin enough time in the rest of English fiction. Just as anyone who persists in calling *Tom Jones* the greatest novel in the language must have had a thin enough time already.

Gibbon predicted that " *Tom Jones*, that exquisite picture of human manners, will outlive the palace of the Escurial and the Imperial Eagle of the House of Austria." In its day such a pronouncement was brave to the point of blasphemy. To-day the prophecy has been fulfilled, though History (which was probably under some sense of obligation towards Gibbon) has dragged in a world war and a revolution to justify him.

TOBIAS GEORGE SMOLLETT

Smollett was a Scotsman. He was red-headed. He thought Scottish scenery better than English. And he had the natural Scottish talent for detecting and proclaiming the defects in English character. Out of the last he got his living and his reputation ; and what we call English fiction got one of its best story-tellers.

Smollett is one of those characters in whom the eighteenth century seems to have been richer than any other ; men who contained in their brief but intense lives the whole essence of their time. His arrival in London, a surgeon's apprentice, all rawness and r's, with *The Regicide*, a tragedy in verse—an excellent name for it— under his arm ; his search for a patron ; his temporary failure ; and his lasting bitterness, might be the picture of any literary aspirant of the period.

But there was a difference. He came to town a very callow country calf, and within a few weeks there was blood on his horns. For Smollett had one of the worst tempers in the history of English literature. And it was an angry mind that chased his body through anxiety and anguish and antagonism to a grave abroad at the age of fifty-one.

It was this angry mind of his that led him to publish *The Regicide* by private subscription as soon as he had become famous as the author of *Roderick Random*. It was this angry mind that led him to preface the work (which was still a failure) with the words :

I was taken into the protection of one of those little fellows who are sometimes called great men, and, like other orphans, neglected accordingly. Stung with resentment, which I mistook for contempt, I resolved to punish this barbarous indifference, and actually discarded my patron, consoling myself with the barren praise of a few associates who, in the most indefatigable manner, employed their time and influence in collecting from all quarters observations on my piece which, in consequence of those suggestions, put on a new appearance almost every day, until my occasions called me out of the kingdom.

It was the same malice in his soul that made him introduce Lord Lyttelton, the patron who had picked him up and dropped him quite reasonably when he discovered that there was very little to patronise, as Lord Rattle or Gosling Scrag ; and Garrick, who had failed as unforgivably in his appreciation and discernment of Smollett, as Mr. Marmozet.

It was his restless temper that set him up as a physician, and urged him to quarrel with his women patients and compelled him to write a book exposing the Bath Waters while practising as a doctor in the town.

It was a spirit on edge that led him to write " that the first work of his that he had left under the protection of a patron was retrieved by pure accident (I believe) from the most dishonourable apartment in his lordship's house."

And it was a spirit in flames that led him, on no real foundation, to write in the *Critical Review* of Admiral Knowles that " he is an admiral without conduct, an engineer without knowledge, an officer without resolution and a man without veracity " ; all of which cost Smollett exactly one hundred pounds and three months' imprisonment.

But it was unquestionably just this aggregate of mental furies which had made the obscure surgeon's apprentice into a great novelist.

Smollett's schoolmaster, comparing him with boys of "superior decorum and propriety," said of him, "give me before them all my own bubbly-nosed callant with the stane in his pouch." Fortunately there exists an English version by Sir Walter Scott of this remark. It runs : " Our Southern readers must be informed that the words contain a faithful sketch of a negligent, unlucky, but spirited urchin, never without some mischievous prank, and a stone in his pocket ready to execute it."

A mischievous prank that involves the old Scots pastime of Tossing the Brickbat seems a trifle heavy going to the modern mind. But it was really the whole secret of Smollett's literary method. He was the artist of the flying brickbat and the broad wink. And to appreciate his novels it is necessary to throw off two of the heritages of the nineteenth century, a sensitive conscience and a kind nature, and to recover two of the heritages of the eighteenth century—jocularity, and complete inhumanity towards such unpopular persons as the watch, schoolmasters, priests and parsons.

Smollett, we have said, was a distilled bottle of the essence of his time. And the whole of Smollett condenses in one place into a single drop of picturesque prose. That place occurs in *Roderick Random* :

> At length it was proposed by Bragwell that we should sweat the constable, maul the watch, and then reel soberly to bed.

No entire novel of Smollett's ever proceeded quite so perfectly as that single sentence. No novel could. But they all came near to such picaresque perfection.

Smollett's mind as a mind was, on the whole, a poor drabbity affair. It was never high-flying like Fielding's, or high-falutin like Richardson's. It never soared above a servant girl's attic bedroom. Smollett moved in low places, not as Fielding, the gentleman gone rogue, but as though he were a natural part of the furniture of social grossness.

That he was descended from the Lairds of Dunhill gave him sufficient Scottish pride to declare : " The low situations in which I have exhibited Roderick I never experienced in my own person." But that is hardly to the point. The charge brought against him is not that he was disreputable in person but that he was debased in mind. And it is not a pleasing thought that Smollett should have *invented* the vices of young Roderick. Spontaneity is the first absolution of sin.

Life, moreover, was combed by the author for so many of the burrs and snarls where Smollett had stuck to it that anyone may be forgiven for believing that it had been combed clean. If Smollett did not like to be pointed out as the young man who had fought and fornicated all the way between Scotland and London he had no more than himself to thank for the notoriety.

Roderick Random remained in the public mind the Autobiography of a Super-Scamp. Smollett's hero was born of a good family in the North, apprenticed to a surgeon, came South, went on board a man-of-war as surgeon's mate on the expedition to Carthagena. Which is exactly what happened to Smollett. And because some of the events were so conspicuously alike, everyone thought that the two careers of character and author must be identical. For if any author starts writing autobiographically, the public will always show its appreciation of the confidence by continuing to read autobiographically long after the author has ceased to talk about himself.

And so it is that the characters in Smollett's novels have all been so neatly pinned out with the names on little tabs beneath. "Scrap" (brother of Fielding's "Partridge") = John Lewis, Bookbinder of Chelsea; "Sheerwit" = Lord Chesterfield, and so on ; together with many that a child could see had their origin in the whole monstrous brood of Father Adam and not in this one eccentric son of his, or that.

Such a character as Commodore Hawser Trunnion, for example, bursts into English fiction with the blaze of art and not of nature. He is a model, not a faithful copy. He is the model after which a roaring, stampeding, blaspheming procession of choleric sailors, from those of Marryat to those of Jacobs, have been taken.

In quoting the passage which introduces Trunnion (which if you like, you will like all Smollett) I make no apology for length. I could wish indeed that it were twice as long. Or that there was no need for me to quote any of it to be understood.

At that instant, Mr. Pickle's ears were saluted with such a strange noise as even discomposed the muscles of his face, and gave immediate indications of alarm. This composition of notes at first resembled the crying of quails and the croaking of bull-frogs ; but, as it approached nearer, he could distinguish articulate sounds pronounced with great violence, in such a cadence as one would expect to hear from a human creature scolding through the organs of an ass. It was neither speaking nor braying, but a surprising mixture of both, employed in the utterance of terms absolutely unintelligible to our wondering merchant, who had just opened his mouth to express his curiosity, when the landlord, starting up at the well-known sound, cried,

" Odds niggers, there is the commodore with his company, as sure as I live " ; and with his apron began to
wipe the dust off an elbow chair placed at one side of
the fire, and kept sacred for the ease and convenience
of the infirm commander. While he was thus occupied,
a voice still more uncouth than the former bawled
aloud " Ho ! the house, ahoy ! " Upon which the
publican, clapping a hand to each side of his head, with
his thumbs fixed in his ears, rebellowed in the same
tone, which he had learned to imitate, " Hilloah ! "
The voice again exclaimed " Have you got any attor-
neys aboard ? " and when the landlord replied " No,
no," this man of strange expectation came in, supported by his two dependents, and displayed a
figure every way answerable to the oddity of his
character.

He was in stature at least six feet high, though he had
contracted a habit of stooping, by living so long on
board ; his complexion was tawny, and his aspect
rendered hideous by a large scar across his nose, and a
patch that covered the place of one eye. Being seated
in his chair with great formality, the landlord com-
plimented him upon being able to come abroad again ;
and having in a whisper communicated the name of his
fellow guest, whom the Commodore already knew by
report, went to prepare, with all imaginable despatch,
the first allowance of his favourite liquor, in three
separate cans, for each was accommodated with his
own portion apart, while the lieutenant sat down on the
blind side of his commander ; and Tom Pipes, knowing
his distance, with great modesty took his station in the
rear.

Having thus seen Trunnion in his lusty lustful prime

we should know also his tombstone : that is if we have not made it the goal of a pilgrimage already :

Here lies
Foundered in a Fathom and a Half
The shell
Of
Hawser Trunnion, Esq.
Formerly in command of a Squadron
In His Majesty's Service
Who broached to, at Five p.m. Oct. X.
In the year of his age
Threescore and nineteen.

He kept his guns always loaded
And his tackle ready manned
And never showed his poop to the enemy
Except when he took her in tow ;

But

His shot being expended
His match burnt out
And his upper works decayed
He was sunk
By Death's superior weight of metal

Nevertheless

He will be weighed again
At the Great Day,
His rigging refitted,
And his timbers repaired,
And, with one broadside,
Make his adversary
Strike in his turn.

That typical passage of Smollett, dense with amusing invention, is the epitaph of John Bull afloat : a national, not a personal affair. And it is curious that Scott, who was so deeply impressed by the English nationality of Fielding's genius, should not have noticed that it was the Scotsman, Smollett, who built the new English hero for the new English novel. The nautical novel has, it is true, never been more than a side show in the street of fiction. It first came in the childhood of the art, and has remained very largely for the childhood of the reader. Smollett's greatest debtors are not those who write about the sea— Conrad, for instance, owed him nothing, despite the fact that he thought he did—but those who learnt from him to write interestingly in fiction about almost everything else.

Dr. Baker remarks that " Fielding had dealt in character as well as in characters. Smollett's concern was the superficial features of temperament, mannerisms in which men differ, not with the deeper human qualities that unite them." It is an excellent distinction. It is as much as to say that Smollett's characters, even his Roderick Random, Peregrine Pickle, and Humphry Clinker are flat characters to be looked at and laughed at, but not to be walked round and examined.

It is not, however, completely true. For Fielding had his crowded background of flat characters such as Mr. Supple the curate, Mr. Thwackum the divine and Mr. Square the philosopher. But that may have been merely that the eighteenth century was one of three moments— Scott brought in another, and Dickens the last—when minor characters enjoyed all the rights of full citizenship in fiction.

And we should remember that even though Trunnion and Bowling and Strap and Pipes may be no more than flat characters—they certainly only present one face to the world—they are so substantial that we could spend a whole evening in their company without ever suspecting that, like Scandinavian fairies, they are knife edges of which only the broad side of the blade should ever be looked at.

Perhaps the flattest and thinnest of all the flat characters in fiction are those unfortunate women in the novels of the eighteenth century who stray upon the stage like a dancer in a musical comedy whenever the producer feels that the strain of asking the human mind to work consecutively has grown too great.

These women with a past who are always so eloquently and reminiscently aware of it, are the most tantalising butterflies of fiction. And the eighteenth century author plunged about after them like a kitten. The inordinate length of *The Memoirs of a Lady of Quality* makes one ask whether Smollett had the slightest interest in the original story of Peregrine Pickle. Miss Williams again simply steps from the printed page in *Roderick Random*, accosts the author and goes off arm in arm with him for three, long, seamy chapters while the unfortunate reader sits and waits like an anxious wife for his return.

The Lady of Quality, however, had one justification for existence, that silly Miss Williams, the sister of Fielding's Miss Matthews, had not. When *Peregrine Pickle* appeared, the public with its preference for scandal over literature greedily absorbed it more for the sake of the rumoured relation to Lady Vane, Smollett's benefactress, than for the sake of Peregrine Pickle, the Young Man of Bad Quality.

Seven years later when the second edition appeared, and the scandal was about as exciting as *l'affaire Putiphar*, people began to see how good the rest of the book was. And there being no profit in continuing to boast of it,

Smollett industriously began to repent it publicly, and announced that he "had expunged every adventure, phrase and insinuation that could be construed by the most delicate reader,"—i.e. the most delicate reader that Smollett could imagine—"into a trespass into the rules of decorum ".—probably very much to the annoyance of Lady Vane, whose life does not suggest that shame ever came between her and her sleep, and who probably preferred being reviled to being ignored.

Her career, indeed, is remarkable enough to merit some passing memorial. She married Lord William Hamilton when she was seventeen. A benevolent providence excused his lordship's obligations two years later. Then she married the unfortunate Viscount Vane when she was twenty. The rest of her life was as beautiful as it was brief. She was seventy-five when she died.

It is not altogether clear why *The Memoirs of a Lady of Quality* should have been so steadily and ruthlessly condemned. They may be poor fiction, butting in and staying on like an insensitive uninvited guest, but they are reasonably good Smollett.

The objections to Miss Williams go deeper. She was mother—or Moll Flanders was—of a tainted brood of young women with hearts of gold and a powerful narrative style, who are forced usually by their good looks and by the black looks of Fate, into careers which give them unique opportunities both to display their generosity and to acquire material for reminiscence.

In the famous second edition of *Peregrine Pickle* Smollett owns with contrition that in one or two instances he did give way too much to suggestions of personal resentment. But he defies the whole world to prove that he "was ever guilty of an act of malice, ingratitude or dishonour," a remark that leads one to

EF

wonder whether Smollett had the least notion of what the
rest of the world meant by any of those things. Which was
very much what Hazlitt was hinting at when he said
" that there was a *crude* conception of generosity in some
of his (Smollett's) characters " ; a generosity of which
Fielding's were incapable.

During his middle years Smollett was working with
that energetic vivacity of mind that at the time is so
difficult to distinguish from genius. The cry of " over-
production," which is the tribute that the half sterile
always pay to the fully fertile, was raised. Smollett was
accused of having " journeymen authors ready to turn
out tragedy, comedy, farces, history, novels, voyages,
treatises on midwifery and in physics, and all kinds of
polite letters."

Certainly in the twenty-three years between 1748, when
he published *Roderick Random*, and 1771, when he published
Humphry Clinker and died, he wrote enough to establish a
myth of the magnitude, if not the mystery, of the myth of
Bacon.

He followed *Roderick Random* three years later with
Peregrine Pickle. Two years later he published *The Adventures of Ferdinand Count Fathom*, which, if he had not published *The Adventures of an Atom* would have had the distinction of being his most unpleasant work. Another two
years, and he had translated the whole of *Don Quixote.*
The year following he became editor of the *Critical
Review*, worked hard and was imprisoned for his too
active editorship. There he wrote *The Adventures of Sir
Lancelot Greaves.* But hard as he had been working he
found to his disgust that someone had been working
harder. Hume had already published two volumes of his
History of England. Smollett therefore accepted the

challenge that Hume had no thought of issuing, read three hundred volumes in two years (so he said), produced four volumes of his history, cornered the market and published another four volumes seven years later. The year after the last volume was published he produced *A Compendium of Authentic and Entertaining Voyages*, in seven volumes, and after two years of rest another compilation of similar hugeness and uselessness, *The Present State of All Nations*, in eight volumes. During all this time he was a leader writer on the Tory paper, *The Briton*, and on the staff of the *Critical Review*.

But strain as he could, Smollett never managed to run level with life. He was perpetually in debt, troubled by enemies and irreparably damaged by the death of his daughter. By the year 1763 he would have needed two years' start to keep ahead of his affairs.

We might call his youth romantic for want of a better name ; and his middle age tragic for want of a worse one. For his whole existence was fitting into just those moulds that Fielding had fitted some fifteen years or so before. When it seemed at last as though Fate had decided that Smollett should conform to the popular impression of a novelist as a human factory working sweated hours on low pay, Smollett went abroad, a broken man too ill to do more than to write two volumes of *Travels through France and Italy*.

Sterne in his *Sentimental Journey* made the work more famous than it ever would otherwise have been by referring to the author as the learned " Smelfungus " who, " set out with spleen and prejudice, and every object he passed by was discoloured and distorted." Thus when Smollett came back to England he saw Bath through eyes still discoloured and distorted. He went up to Scotland with the spleen and jaundice working at such a pitch that everything even in his native land was productive of " misery and disgust." He temporarily eased the fever of his feelings by a virulent political allegory, *The History and Adventures of an Atom*. Then with that foreknowledge of death that is the privilege of men who have known life well, Smollett set out for perpetual exile in Italy.

A dying man, he could do no more than write his masterpiece, *Humphry Clinker*. Hazlitt declared this work to be " the most pleasant gossipy novel that was ever written," and Thackeray described it as " the most laughable story that has ever been written, since the goodly art of novel writing began." But Thackeray, it should be remembered, was prejudiced against Dickens.

Certainly there is no novel in the language that would seem to have been written more completely free of the shadow of madness and death than *Humphry Clinker*. Yet Smollett when he wrote it was never free from the fear that he was losing his reason, and never in doubt that he was dying.

It is after all only just a novel. It was a travel book in design, and a letter-book in form. This opened mail-bag of letters from different people about the same events is simply an opportunity for Smollett to reveal the only psychological discovery that he ever made : that different people have different minds. It was as remote from a book of travels as Mr. Belloc's *Path to Rome* is remote from a Baedeker. Jaundice and spleen are still its principal constituents, and Smollett saw the defects of this world with the acute eye of a sanitary inspector. His work is truly excellent journalism. Consider, for instance, this admirable piece of sensational writing on the pollution of the nation's food.

The bread I eat in London is a deleterious paste, mixed up with chalk, alum and bone-ashes ; insipid to the taste, and destructive to the constitution. The good people are not ignorant of this adulteration ; but they prefer it to wholesome bread, because it is whiter than the meal of corn, thus they sacrifice their taste and their health, and the lives of their tender infants, to a most absurd gratification of a misjudging eye ; and the miller, or the baker, is obliged to poison them and their families, in order to live by his profession.

Humphry Clinker is full of such passages, which have as little to do with fiction as with travel. The book is pure Smollett, recognisable as he was to his mother who had not seen him for years, by the twinkle in his eye. When it appeared, the author was out of all favour in England. And Smollett, who had made more men amused or angry than any other author of his time died in the sad limbo that lies midway between neglect and unpopularity.

His widow continued to live on near his foreign grave, supporting herself obscurely and with difficulty ; a shadowy, retreating figure the whole of whose private fortune had been spent by her husband ; a woman who in heaven must have found much to talk about with the first Mrs. Fielding.

LAURENCE STERNE AND HIS FRAGMENT OF LIFE

It would be possible to write a far larger and more comprehensive history than this outline of outlines, yet do no more than touch on the strangely vegetating figure of the Yorkshire Parson, Laurence Sterne. He had a mind which was so peculiarly and richly and vexatiously his own that, though he was later in life imported to London because of it, no one of talent was fool enough to try to model his own style on Sterne's.

And so no school of *Tristram Shandy*—just as there was no school of *Alice in Wonderland*—ever grew up. *Tristram Shandy* was a work which, once done perfectly and by one man, needed never to be done again. And though we may deplore its morals with Hazlitt, its " stupid disgustingness " with Coleridge, its " bawdry and pertness " with Goldsmith, and even its very oddity with Dr. Johnson, there are qualities that, sooner or later, persuade us that of its solitary kind it is perfect. And the greatest of these is charity.

For what did grow up as a result of *Tristram Shandy* was the novel of sentiment—a term that soon grew to mean so much that it came to mean nothing at all.

Sterne's family crest was a starling : a singularly applicable bird. Sterne's great-grandfather was an Archbishop : a poorer choice of Fate's. And Sterne in his major writings—his minor works, excellent sermons, served their purpose in York Minster in their own day—lived up to his arms rather than to his ancestor.

Tristram Shandy stands out, a lonely and lavish monument to the idleness of the eighteenth century parson. It was composed, starling-wise, of bits that Sterne had caught from Rabelais and Cervantes and Burton's *Anatomy of Melancholy* and Locke's *Essay concerning Human Understanding*, and Bacon and Montaigne and any number of military treatises that supplied the gabions and bastions and sally-ports of Captain Shandy's conversation.

Indeed, had Sterne not been hailed for a genius he might have been hanged for a thief. His book is a madly unalphabetical and deliberately disarranged catalogue of the respectable learned works in the Library of York Minster, cemented with genius to an equally illogical and jumbled catalogue of the disreputable and amusing works in the library of Skelton Castle ; the original of Crazy Castle, where the *fin du dixhuitième siècle* " *Demoniacks*," originators of the popular Hell Fire Movement, once held their Young Men's Assemblies.

As for anyone's hanging himself who read Richardson for the plot, so anyone should be straightway confined who attempted a second time to read Sterne for that purpose. His mind is so exorbitantly loaded with information and imagination that the slightest push administered by a new idea destroys the equilibrium of narrative. And it is so inquisitive a mind, so everlastingly subject to new attractions, that even stray words sweep him continually away in an instant into a new corner of his mental universe, to revolve for a space a rejoicing, glittering satellite to one of his own thoughts.

If a reason, other than the simple and sublime fact of his being Laurence Sterne, can be found for this vagary, it is that during his early life he had amassed so great a store of something like learning, yet had so little opportunity in

the Yorkshire parishes of Sutton-in-the-Forest and
Stillington of trying it on anyone. It would be as wrong to
imagine that Sterne ever allows himself to be accidentally
diverted in his thoughts as it would be to imagine that a
man who knows the tricks of Hampton Court maze is at
fault for not marching straight ahead as inflexibly as a
Roman. The only difference is that Sterne is like a man
who walks in the shapes of a maze even though the walls
of the maze are not there. And it is necessary only to remember the strange disorder in which Life, with its angles
and malformations, is laid before us to see that Sterne's
method is at least as true to the passage of life as the un-
bending roadway, mapped out with the ruler of Time, that
the ordinary narrative novelist follows.

The popularity of *Tristram Shandy* has been fluctuating
but, on the whole, declining since the first enthusiasm,
when it appeared in 1760. Even in its own day, however,
Walpole referred to its " very tedious performances " and
remarked that, " It makes one smile two or three times at
the beginning, but in recompense makes one yawn for
two hours." True, the book is now more perfectly assured
of immortality than any cautious critic or publisher would
have cared to predict in its own time ; even though
Garrick—who was the Mr. Baldwin of his day for recommending semi-officially whatever reasonably good book
he had last been reading—was tremulously excited by
and about it.

But *Tristram Shandy* has tended more and more to be
read with an anticipation of delight, the quality of giving
almost as much as we are getting, that we bestow on books
that have become acknowledged literary curiosities.

No one, I believe, who is not more than a little interested in writing has ever been more than a little interested
in reading *Tristram Shandy*. Johnson declared that it would

not last. And though it is usual to regard this as one of the Doctor's critical howlers—like his inability to see more than raffishness in Fielding—perhaps Johnson was saying something nearer the truth than is generally realised.

That is not to say that Johnson did not display a slight pettishness of temper in his attitude towards Sterne. He, as the devout churchman, outside Holy Orders, could hardly be expected to have been proud of the sentimental Epicurean within the Church.

And when he made the remark, " Anyone who has a name, or who has the power of pleasing, will be very generally invited in London. *The man, Sterne*, I have been told has had engagements for three weeks," we see the darkening frown of the everlasting Churchwarden over a poor one of the Cloth whose dignity is not so great as his counsel's. When Goldsmith quite stupidly bleated out, " And a very dull fellow," and so provoked Johnson's " Why, no, Sir," we are not quite certain whether Johnson was paying a tribute to Sterne or merely disagreeing, as he invariably and conscientiously did, with Goldsmith.

It is a strange thing that *Tristram Shandy* should ever have been a success ; only a mixture of Yorkshire persistence and author's pride got it printed at all. Dodsley, the cleverest publisher of his time, rejected it, despite the author's charming letter which accompanied the MS., explaining that " the plan, as you will perceive, is a most extensive one—taking in not only the weak points, the sciences, in which the true point of ridicule lies— but everything else, which I find laugh-at-able in any way."

On the whole, we can only sympathise with Dodsley. He was on the point of retiring, and experiment is no part of the business of retirement. He had seen the rise of English prose fiction and he could hardly be expected to be enthusiastic about the rise of an English prose freak.

For Sterne was not only revolutionary but reactionary. Literature, which had been steadily progressing, now looked like suffering a set-back. A table of laws as unyielding as the original Mosaic ones of stone had been drawn up, and Sterne, like Moses, had broken them.

It has been wondered often enough, whether or not *Tristram Shandy* was a parody of the prevailing novel. And the answer would seem to be that it was about as much a parody of *Tom Jones* as *Alice in Wonderland* is a parody of *The Cloister and the Hearth*. It was a joke. But it was not a bitter joke. A parodist is usually a man whose wit has developed beyond his compassion—there must, it is true, be compassion there if the parody is to stick—and Sterne's compassion was always at melting point. There were fragments of parody like the fragments that a caddis collects around it—Dr. Slop, for example, was Dr. Burton, the obstetrician, of York—but parody was not the prime excuse for the book. Turn to the Dedication :

To the Right Honourable
MR. PITT.

SIR,

Never poor Wight of a Dedicator has less hopes from his Dedication, than I have from this of mine ; for it is written in a bye corner of the kingdom, and in a retired thatched house, where I live in a constant endeavour to fence against the infirmities of ill health, and other evils of life, by mirth ; being firmly persuaded that every time a man smiles—but much more so, when he laughs, it adds something to this Fragment of Life.

I humbly beg, sir, that you will honour this book, by taking it—(not under your Protection—it must protect itself, but)—into the country with you ; where, if I am ever told that it has made you smile ; or can conceive that it has beguiled you of one moment's pain—I shall think myself as happy as a minister of state ;— perhaps much happier than anyone (one only excepted) that I have read or heard of.

> *I am, great sir,*
> > *(and what is more to your Honour)*
> > > *I am, good sir,*
> > > > *Your Well-wisher, and*
> > > > > *most humble Fellow-subject,*
> > > > > > THE AUTHOR.

Those are not the words of a literary surgeon, whose words cure only by being cutting. There is none of the orgy of chastisement that we find in Fielding's Prefaces ; none of the thick stick laid across fat shoulders. Sterne, indeed, preferred the method of the sugar-stick to the thick stick, and introduced a sob where Fielding would have provoked a yelp.

Sterne's love-letters have their own sweet devoted charm and reveal a lot of the man. Unfortunately, they are not all written to the same woman ; a defect more distracting to the reader, doubtless, than to the author.

Admittedly the letters that Sterne wrote to his wife, Lydia, before marriage are at least as delightful as those he wrote to Eliza after his marriage. But there is an all too human falling off in the Lydia correspondence. Thus we find him assuring his *fiancée* that they would " be as merry and innocent as our first parents in Paradise," and later warning her as his wife, " not to forget your luggage in changing postchaises." It is a melancholy remark : it drains all the dew out of Paradise. But if Mrs. Sterne really was a luggage-losing kind of woman, she was hopeless ; and we can excuse Sterne his devotion to Eliza.

The love-letters, or at least the loving letters, of Sterne are important because in them Sterne for the first recorded time in the language uses the word " sentimental " ; a word that later came to be used very much as the word " psychological " is used now. By meaning too much, it grew to mean very little. And the only clarity it acquired in the course of years was that it finally meant something appreciably different from its original intention.

In 1749 Lady Bradshaigh wrote to Richardson : " Pray, Sir, give me leave to ask you (I forgot it before) what, in your opinion is the meaning of the word *sentimental*, so much in vogue among the polite, both in town and country. . . . I am frequently astonished to hear such a one is a *sentimental* man ; we were a *sentimental* party ; I have been taking a *sentimental* walk." Had Sterne been asked, however, he might have replied, in less asphyxiating English of course, with a phrase that, as Mr. Priestley has suggested, might be raped from Hollywood, to describe the intention of a sentimental author, namely, " the making of dimples to catch the tears."

Part of this trouble in definition is caused by the fact that in its day " sentiment " merely meant any indulgence of the emotions for their own sake, and to-day it obstinately means any over-indulgence for the reader's sake. And the real contribution of sentiment to the novel is not that it taught writers what kind of novel to write, so much as that it gave them an excuse for writing at all. It was the first justification of art for art's sake ; agreeably disguised as art for heart's sake.

It is remarkable that Sterne, the founder of sentimental fiction, should not have been a true sentimentalist himself. He was above all things an artist ; and artists cannot allow those emotions which affect their art to get out of hand. In the true eighteenth century manner he regarded indulgence of any kind as one of those extravagances which are good in moderation, and he chose to indulge in the tittering laugh and the wet handkerchief.

Thackeray, who was really much more a slave to his emotions than Sterne, was naturally suspicious of him for it. His comment on Sterne was : " He goes to work systematically and of cold blood ; paints his face, puts on his ruff and motley clothes, and lays down his carpet and tumbles on it." Thackeray (who may have been thinking in the back of his mind of Dickens as he wrote it), remarked also that Sterne " used to blubber perpetually in his study, and finding his tears infectious, and that they brought him a great popularity, he exercised the lucrative gift of weeping."

But Thackeray came of a wet-eyed generation, who as children, had shared all the misfortunes of Amy Robsart, and who, when they put away childish things, were to weep as copiously at the bedside of Colonel Newcome. If Thackeray had lived when Sterne was alive, he would have seen what a civilising thing is a tear.

That, however, is no reason why we need pay it more than its due of attention *now*, why we need regard poor Maria and the Lyons donkey in the *Sentimental Journey*, and ignore Widow Wadman and Uncle Toby and Corporal Trim in *Tristram Shandy*.

Uncle Toby, indeed, deserves a statue in every literary institution in the country. For he was the first considerable character in English fiction to live without movement. The Epic of the Open Road was already changing

into the smaller and finer Lyric of the Closed Room.
Psychology had come in at the window and the coach-
men and Tom Joneses has gone out of the door.

The Rape of the Locke in *Tristram Shandy*, where Sterne,
paraphrasing Locke's *Essay Concerning Human Understanding*, shows Uncle Toby (who was " puzzled to
death " by it all) being taught the philosophy that
" whilst we receive successively ideas in our minds we
know that we do exist," is really an actor in the historic scene of a psychological, or sentimental, novelist
battering the peg, on which he proposes to hang
his fiction, into the thick skull of an unsentimental
character.

We have said that Sterne left no school, though his
influence was discernible as far away as Meredith. But
he left one ardent pupil in the Scotsman, Henry Mackenzie, who published in 1771 a novel, *The Man of Feeling*,
which only the greater glory of Scott has saved his fellow
countrymen from the task of arduously admiring ever
since.

It is a book of that supercharged archness of sentiment
that Sir James Barrie has so successfully revived. The
author could burst into tears as easily as Alice. Morley
made the joke that " no book so copiously watered with
tears could be called ' dry,' " and gave an index of forty-
seven instances of them. Though that, perhaps, is a
harsher criticism of a man of letters temporarily gone mad
and turned ledger-clerk, than of Mackenzie's lachry-
mosity. Nevertheless some of the downpours and drizzles
in Mackenzie's Vale of Tears are remarkable enough to
deserve perpetuity. For instance :

Harley kissed off her tears as they flowed, and wept
between every kiss,

is as much a tribute to the hero's caudal nimbleness of neck (incommoded as he was with his own paroxysms) as to his warm-heartedness.

The truth is that Mackenzie was writing of tears and kisses as a poet might write of them ; in the abstract. Just as any decadent eighteenth century poet, who earned his keep, saw wherever he walked a ruined Gothic tower with gibbous moon tingeing the obfuscation of a lettered urn and spires, dim discovered, discernible through a rift in the tower, so Mackenzie saw his tears and kisses everywhere.

And it should be borne in mind that it is the method which is outmoded : not the grief, which is necessarily insincere. Mackenzie was striving to produce an effect, not to report one.

A thesist has yet to write an essay on The Tear in Prose Fiction. Chronologically, its chief moments will coincide with those of the Emancipation of Women. The spirit that dragooned the women of Great Britain into demanding a vote also abolished, when it abolished one of the ancestral freedoms of women, one of the most satisfying set-scenes of the novel—the heroine in tears and the hero on his knees beside her. And the tear cannot even be said now to be on the other cheek. For no hero can go wet-eyed in a world of dry-eyed women.

The Man of Feeling is very much the novel that *Tristram Shandy* might have been, had Sterne whispered its plot into the purifying ear of Samuel Richardson. It is *Tristram Shandy*, without just the cock-snooping impudence of mind that added such relish to the Yorkshire parson. Mackenzie in his *Anecdotes* remarked :

Sterne often lacks the dignity of wit. I do not speak of his licentiousness, but he is often on the very verge of buffoonery, which is the bathos of wit, and the fool's coat is half upon him.

That is a clear, if obvious criticism : to say that Sterne lacks dignity is rather like announcing the discovery that Scott lacks conciseness. But at any rate the remark exactly explains the aims and prejudices of Mackenzie. And his aims and prejudices were truly at one with the public's.

Mackenzie's weeping, rambling, anonymous work with its Perennial Prose Prostitute episode, and the frequent references to " sweet sensibility " and " sadness " and " death," was so popular that it preserves from the oblivion of decent ecclesiastical history a young clergyman, Mr. Eccles of Bath, who made a manuscript copy of *The Man of Feeling*, and declared himself to be the author. Mackenzie's publishers were driven finally to expose Mr. Eccles. And the waters of the neighbouring Avon, appreciating the truly artistic nature of the century through which it was flowing, and its reeds possibly still whispering of a previous literary scandal on its banks, rose up and drowned the poor young man.

Scott admired Mackenzie, as well he might. For Mackenzie, who felt very much as Smollett did about Scottish scenery, was an inspired catalogue of the hills as well as of the pains of his native country. And Scott got a reputation for doing that kind of thing rather well himself at a later date.

Scott also got a reputation for his portraits ; portraits of silver-headed age. They were Mackenzie's too. Hitherto the best portraits in fiction had generally been only of the worst people.

Mackenzie's contribution to literature indeed is considerable. The only flaw in it is that *The Man of Feeling* is nowadays unreadable to nine out of ten normally curious readers. The remark made by Christopher North in 1822 that " Henry Mackenzie will live as long as our tongue, or longer," is at once a garland round an author's head and a noose round a language's neck.

THE MAJOR MINOR NOVELISTS

The years between 1751, when Fielding published *Amelia* and stopped writing fiction, and 1778, when Fanny Burney giggled over the popular mystery of the publication of *Evelina*, saw the production of the major minor fiction of English literature—*Rasselas*, *The Vicar of Wakefield*, and *The Castle of Otranto*. It was minor fiction because none of the authors—Johnson, Goldsmith and Walpole—was naturally a novelist. And it was major fiction of its kind because all three were men of genius.

Johnson was about as natural a novelist as Dean Inge. He was a moralist of rare serenity of conviction and rare severity of code ; again like Dean Inge. He wrote his one novel *Rasselas*, as the Dean of Saint Paul's writes his newspaper articles, with complete lack of regard for the prevailing form of such pieces of writing. The remarkably satisfying result in each case is due solely to the underlying intelligence.

It is one of the pieces of good fortune of literary history that we possess so exact an account of the fantastic events that lead to the publication of *Rasselas*. Towards the end of January, 1759, Johnson's mother died, and Johnson, in his usual condition of urgent insolvency, had to pay the expenses of the funeral as well as other outstanding debts.

With the sublime competence which was his he wrote *Rasselas*. He sat down in his Gough Square garret and, in the evenings of one week, sent it to the press in portions as it was written, and did not take the trouble to read it until he revised it for a second edition. Dodsley paid him altogether £125 for it ; enough to bury a whole family. It is in such episodes as the writing of *Rasselas* that the true greatness of Dr. Johnson can be measured.

Ten days after the funeral, Johnson, who must in reality have been pricked at a thousand points by the little devils of debt and doubt, wrote : " My mother's debts, dear Mother, I suppose I may pay with very little difficulty." Three months later *Rasselas* was published, Dr. Johnson was temporarily solvent again, and the cruel system that puts genius to the tread-mill was once more vindicated.

Rasselas, indeed, is one of the best answers to the "Pensions-for-Poets" kind of talk that not infrequently breaks out. A mind like Dr. Johnson's is rare, but sloth such as Dr. Johnson's is common. And Johnson was an author who worked with zest only when the bailiffs of Fate were greedily pressing for an early settlement of account.

The spectacle of Dr. Johnson telling a story is rather like that of an elephant herding sheep : something much smaller could do it far better. In *Rasselas* he simply drove his characters into the Happy Valley, denied them the normal pleasures of a life of fiction, and set them all talking in epigrams. Had anyone of them found himself temporarily at a loss for a wise saw, any of the others or even " the solemn elephant " in the first chapter could easily have filled the gap. For living as they did in such un-natural association, their style of conversation became very much like each other's—and like Johnson's ; just as St. Joan and Tanner and Major Barbara and King Magnus all speak at times very much like Mr. Shaw.

Thus, in *Rasselas* Imlac would remark that, " Human life is everywhere a state in which much is to be endured, and little to be enjoyed," and Nekayah would say that, " Those who marry late are best pleased in their children, and those who marry early in their partners." And so they continue this intellectual competition—very stimulating to the reader—with Imlac scoring four to the princess's one.

Some of Imlac's remarks are notably good. For instance : " Man cannot so far know the connexion of causes and events as that he may venture to do wrong in order to do right " ; and " How comfortless is the sorrow of him, who feels at once the pangs of guilt and the vexation of calamity which guilt has brought upon him " ; and " To hear complaints is wearisome alike to the wretched and the happy " ; and " That you have been deprived of one pleasure is no very good reason for rejection of the rest."

Rasselas indeed might be described as the most ambitious of the *Rambler* essays. It was an essay written by a philosophic mind in sadness ; which is probably the very saddest kind of mind. There are some who can see no beauty in Johnsonian prose—and admittedly, parts of *Rasselas* do read as though Johnson had recently been studying Dr. Johnson too closely—just as there are those who find no elevation in the thoughts which do sometimes give a rather captive-balloon effect of striving to rise. But Johnson proved to conviction that the new and adaptable form of prose fiction could suit the philosopher and the moralist as well as the mischievous man of the world and the mountebank.

In short, Johnson in 1759, taught the English novel to be intellectual ; a lesson that for natural reasons has rarely been applied since.

*   *   *

In 1764 Walpole taught the novel the fascination of mystery ; a lesson that, like scripture in a church-school, has all but swamped the whole syllabus of fiction.

Walpole's *Castle of Otranto* is the sort of work that a contemplative devil, with his back against one tombstone and his feet upon another, might have scribbled while waiting for the dawn-cock to crow. It is astonishing that Walpole ever wrote anything that resembled a novel at all : it was the most nearly vulgar lapse in his life.

He was, of course, quite unfitted to write a novel in the great tradition. Walpole embraced mankind with the affectionate intimacy of a man handling a bargepole. All those qualities of polished, even French-polished, wit, supercilious elegance and a pretty fancy, which make Walpole's letters the first in the language, are the very qualities to pursue with a pitchfork in fiction.

As well expect Mr. Max Beerbohm to write a novel in the manner of *The Good Companions*, or Mr. Lytton Strachey to write the " official " biography of Mr. Henry Ford as to expect Walpole to write an English novel. His upbringing was against him. He never knew what it was to be poor, as Fielding and Smollett before him did, and so was denied the commonest of the profound experiences of mankind.

His father, Sir Robert Walpole, has come down through history as one of the most generous and ungrudging of parents who ever benefited their children at someone else's expense. And Horace, the sickly infant, went through the world on a row of sinecures like stepping-stones, never meeting in the flesh the great democracy of fiction, and quarrelling with the aristocracy who happened to share the stepping-stones with him.

It would be a rash thing to say, as has often been said, that Walpole was serious, with other than the simple and sublime seriousness of the story-teller, when he wrote his little novel of a beautiful virgin and a distraught Italian nobleman who spends his time crying to the heavens for an heir : of monstrous armour and Plutonic plumes : of melancholy spectres and everlasting underground passages.

It would be as rash as to conclude that the novelist of the twentieth century is really a nervous, logical creature, obsessed by the fear of sudden and violent and clue-strewn death.

We see Walpole as a pale prancing maypole, sidling through the circumambient Gothic gloom. But the gloom was purely local. It was even a local industry. Strawberry Hill was a factory of the fantastic, where His Serenity, the Landgrave of Strawberry, could gaze on more than Gothic grotesques in considerably more than Gothic comfort. And if Walpole chose Strawberry Hill for a toy merely to indulge an idle whim, it is not too much to suppose that *The Castle of Otranto* was no more than another personal indulgence : and not the prayer uttered to Heaven for which it has sometimes been taken.

Walpole describes how he came to start his novel :

I waked one morning in the beginning of last June from a dream, of which all I could recover was, that I had thought myself in an ancient castle, (a very natural dream for a head filled like mine with Gothic story) and that on the uppermost banister of a great staircase, I saw a gigantic hand in armour. In the evening I sat down and began to write, without knowing in the least what I intended to say or relate. The work grew on my hands, and I grew fond of it. Add, that I was very glad to think of anything rather than politics. In short, I was so engrossed with my tale, which I completed in less than two months, that one evening I wrote from the time I had drank my tea, about six o'clock, till half an hour after one in the morning when my hands and fingers were so weary that I could not hold the pen to finish the sentence, but left Matilda and Isabella talking in the middle of a paragraph.

A dream is an old excuse for letting imagination into the mind. From Jacob to Coleridge it has been an excuse that has been accepted whenever the mind behaves more extravagantly than its owner feels that he can safely afford.

When *The Castle of Otranto* was first published, Walpole could not even bring himself to confess that his sleeping mind was so prodigal and profuse in its disorders. The first edition bore a preface with place, date and fake written all over it. In it is described how Walpole came upon the work in the original Black Letter Italian " in the library of an ancient Catholic family in the north of England," and how he is convinced that even the story itself " is founded on truth."

And Walpole would never have confessed had not the leg he was pulling suddenly come clean away in his hand, and he been forced to explain how it came to be in his possession. He confessed with just that disarming obliqueness of the moral sense that was his. Like a bogus company promoter, he explained that he had intended all the time to come forward if the scheme succeeded, and to remain in decent obscurity if it fell flat. And he went on to explain that the story was an attempt to blend ancient with modern romance, to build a nest, even though it were a mare's nest, of imagination, in the tree of nature.

One canon of composition he enunciates is so thoroughly the product of a wakeful, rational mind, and the whole story is so obedient to the canon, that we see the dream and the excuse dissolving before our eyes.

Walpole remarked that he had observed that " in all inspired writings, the personages under the dispensation of miracles, and witnesses of the most stupendous phenomena, never lose sight of their human character ; whereas in the productions of romantic story, an improbable event never fails to be attended by an absurd dialogue. The actors seem to lose their senses the moment the laws of nature are suspended."

Thus Walpole suspended the laws of nature, establishing romantic lore in their place, and gave to the characters an eighth sense, a sense of their momentous responsibilities in behaving exactly like a party of tourists— observant but scarcely surprised—on a conducted tour through the suburbs of Hades. So we get such a typical passage as this :

" I tell you," said Manfred imperiously, " Hippolita is no longer my wife ; I divorce her from this hour. Too long has she cursed me by her unfruitfulness. My fate depends upon having sons, and this night I trust will give a new date to my hopes."

At those words he seized the cold hand of Isabella who was half dead with fright and horror. She shrieked and started from him. Manfred rose to pursue her, when the moon, which was now up and gleamed in at the opposite casement, presented to his sight the fatal helmet, which rose to the height of the windows, waving backwards and forwards in a tempestuous manner, and accompanied with a hollow and rustling sound. Isabella, who gathered courage from her situation, and who dreaded nothing so much as Manfred's pursuit of his declaration, cried :

" Look, my lord, ' see, Heaven itself declares against your impious intentions.' "

" Heaven nor Hell shall impede my designs," said Manfred, advancing again to seize the princess. At that instant the portrait of his grandfather, which hung over the bench where they had been sitting, uttered a deep sigh, and heaved its breast. Isabella, whose back was turned to the picture, saw not the motion nor whence the sound came, but started and said :

" Hark, my lord, what sound was that ? " and at the same time made towards the door. Manfred, distracted between the flight of Isabella, who had now reached the stairs, and yet unable to keep his eyes from the picture, which began to move, had, however, advanced some steps after her, still looking backwards on the portrait, when he saw it quit its panel, and descend on the floor with a grave and melancholy air.

" Do I dream ? " cried Manfred, returning, " or are the devils themselves in league against me ? Speak, infernal spectre ! or, if thou art my grandsire, why dost thou, too, conspire against thy wretched descendant, who too dearly pays for "—ere he could finish the sentence, the vision sighed again, and made a sign to Manfred to follow him.

" Lead on ! " cried Manfred ; " I will follow thee to the gulf of perdition." The spectre marched sedately, but dejected, to the end of the gallery, and turned into a chamber on the right hand.

Manfred, it might be objected, speaks a little too much in the grand manner, at least to modern ears. But it should be pointed out that he was a foreigner and a Catholic, and so naturally excitable and not altogether responsible for his actions. And few of us know exactly how we should behave if we had just arranged to rape a girl, and our dead grandfather, sedate and dejected, were to get down from a canvas on the wall and go and shut himself up in another room. Considering the enormity of the old gentleman's behaviour, Manfred kept his nerve, to say nothing of his temper, remarkably well. He was apparently less anxious than most men are who are called on merely to assist a conjurer on a concert hall stage.

Scott spoke of the " wild interest " of the story of *The Castle of Otranto* ; and I believe that if we had not all of us been brought up with the criticism that it is " creaky " already in our minds, we should find it infinitely more exciting than most of our modern " thrillers." At least we should until within a page or two of the story's close.

For it is one of the incidental enslavements of the rational mind that only those miracles which are no more than ingenious illusions shall be admitted ; and even then the last chapter must contain a full confession by the Almighty as how he contrived to appear miraculous.

Thus it is that the modern mind is apt finally to feel more than a trifle cheated when God (or the Devil) remains obstinately silent about his means, and ostentatiously showy about his manifestations. But at the actual moment of reading, the mind is feverishly fascinated.

It is not an accident that a whole saga of the supernatural came to be written towards the end of the eighteenth century. The supernatural trespasses into the rational world in two distinct states in the evolution of the human mind. The first is when unaccountable and unearthly beings are found everywhere among men, as unnecessary as poppies in a cornfield. That is the superstitious period. The second is when unpredictable messengers appear with calamitous warnings, or tremendous tidings, or helpful and sometimes purely temporary advice. That is the religious period. For the first and last test of a Christian miracle is not whether it is wonderful but whether it is useful.

Obviously then, there is no riot of bizarre amusement to be had from the religious miracle. Once miracles are accepted and put into literary form the phantasy becomes merely that grosser thing—religious propaganda. The miraculous events in *The Castle of Otranto* are all palpably miracles of superstition, and not of religion. And they are not the products of the uneasy belief that is to be found in the childhood of the race, before superstition has had time to crystallise itself into religion, but the uneasiness that flourishes again in the decay of religion.

In the eighteenth century everyone had a sense of the religious tradition, but few the spirit of religious faith. So God floated out of the Churches and ghosts floated into the home. And from Walpole onwards came a stream of terrifying writers : Clara Reeve, Mrs. Radcliffe, " Monk " Lewis and the rest, who created a superstition of singular density, and no little literary effectiveness— to those left with sufficient religious instinct to enjoy it.

But Walpole was not a pumpkin-spectre out to frighten yokels. He foresaw his successors as little as he foresaw his success. And there is no reason to believe that he saw the real significance of what he had done for fiction.

He seemed to think that because he had taught his characters to behave with that admirable detachment and suspicion that Gideon displayed before the miraculous fleece, he had instituted a new kind of romance. It is necessary only to remember Gulliver's behaviour before the Houyhnhnms to see that Manfred had been rather seriously anticipated.

But what Walpole did do was the infinitely more important thing of changing the story from a mere string of events into a cat's cradle of ingenious complexity ; to lay out a plot like a pattern and not merely uncoil it like a rope. And he did this, not because of any superior intelligence in his mind but because the nature of his plot compelled him.

If you write a story with a skeleton in the cupboard in the first chapter you must, sooner or later, explain how it came to be there, and the story will move forward with this as its purpose. And so when Walpole begins with a miraculous helmet, crushing a bridegroom to death on the first page, we know that we shall have to hear more about the helmet, and that we shall be given some reason, no matter how unreasonable, for its behaviour. Each chapter, thereupon, assumes a new responsibility, earning its keep, not merely by adding to the length, but to the purpose, of the novel.

Tom Jones, for example, could have stretched to twice its length, with no damage or improvement to itself, only providing that Tom's endurance could support the strain of forgetting his Sophia in the simplest way he knew, and that the reader's patience could endure him for so long.

*   *   *

The third major piece of minor fiction of the period is *The Vicar of Wakefield*. It is the typically repentant product of a man who has crowded the greatest wildnesses of his life into the early years. There is a kind of innocence that is so closely akin to idiocy that we may be forgiven if we call it by its harder name. And the idiotic incumbent of Wakefield reveals just those deficiencies of intelligence that made his author one of Fortune's gifts to the trickster and the cheat.

The Vicar of Wakefield is usually exhibited as the most successful of Johnson's god-children. But Johnson found it in circumstances that were likely to commend it. The description that he has left of the incident is this :

> I received one morning a message from poor Gold-smith that he was in great distress, and as it was not in his power to come to me, begging that I would come to him as soon as possible. I sent him a guinea, and promised to come to him directly. I accordingly went as soon as I was drest, and found that his landlady had arrested him for his rent, at which he was in a violent passion. I perceived that he had already changed my guinea, and had got a bottle of Madeira and a glass before him. I put the cork into the bottle, desired he would be calm, and began to talk to him of the means by which he might be extricated. He then told me that he had a novel ready for the press, which he produced to me. I looked into it and saw its merit ; told the land-lady I should soon return, and having gone to a book-seller, sold it for sixty pounds. I brought Goldsmith the money, and he discharged his rent, not however with-out rating his landlady in a high tone for having used him so ill.

In a room with the shadow of the bailiff on the blind a man would find merit in sixpence. That is not for one moment to pretend that *The Vicar of Wakefield* was devoid of merit. The simple sentiment of the story is obviously sincere ; it goes straight to the heart of the public like the picture on a sublime tradesman's calendar.

No one, I suppose, could fail to see the charm of the nincompoop old vicar ; no one, that is, who can put his common sense in his pocket for a space. But the trouble is that Goldsmith's picture of an honest man was no more than that of a fat, affectionate pig, politely handing the fatal knife to a pig-sticking destiny.

That was at the back of Goldsmith's mind because it had been at the back of his life. Goldsmith was a pawn of Fate who began the game with a gambit. When his family did contrive to send him to college in Dublin he played the fool so strenuously that his tutor, poor desperate man, broke into his rooms and boxed his ears in the middle of an uproarious party. The disgrace was too great; Goldsmith sold his books and, with his ears still singing with shame, left Erin never to return.

At least, it is what he intended. But being the weak, asinine creature that he was, he dawdled on in Dublin, plying his sacred trade of idler, until he had only a shilling left. Then the family appeared and Goldsmith had to be reconciled with his tutor. It was all a part of the shifting design in his patternless life.

The next years show us Goldsmith wandering about the world from Edinburgh to Padua, being arrested and robbed and cheated and tricked, playing his flute for pence, spending the money that his family with saintly patience continued to send him, now in Leyden, now in Italy, and behaving in general as though Life had really created him to see if for one character at least she could not behave as generously and variously as fiction. But patternless as the life was it was all of a piece; like needing a patron and ridiculously mistaking his manservant for him, and then spurning the patron on the entirely false assertion that " book-sellers are the best patrons " ; behaving like a Duke in the intervals of living like a pauper ; earning a prosperous living, yet dying in debt to the tune of £2,000.

Goldsmith is one of the few inspired loafers in history ; a man who learned more from idleness than most men do from industry. Since loafing was his apprenticeship to life, and he was so diligent, we may forgive him that for its sake he was also a liar, a cheat and a thief. He was the pickpocket in leading strings. His mother had always had great faith in her son's ingenuity as a writer. And her proof was not long lacking. For young Oliver was fertile in reasons for her giving him money.

For example, there was his old story of how he embarked upon a ship for America, paid his fare, sent his kit, his valuable kit, on board and then missed the vessel. The only thing that makes the story even worth repeating, now that its original purpose of getting money is pointless, is that there certainly is something that rings true about Goldsmith's not knowing the name of the ship.

For there is another story of how he first arrived in Edinburgh, took his luggage to his rooms and left to explore the town, only to find he had failed to note the number or street of his lodgings. By chance, it is said, he met the porter who had carried his luggage : which saved him. And the little vignette of An Irishman in Scotland was complete.

But in matters of money Goldsmith is hard to blame. His was a nature of lavish habits, for which money was essential. When he came to have it later in life he spent it. And probably he quite sincerely could not imagine that there were people in this world who liked to have money by them, at rest as well as in motion.

Goldsmith's generosity, indeed, has become one of the great historical attributes, like Smollett's temper and Sterne's wit and Sidney's grace.

To have been a friend of either Goldsmith or Johnson would have been to be as immune from the fear of actual hunger as any man possibly could be. The only difference between Goldsmith's generosity and Johnson's was that Johnson knew the value of money and deliberately made himself forget it upon occasion, and Goldsmith never knew.

One of the unfading scenes of sentimental history is that
of the crowd of indigent mourners, pauper dependents on
a debtor, who thronged Goldsmith's staircase in Brick
Court when he died. And the scene is still affecting even
though the grief of a beggar when his benefactor dies is
necessarily not above suspicion.

It would be easy criticism to say that the simplicity of
The Vicar of Wakefield was the same simplicity which led
Goldsmith to give away his money and his coat and his
breakfast, and behave always as though St. Anthony were
holding out a hand from every doorway. But that would be
misleading, because it would overlook such a piece of
work as *She Stoops to Conquer*. Goldsmith was perpetually
puzzling his contemporaries by suddenly shining through
the mists of his own mind like a sun, and then as suddenly
taking cover again. And he puzzles us still more. *She
Stoops to Conquer*, for example, is the product of a man who
has seen through all the follies of mankind. And seeing
through a folly is usually halfway to overlooking it.

In *The Traveller* and *The Deserted Village*, on the other
hand, Goldsmith still believed in Human Folly and
Human Frailty and Human Despair and Human Regret
and Human Pride : and wrote about them in the manner
of a yearning and pessimistic preacher. In *She Stoops to
Conquer* and *The Good Natured Man* the moralist has
given place to the Epicurean ; and the soft, serious
things of life are all deliciously played upon by the comic
spirit.

Not that Goldsmith's was a consistent and chronological
pilgrimage from pessimism to comedy. On the contrary,
it was a hesitating jay-flight between one mood and the
next. And it so happens that *The Vicar of Wakefield*, which
is that part of Goldsmith that concerns us, was written in

a moment when Life outside was a forbidding grey, and everything within was a delicate shell pink.

" With that sweet story of *The Vicar of Wakefield*," wrote Thackeray, " he has found entry into every castle and every hamlet in Europe. Not one of us, however busy or hard, but once or twice in our lives has passed an evening with him and undergone the charm of his delightful music."

Such an utterance illuminates more of the kindly soul of Thackeray than of his subject. At the least provocation Thackeray's heart was ready to overflow ; and his pictures of every king and peasant from Novaya Zemlya to Gibraltar all greedily poring over Goldsmith, and of Scrooges indulging themselves with their solitary feast of pathos, are the product of a mind that carries more than a fair handicap of sentimental lead.

Scott said : " We read *The Vicar of Wakefield* in youth and in age—we return to it again and again, and bless the memory of an author who contrives so well to reconcile us to human nature." And that is very fairly put. Scott had fewer of that sort of books to which a man may return again and again than Thackeray had. And there was intelligence as well as affection in naming youth and age as the best times for reading about the Vicar.

The subject of *The Vicar of Wakefield* rather obviously is Marriage : the characters in the story are a wife, sons and daughters and the spectre of poverty. Now, though Goldsmith was extremely well equipped to describe the latter, he had as a bachelor no qualifications at all for writing about the former. And his novel in consequence is very much what a well disposed hermit might imagine marriage to be like. It is a mixture of nonsense and realism ; an Arcady in which a writ of impeachment could still be served.

Gꜰ

Its chief merit is that it is constantly interesting ; and its popular appeal is due to the fact that it is made up of small, separate scenes, sufficiently short to be appreciated as a whole by a simple mind.

It is, indeed, the product of a mind working as a dramatist's mind works, in moments and divisions of activity. And such a passage as :

"Where, where are my children ? " cried I, rushing through the flames and bursting the door of the chamber in which they were confined : " Where are my little ones ? "—" Here, dear papa, here we are," cried they together, while the flames were just catching the bed where they lay. I caught them both in my arms, and conveyed them through the fire as fast as possible, while just as I was going out the roof sunk in . . .

is a classic example of the sort of melodrama which was to get out of hand a century later, but which was still a respectable literary device in the eighteenth century.

THE ARRIVAL OF FEMALE GENIUS

Fanny Burney is the first recorded specimen of a now familiar English bird often shot on these shores, the woman novelist, who could write a really admirable novel, yet remain a foolish young thing all her life.

She was favoured as few have been in the moment of her coming : 1778 was the end of one of the most alarming literary droughts in English history. But it would be ungenerous to attribute one of the conspicuous successes of talent merely to an accident of time. For Fanny Burney could write. Indeed, she could not help writing. Like

Richardson's, her soul expanded and expended itself on paper. And it is probable that at any moment her mind was comparatively well emptied ; she certainly behaved at the Thrales' as though it was. When Sheridan, very politely making conversation, asked Fanny, " What, then, are you about now ? " she replied with the fatuity of a coy nursemaid, " Why, twirling my fan, I think."

By the age of sixteen she had written enough to make a bonfire of her writings, which included a complete novel. The reason for the conflagration is said to have been that her stepmother had admonished her to guard her mind against such gaudy toys of invention. That may have been the reason : for Fanny in the flesh had the spirit of a fly. But—so far as I know, there is no tangible evidence to support the theory—it seems far more likely that the second Mrs. Burney's disparagements had sent Fanny back to reading her own *juvenilia*. And the rosy prose fiction of thirteen and fourteen doubtless had a strangely flaccid look in the white light of the eyes of sixteen.

At any rate, Fanny burned her romances, put authorship resolutely behind her, and began to keep a diary. Probably something of the kind was absolutely necessary. Fanny would simply have disappeared out of existence if she had not been living a robust life on paper as well as a bashful life on earth. And soon she was secretly at work on *Evelina*, writing as industriously and cautiously as Pamela. " The fear of discovery or of suspicion in the house," she tells us, " made the copying extremely laborious to me ; for in the daytime, I could only take odd moments, so that I was obliged to sit up the greater part of many nights, in order to get it ready."

She preserved an elaborate anonymity, which was probably more fascinating than necessary : it was as though a little peninsula of romantic fiction had at last managed to obtrude its nose into the world of fact. She offered the first two volumes of her book to the fashionable Dodsley, in Pall Mall, under no signature, and asked that the reply should be addressed to Mr. Grafton at the Orange Coffee House in Pall Mall. Mr. Dodsley's reply restored the geographics of fact. He answered (as any self-respecting publisher was bound to answer) that he would not stir a finger without knowing the author's name. Fanny, therefore, made one more effort to impose romantic fancy on unromantic, manuscript-rejecting Life. And she beat Life at its own game. She dressed up her brother Charles in a disguise and sent him off, bearing the manuscript, to Mr. Lowndes in Fleet Street. Thereafter the impatient Mr. Grafton called for his letters at the Orange Coffee House, with almost feminine nervousness and frequency. And he finally received the reply that as soon as the book was finished there was a publisher waiting to receive it.

Probably the original plan of *Evelina* seemed unnecessarily long to Fanny about that date. Certainly she wrote : " I had hardly time to write half a page in a day ; and neither my health nor inclination would allow me to continue my *nocturnal* scribbling, for so long a time, as to write first, and then copy, a whole volume." But the question whether to write only two parts or persevere with a concluding one usually ends with the completion of the third, and a year later, in 1778, Mr. Lowndes had paid her £20 for the entire work, a sum which caused Fanny " boundless surprise at its magnificence."

Fanny was soon enjoying the highly practical pleasure of hard cash and that purely æsthetic pleasure (to an artistic mind such as hers) of watching everyone wondering who the author of *Evelina* really was. And the romantic little soul of Fanny is again revealed when she and her stepmother, who, like a sensible woman, disapproved not

of authorship but only of unsuccessful authorship, visited
Mr. Dodsley to inquire about the indentity of the author
of *Evelina,* and the poor bewildered bookseller replied
that he knew nothing except that " it was a page torn
from life."

The extraordinary thing is that everyone should have
thought the novel was by a man. One has only to compare the sweet vaporous morality of *The Vicar of Wakefield* with the acidulated comment of *Evelina* to detect the
difference in the sex of the two authors.

From the publication of *Evelina* onwards Fanny's career
was so remarkably successful that it was quite impossible
for her ever again to write anything so good. She appears
to have kept respectable people awake almost as out-
rageously as the air-raids did later. Indeed, her very
reputation hangs on the fact that she made half fashionable London insomniomaniacs when *Evelina* was first out.
Joshua Reynolds, for instance, who started it and was
" too much engaged to go on with it," was " so caught
that he could think of nothing else, and was quite absent
all the day, not knowing a word that was said to him ;
and, when he took it up again, found himself so much
interested in it, that he sat up all night to finish it." While
this tribute is revealing, as much of Sir Joshua's memor-
ably excitable mind, as of Fanny Burney's genius, it is
well to remember that for the past ten years or so there
had been nothing published that could keep even a wakeful man from sleep. But Fanny was always hearing of her
successes, and was the recipient of as many bouquets during her lifetime as Congreve. Like Congreve she got to
know everyone. But unlike Congreve, whose magnificence
commanded praise even from Dryden, she was a pet whose
helplessness educed flattery even from Johnson. Everyone
in the presence of an author has said harmless, happy,

helpful things that he would not repeat on paper for the price of his soul. The fact is that no one would expect him to. Thus when Johnson declared that he was too proud to eat earthly food when sitting next to Fanny Burney, we know that it is Johnson, the ponderously agreeable luncheon guest, and not Johnson, the mentally alert critic, who has spoken. The flatteries that were paid Fanny, indeed, are so numerous as to make one wonder just what her contemporaries really thought of her. A deep respect for the intelligence of anyone simply freezes words of flattery in the throat. Yet Johnson and Sheridan and Burke and Sir Joshua Reynolds and Mrs. Thrale were all raiding the flowershops of the imagination for bouquets to throw to her ; until on one occasion Fanny felt so over-powered that she would like to have been able to " poke herself under the table."

Evelina itself is startlingly intelligent, so intelligent, in-deed, that it should have educated Cadell, the publisher, who eleven years later was so snubbing to the shy soul of Jane Austen. It should have warned him that alone among the arts the novel was the one which suited the feminine genius perfectly, and that more would be heard of it pres-ently. For a novel does not require rhetoric or the exercise of reason ; two things at which men are conspicuously better than women. But it does require acquaintance with life and interest in other people ; which is exactly what most women possess more abundantly than men. It would be possible for instance to comb and recomb *Evelina* for stretches of fine writing, or rich purple thoughts, or passages pregnant with penetration or observation (other than that which accompanies the formula of a rather ungracious female wit) and find none of them.

Yet it would be hard to know exactly how to improve it in any particular. Had Fanny Burney lived thirty years later she would have displaced several reputations. As it is, she remains trapped in the notoriety of the century, a century of rakes and wenches and elegant postchaises and dinner at four o'clock and a dirty navy. Another generation and she would have been ageless. As things were planned, however, she is merely the most wide-eyed, pert, nervous, provocative reporter who strayed unsoiled through the refined raffishness of the eighteenth century.

True, she did drift on, a woman with a splendid past always before her, into nearly the middle of the nineteenth century. The Queen adopted her and gave her full use of the royal backstairs. M. d'Arblay married her and set her up in a house of true French fussiness after Fanny came down the royal backstairs for the last time. Henceforward she was as industrious as she was unsuccessful. She died finally in Lower Grosvenor Street, her disordered mind surrounding her with phantoms peopling the reign of Queen Victoria with the spirits of Dr. Johnson's circle.

JANE AUSTEN'S UNHEAVENLY
WORLD

It would seem impossible to overpraise the singular genius of Jane Austen. But with alarming accumulation of hyperbole it has been done.

Though well intentioned, it probably began unintentionally. Lord Macaulay started the trouble with his slightly silly remark that " while Shakespeare has left us a greater number of striking portraits than other dramatists put together, he has hardly left us a single caricature," and that though " Shakespeare has had neither equal nor second " (here the silliness begins), " among the writers who, in that point in which we have noticed, have approached nearest to the manner of the great master, we have no hesitation in placing Jane Austen."

This remark would be perfectly true if it were not that in just such miraculous characters as Mr. Collins, Mrs. Bennet, Sir John Middleton, General Tilney, Mr. Woodhouse, Admiral Croft, and so forth, the supremacy of Jane Austen is most conspicuous. And a caricature does not cease to be a caricature because it has been done skilfully.

Macaulay (now speaking absolute common sense) added, to his previous unfortunate remark, the comment that Jane Austen " has given us a multitude of characters, all, in a certain sense, commonplace, all such as we meet every day. Yet they are all perfectly discriminated from each other as if they were the most eccentric of human beings. . . . And almost all this is done by touches so delicate that they elude analysis, that they defy the powers of description, and that we know them to exist only by the general effect to which they have contributed."

Macaulay certainly knew his Jane ; he very nearly knew her by heart. For she herself said as much when she spoke of her books as "little bits (two inches wide) of ivory on which I work with so fine a brush as produces little effect after much labour." And if only people would remember that the miniature is no more than one of the charming younger sisters of art, some of the worst excesses of rabid Janeism would be avoided.

The limitations of Jane Austen's vision are as remarkable as its brightness of definition. Only a mind of unique certitude and self-possession could have cut out so much of life and then made so much of what was left. But it is well to remember that what is left is no more the whole of Life than Mozart is the whole of music.

It is usual to illustrate the degree of Jane's natural limitations by pointing out that though she lived through the whole scarlet and sensational period of the French Revolution, and actually shared a roof with a widow whose husband had been guillotined, she does not refer to it once.

This, however, is not the final conviction that it has sometimes been taken for. The Great War and the Russian Revolution contributed nothing, or next to nothing, to the *contemporary* fiction of our time. Not that Jane's mind necessarily turned away from anything so ungenteel as heads in a basket and a dead man in a bath, and the other lurid paraphernalia of Revolution. For she had something of the coarseness of the century which was so extremely well-mannered that it could talk about everything. But she certainly was on the side of God and his angels against Godwin and his Radicals. And if

Godwin's disciples were too raffish for her, probably she could not trust herself to find a name for the *arrivistes* who departed the Parisian scene as rapidly as they came.

But the boundaries of Jane Austen's mind may, within limits, be mapped out by saying that she cared less about the Battle of Trafalgar than she did about Marianne Dashwood's twisting her ankle, that she said she would read Southey's *Life of Nelson* only if her sailor brother, Frank, were mentioned in it, and that the death of Sir John Moore—and this was enough to make her a national leper—left her unmoved.

It was not, however, merely what lay across the Channel that was foreign to her and her interests, but what lay within the heart as well. There is the famous passage in which Charlotte Brontë, with more heart than head, condemns her natural opposite, whose heart was the size of a humming bird's and whose head was as hard as a hailstone :

Anything like warmth or enthusiasm—anything energetic, poignant, heartfelt is utterly out of place in commending these works : all such demonstration the authoress would have met with a well-bred sneer, would have calmly scorned as *outré* and extravagant. She does her business of delineating the surface of the lives of genteel English people curiously well. There is a Chinese fidelity, a miniature delicacy in the painting. She ruffles her reader by nothing vehement, disturbs him by nothing profound. The passions are perfectly unknown to her ; she rejects even a speaking acquaintance with that stormy sisterhood. Even to the feelings she vouchsafes no more than an occasional graceful but distant recognition—too frequent converse with them would ruffle the smooth elegance of her progress.

Her business is not half so much with the human heart
as with the human eyes, mouth, hands, and feet. What
sees keenly, speaks aptly, moves flexibly, it suits her to
study ; but what throbs fast and full, though hidden,
what the blood rushes through, what is the unseen seat
of life and the sentient target of death—this Miss
Austen ignores. She no more, with her mind's eye, be-
holds the heart of her race than each man, with bodily
vision, sees the heart in his heaving breast. Jane Austen
was a complete and most sensible lady, but a very incomplete and rather insensible (not senseless) woman.

Unfortunately it has become customary to say " Poor
Jane ! " instead of " Bravo, Charlotte ! " after that
diatribe.

There *is*, nevertheless, a portrait of Jane Austen, which
could be constructed, that is at least as credible as the
face with Madame de Sévigné's smile beneath Homer's
brow, crowned with a lace cap, which has with variations
been imposed on our imagination. And the portrait is
that of a smug little face seen pressed close behind a
muslin window curtain. I do not say that it is the true
portrait. Indeed, I would say that it is as untrue as the
other ; which is to say that it is not true at all. It is
merely in the manner of a corrective. It is, however,
worth remembering that the one description of Jane
Austen that is cherished is that of a "clear brunette with
a rich colour . . . full round cheeks, a mouth and nose
small and well-formed, bright hazel eyes, and brown
hair, forming natural curls round her face "—the very
portrait of a village quiz.

To link Jane Austen's name with the names of Homer
and Shakespeare and Cervantes and Scott, as one of her
earlier commentators has rashly done, is simply to

invite Folly to play with fire. Upon investigation, the comparison collapses as utterly as if we were to search for a troop of feminine counterparts to Fielding or Smollett.

It has often been said that Jane Austen, as a writer, rose superior to the natural walls and barriers of her sex ; that she becomes a kind of unseen, all-seeing, sexless Ariel. It is doubtful, however, whether this means very much more than that she writes so well that, if you had not known her to be a woman, you might take her ability to be that of a man. True, no man ever had just that patience of observation, that ear for absurdity, that eye for incongruity, that sense of mischief and minutiæ ; and certainly none had the opportunity for exerting their talents that Jane had. She is perfectly feminine in her range of experience ; and in her competence of reporting feminine experience, perfectly masculine.

But competence alone is no more than a ticket entitling the holder to travel first-class to Perfection ; it is not the journey accomplished. Sooner or later when competence is mentioned, some reference must be made to the materials. And when once we step beyond speaking of Jane Austen's competence, we become uncomfortably aware that another step would take us clean off the map. For the boundaries of her mind, as distinct from its depths, are such that no more than a fragment of human experience, the size of a hencoop, is enclosed.

Misjudgments of Jane Austen usually arise from two simple errors. Those who decry her have generally searched for things utterly outside her scope and so been disappointed, and those who applaud her extravagantly are usually those who are content with something alarmingly less than the whole of normal adult range of life.

It is one of the great commonplaces of criticism that

minds like Homer's and Shakespeare's and Cervantes'—
Scott perhaps should not be included by the earlier critic
—exhibit no obvious boundaries, and reveal no peculiar
landmarks.

It is the whole of life that beats back at us from them.
Homer has somehow contrived to avoid putting his foot
through the scenery of the Odyssey as, say, Thackeray
is always putting his foot through his novels. At the end of
Hamlet and *Don Quixote*, we are convinced that we know
more of everyone, including ourselves, and excepting the
author. But Jane Austen is for ever unintentionally breaking through. I do not refer to her archness, which is as
much a part of her novels as it evidently was of her, but
rather to moments when we realise that we have caught
her completely off her habitual guard. And when it is so,
we become aware of the natural limitations of a character
so lively that its size is deceptive. I do not suggest that
these limitations are necessarily those of a small mind.
Nevertheless, in a greater mind no hint of, say, anything
so trivial as dislike of noisy children would, as in *Sense
and Sensibility*, trickle through, leaving in the reader's
memory the image of a shadowy spinster with nerves and
teeth set permanently on edge.

There are any number of ways of looking on life ; and
the way of the humorous spinster is one. Jane Austen,
indeed, showed that it could be a remarkably good one.
Regard Jane as the greatest spinster in letters and you
have said too little. Regard her as one of the great masters
of fiction and sooner or later you will have to make excuses
for her.

Jane certainly showed that a maiden lady in a small
village could know as much about human nature as the
philosopher on the highest hill. The wise second chapter of
Sense and Sensibility, in which cupidity reduces the generosity

of a will to terms so low and disgusting that we seem to hear the dead benefactor turning over and over in his grave like a bobbin, is one of those scenes that glow with the luminosity of disillusion. Jane Austen, indeed, seems to have been born disillusioned. Had she lived longer she might have grown philosophic. As it is she was always better at painting a human weakness than a human virtue—a peculiarity of old maids. Indeed, that habit of hers of never looking up at a saint or down at a sinner, but only straight in front of the curate, is what destroys any claim to absolute greatness that can be made for her.

The destruction of Janeism could be continued on other counts still without detracting in any way from discerning appreciation of her books.

Her plots are childlike where they are not absurd ; *Lady Susan*—the only startling one among them—is very much what might have resulted had the strenuously irregular " Colette " handed over one of her earlier novels for dialogue by the author of *Sandford and Merton*. Jane Austen is never lyrical ; she is not even religious. The beginnings of her novels are dull to disappointment, and her prose is among the most unmusical in the language ; Alice Meynell called it a " mouthful of thick words."

Jane Austen could not draw a man that is recognisable as other than the sort of man an unmarried woman sees. She knew passion as the canary knows the cat ; as something to be avoided. Her landscapes, though popular, are mere green crêpe and stiff cardboard. As for example :

Cleveland was a spacious wooden-built house, situ-ated on a sloping lawn. The pleasure grounds were tolerably extensive ; and, like every other place of the same degree of importance, it had its open shrubbery, and closer wood walk ; a road of smooth gravel, winding round a plantation, led to the front . . .

Spacious house, situated on a sloping lawn, delightful gardens, gravel-drive . . . many estate-agents have said more. And this deficiency of physical observation in remarking any distinguishing things, sometimes makes us wonder whether Jane Austen had any eyes at all to use, or whether she merely relied on the quivering antennæ of her intelligence—which were of no use in informing her of inanimate things.

Elsewhere in *Sense and Sensibility*, we find a vivid demonstration of her essential weakness and her strength. First we have the masterpiece of inefficient description :

Miss Dashwood had a delicate complexion, regular features, and a remarkably pretty figure. Marianne was still handsomer. Her form, though not so correct as her sister's, in having the advantage of height, was more striking . . .

and so on, till even a rural policeman might be forgiven for believing that his description of the missing and the dead had more of accuracy and more of art.

Then comes the change from utter inefficiency to complete and perfect competence, when Jane stops saying pleasant things about someone's face and begins saying unpleasant things behind someone else's back.

Brandon is just the kind of man . . . whom everybody speaks well of, and nobody cares about ; whom all are delighted to see and nobody remembers to talk to.

Alice Meynell, again, spoke of the essential meanness of Jane Austen's art and called hers an unheavenly world. Certainly it was a world that was brightened by a bachelor as by a beacon, and lit up for pages by a legacy.

It has been added to most comminations of this kind, that Jane is often callous, with the calculated callousness of the cad. And in support of this it is usual to quote the letter in which she writes :

> Mrs. Hall, of Sherborne, was brought to bed yesterday of a dead child, some weeks before she expected, owing to a fright. I suppose she happened unawares to look at her husband.

It *is* an ugly remark. A sensitive mind to which a dead baby is a disgusting, chastening and even a terrifying thing, could never have harboured that genuinely comic afterthought. And that is not the only letter which has about it that same gnattish humour. But such letters are magnificently misrepresentative of the whole.

There are letters to Jane's favourite sister, Cassandra, as for instance the one in which she says : " I have now attained the true art of letter-writing, which we are always told is to express on paper exactly what one might say to the same person by word of mouth. I have been talking to you almost as fast as I could the whole of this letter," which persuade us that here is the perfect letter-writer corresponding with the perfect sister.

It has also frequently been observed that Jane Austen is obsessed by money. She is. And in very much the way in which a railway time-table is obsessed by trains. It was her subject. She had the unsentimental sense to see how far marriage is at the mercy of money. The real strangeness is not that her characters talk about it so much, but that they talk about it in such terms. It simply means that the novels of Jane Austen are a chapter in the domestic and marital economics of a system that has been supplanted.

If ever there were a woman designed for spinsterhood it was Jane Austen. She wore the cap of middle age early in life ; and she wore it from youth in her books. She could never have found a man within reach who was mentally her equal. And since she gives no hint of passion in her nature she could hardly be expected to have committed the indiscretion of misalliance. Her life is so placid and uneventful, even where it is known, that it has scared off the biographers and turned them, for the most part, into commentators on her books.

Her nephew, in his *Memoir*, purely as an afterthought, mentions two faint, male figures, one of which faded out shortly afterwards in death, who attempted the unequal match with Jane Austen, probably without even glimpsing the mind that lay within, and (so the nephew again assures us) without deeply disturbing his aunt's tranquillity of emotion.

All that we know of the physical Jane was that she was brought up in Steventon Parsonage, an island of local culture, where charades and cribbage and *bouts-rimés* and " miles of fringe and acres of carpet " were all worshipped, and where the rest of the world was Ultima Thule, seen across seas of mud, where every billow was a cart rut.

Jane Austen's life, apart from the fact that her books were written in it, is one of the sweet blanks of literature. It was a life in which the peaks of experience were no more than emotional molehills. And it was a life that seems to have been crowded imperatively forward.

She began her best novel, *Pride and Prejudice*, before she was twenty-one, and finished it within ten months.

Hf

Sense and Sensibility was started as soon as *Pride and Pre-judice* was finished ; and it contained the frame of a tale, *Elinor and Marianne,* that had been written before Jane's maturity, at twenty. The earlier work had been in the form of letters—a trouble that doubtless derived from Samuel Richardson, whom Jane Austen read and liked ; and whom, in making one of her characters say, " It is my duty and also my wish," she imitated. *Northanger Abbey* was begun at twenty-three.

The fate of the three books shows how ill-prepared the public was for fiction that had its roots in the uneventful Monday-to-Saturday life of mankind. *Pride and Prejudice* was refused by return of post ; *Sense and Sensibility* was kept back ; and *Northanger Abbey* was bought in 1803 by a publisher in Bath, who paid £10 for the privilege of denying it to the world and condemning his own powers of judgment and decision by letting it lie by him for years, finally to sell it back for the sum which he had paid for it.

At the age of thirty-four Jane found a publisher who gave her £150—nearly a quarter of the entire sum at which the contemporary world valued her—for *Sense and Sensibility.* And it was not till sixteen years later that she offered *Pride and Prejudice* to a publisher for the second time and saw it accepted.

It has been found convenient to divide Jane Austen's life into two periods of activity. The first produced *Pride and Prejudice, Sense and Sensibility,* and *Northanger Abbey* at Steventon Parsonage ; the second, *Emma, Mansfield Park* and *Persuasion* at Southampton. A period of something like ten years lies between ; and so far as we can tell, without being wise after the event, they did not leave any trace on her mind.

Knowing the sad, quiet life of Jane Austen, we can

almost forgive the excessive praise that she has received ;
it is a post-dated cheque that has been duly honoured.
Throughout her life she chose to remain anonymous, and
so could smile at Fate for not recognising her. Then at
that moment when, with the Prince Regent assuring her
of his regard, it looked as though Jane were at last to be
seen at her real size, she went into one of those mysterious
declines that decimated the century. Her hopes almost
exactly balanced her rewards.

On her deathbed, when she was asked if she wanted
anything, she replied, " Nothing but death " ; the last,
sensible, modest, unreligious expression of a woman to
whom Life had been a joke that she had seen once too
often.

THE REIGN OF TERROR AND THE NOBLE SAVAGE

Walpole's *Castle of Otranto* established the Gothic architecture in fiction. It also established the Gothic archness in romance. Human qualities were magnified out of proportion, until they were distorted out of recognition, like noses in a shadowgraph. Villains remembered Iago and grew viler. Heroes wore the tethered-eagle look in their eyes, and grew more Byronic. Or, as perhaps we should say, Byron wore the tormented Gothic expression on his face, and grew more heroic. The supernatural was caught, hobbled and flogged without mercy.

For half a century in fiction the whole domestic furniture of civilisation was in the hands of necromancy. Doors opened at unseen pressures or unnaturally withheld themselves. Shrieks and reverberations were for ever coming from below stairs like the sounds of some fatal and unsuccessful plumbing operation.

Everything happened in the next room or on another floor. Portraits on the wall frowned, winked and grimaced unceasingly and unnervingly. A cupboard that contained no more than one skeleton would have been accounted empty. Ghosts waited in queues to appear. Those residents who were not ghosts were mostly certifiable.

It is no more necessary to catalogue the novels of this period, in order to depict them, than it would be necessary to enumerate every novel of the kind that followed *Sherlock Holmes* in order to describe detective fiction.

The Renaissance began moderately and grew immoderately. One of the first to attach herself to the movement that was to establish a Reign of Terror in Literature was Clara Reeve, a respectable spinster who wrote her first novel at the mature and unlikely age of fifty-one.

The novel was entitled *The Old English Baron : A Gothic Story*, but it was by no means the unfettered child of fever and romance that *Otranto* was. Clara Reeve, indeed, set out to write a kind of sceptic's ghost-story ; a tale of the supernatural for the plain man. In a modest and disarming Preface she wrote : " We can conceive, and allow of the appearance of a ghost, but it must keep within certain limits of credibility." And she went on to put her finger on the exact weakness in the fiction of the supernatural :

A sword so large as to require one hundred men to lift it ; a helmet that by its own weight forces a passage through a courtyard, into an arched vault, big enough for a man to go through ; a picture that walks out of its frame ; a skeleton ghost in a monk's cowl—when your expectation is wound up to the highest pitch, those circumstances take it down with a witness, destroy the work of imagination, and, instead of attention, excite laughter.

Perhaps it was her age, her unexcitable middle-age, that made Clara Reeve preserve such admirable calm before a ghost. Walpole, who probably disliked more than most men the idea that anyone had been laughing at him, declared that " *The Old English Baron* is so probable that any trial for murder at the Old Bailey would make a more interesting story "—a remark that sounds as rather less than a condemnation to modern ears.

Clara Reeve herself had misgivings that by straining to appear probable, she might have allowed the spirit of the piece to evaporate. And her story shows her to have been right. With the best will in the world it is impossible to create a ghost that is neither natural nor supernatural. But it is desperately and deceptively easy to create one that is merely unnatural. To appreciate any story which contains a ghost as an intrinsic part of it demands a suspension of disbelief, that is so willing as to constitute an original offer of credulity. And Clara Reeve chose the natural possibilities of terror rather than the far more exciting possibilities of the supernatural.

A chest containing a skeleton bound neck and heels together was as far as her macabre fancy took her. Indeed, the only naturally inexplicable event in the whole story is the sound of clashing arms and of a heavy fall somewhere—one of the subterranean plumbing episodes—on a lower floor.

The truth is that Clara Reeve was quite unsuited to her task. In a letter to a friend she wrote : " I have been all my life straitened in my circumstances, and used my pen to support a scanty establishment ; yet, to the best of my knowledge, I have drawn it on the side of truth, virtue and morality." Obviously such a woman had not been designed by Providence to scare the scalps off the simple.

Clara Reeve at fifty-one quite obviously was hardly the Child of her Age. But Ann Radcliffe, who was only thirty when she published her *Mysteries of Udolpho*, was so. If Providence had been ungenerous in Clara Reeve it was prodigal to prodigality in Mrs. Radcliffe. Her pen kept up a perpetual whimper of terror. Her characters move in a world not unlike that of a sick child's nightmare.

All the old familiar alarms of something-up-the-chimney and someone-underneath-the-bed are set out here in elaborate and competent narrative, admirably sustained by the machinery of suspense.

Emily, somewhat ashamed of her terrors, stepped back to the bed, willing to be convinced that the mind only had occasioned her alarm ; when, as she gazed within the curtains, the pall moved again, and in the next moment the apparition of a human countenance rose above it.

One wonders how any woman could bring herself to go to bed in such a house ; the more so because every bedroom seems to have been set square on the footpath between here and Hell. But apparently the characters got used enough to such incidents. They certainly learned to live through them.

Mrs. Radcliffe's pages are loaded with scenery—wild, rocky and romantic, like the blue landscape viewed through a Pre-Raphaelite doorway. It was the sort of scenery that is believed to lie around the Mediterranean ; a strange countryside of papal palaces, ruined monasteries and eremitical retreats. In a word, it was a native Roman Catholic landscape ; and it was a Roman Catholic landscape viewed through an English Protestant telescope.

This whole Romantic Revival or Renaissance of Wonder, indeed, was the child of Protestant reason. The English mind, tired of imaginative restraint, suddenly celebrated a giddy festival of liberty. It turned to those things that had the powerful attraction of mystery. And the weirdest thing that the English mind, moving in the channels of establishment, could imagine was the dark rite of the Roman Church. George Borrow even smelt Roman Catholicism in Walter Scott because the odour of romance was strongly there. And so it is that from Mrs. Radcliffe to that misguided artist, Charles Maturin, the chief actor in the Romance of Terror is the Church of Rome behaving strenuously as those outside it have always

believed, do now believe, and always will believe, that
it has behaved.

The Inquisition provided Mrs. Radcliffe with the material for her best story, *The Italian, or the Confessional of
the Black Penitents*. For there the Church, abstract, awful
and historical, was all the reason that could be needed
to account for any groans that reached the upper air.
And the next great alarmist in literature, Charles Maturin,
in his mysterious masterpiece, *Melmoth the Wanderer*,
drained the Roman Church of all the mystery that it
had accumulated through centuries of maturity in the
Protestant mind.

Charles Maturin contrived to live almost as romantic-
ally as he wrote. When he was a poor curate in Ireland,
an episcopal messenger waited on him with an offer of
preferment. The messenger continued to wait. Then unusual noises were heard, such as should come from no
vicar's clerk. At last in swam Maturin, mazily declaiming
passages from his own plays, his hair all stuck over with
quills like the straws in the March Hare's head. The scene
fades as rapidly as the preferment. We seem to see a vague,
retreating ecclesiastical figure merging into obscurity. But
Maturin, crazy and declamatory, steps right out of the
picture-frame of history and remains before our eyes.

Yet Maturin was not so cracked that he could not write
with at least the easy competence of those novelists who
are remembered to-day because they extracted interest
from the more nearly commonplace. *Melmoth the Wanderer*
begins as well and truly as any novel of the period. Maturin's picture of a miser almost became one of the memorable portraits of fiction. But from the moment when
his hero discovers one of those mouldering manuscripts
that are so common in this, the most illegible period of
English literature, and then has to listen for hours to an

ex-Jesuit's revelations about the Society of Jesus, we are aware that we are watching a novelist who has taken the wrong road and is walking fast in an effort to find himself again. Scott, in a review of *Melmoth*, declared that he had never seen " a more remarkable instance of genius degraded by the labour in which it is employed."

The refrain of the opening chapter in which a penniless and unsuspecting youth visits a solitary and eccentric relative, whose house is rather like a Chamber of Horrors on a Gala Night, is one which with variations has been played until our day. In the opening chapters of story after story we meet a handsome, natural being, hesitant upon the doorstep of one of the lonely Gothic madhouses of romance. The door is opened, and the visitor shining his torch of sanity around him, inspects the interior, until overcome by what he sees, he drops the torch and behaves as wildly as the rest of the Bedlamites. Finally he is shot out of the back door and sits on the top step, a madder and a wilder man. So assiduously was this formula applied in the century of its origin that the romance of terror became so highly developed a thing as to make it doubtful whether Edgar Allan Poe yesterday, or Mr. Julian Green to-day, has added anything to it.

Highly developed ; and highly profitable. Perhaps the most truly typical exponent of it was Matthew Gregory Lewis who soared into celebrity at twenty. Lewis is one of those freakish and fantastic little insects of which the enfolding amber of the eighteenth century is full. The son of wealthy parents, he travelled in Germany and caught there a chronic attack of Goethe while still in his teens.

His gross, ghastly, Germanic mediæval romance *The Monk* won him enough fame to last him through his busy, fussy lifetime, during which he wrote poems and set them to music, and struggled along on an allowance of £1,000 a year. He died in 1818 in his forty-third year, of yellow fever contracted while on a visit to Jamaica where he had been investigating the lot of the negroes and recommending in the manner of his century amelioration, but not emancipation. Such a life is truly the strange product of his age.

He had individual characteristics besides. " How few friends," Scott obliquely remarked of him, " has one whose faults are only ridiculous. . . . Lewis was fonder of great men than he ought to have been, either as a man of talent or as a man of fashion. He had always dukes and duchesses in his mouth, and was pathetically fond of anyone who had a title." Such was the " good-natured fopling," as Lockhart called him, who exploited the popular terror and love of cowled faces in impenetrable shadow that Mr. Edgar Wallace has successfully revived in the present day.

Lewis, indeed, made a fortune out of hiding round the corners of a much frequented by-way of literature and saying " Boo ! " to the public in a hollow, convincing voice.

The Reign of Terror is usually reckoned to have come to an end somewhere about the time of the publication of *Northanger Abbey*. There the arch, Gothic heroine received a humorous, rationalistic jab :

> You will proceed into this small vaulted room, and through this into several others, without perceiving anything very remarkable in either. In one perhaps there may be a dagger, in another a few drops of blood, and in a third the remains of some instrument of torture ; but there being nothing in all this out of the common way, and your lamp being nearly exhausted, you will return towards your own apartment. In repassing

through the small vaulted room, however, your eyes
will be attracted towards a large, old-fashioned cabinet
of ebony and gold, which, though narrowly examining
the furniture before, you had passed unnoticed. Impelled by an irresistible presentiment, you will eagerly
advance to it, unlock its folding doors, and search into
every drawer ;—but for some time without discovering
anything of importance—perhaps nothing but a considerable hoard of diamonds. At last, however, by
touching a secret spring, an inner compartment will
open—a roll of paper appears ;—you seize it—it contains many sheets of manuscript—you hasten with the
precious treasure into your own chamber, but scarcely
have you been able to decipher " Oh thou whomsoever
thou mayest be, into whose hands these memoirs of the
wretched Matilda may fall . . ."

Certainly the legions of demons that had conquered
romance were routed, not so much by an attack of a
more rigid rationalism or of a more religious religion, as
by an attack of the giggles. For it is a part of the convention of the supernatural that no ghost shall appear
ridiculous. And here Jane Austen had defied convention
and raised a laugh at the expense of Hell.

But the truth is, of course, that people did not cease
reading tales of terror from the moment that *Northanger
Abbey* appeared. Everyone, naturally, did not read
Northanger Abbey ; and there are always some people who
find shuddering easier than laughing. Thus, though
romantic parody became a fashion and almost a trade,
romance itself continued as the staple of fiction. Maria
Edgeworth's *Angelina*, or *L'Amie Inconnue*, and Eaton
Stannard Barrett's *The Heroine* could not destroy the
public taste for terror any more than jokes about

greediness could seriously undermine the appetite of school-boys. And so late as the first third of the nineteenth century, the gush of ghosts from the Minerva Press was continuing without abatement.

Mr. Lane, the publisher at the Press, founded the biggest circulating library of his day for the better dissemination of his frights and fictions. It was the sort of literature, like the detective literature of to-day, which is better read on loan than on purchase. Usually such fiction has been written without pains and can be read at least as fast as it was set down. It is rarely necessary to read such books twice. For no one with the best will in the world can be so terrified as he ought to be when he holds a complete dossier of the ghost's movements, before the case. The library alone satisfies the appetite and sharpens it.

And so it was that Hazlitt and Lamb and Macaulay, to say nothing of the unnamed rest of polite society, fattened their imaginations and their fears on the Fashionable Forgotten. Writers from Mrs. Mary Meeke to Mr. Barrett enjoyed a popularity then that might seem enviable even to-day. Theirs was easy and artless stuff to write, as Scott pointed out when he read a batch of such novels, and wrote :

> We strolled through a variety of castles, each of which was regularly called Il Castello ; met with as many captains of condottieri ; heard various ejaculations of Santa Maria or Diavolo ; read by a decaying lamp in a tapestried chamber dozens of legends as stupid as the main history ; examined such suites of deserted apartments as might fit up a reasonable barrack ; and saw as many glimmering lights as would make a respectable illumination.

Now into the midst of so much that was supernatural there came once more the Natural Man, the Noble Savage, an import from France bearing the trade-mark of Rousseau.

Rousseau wore a softer and a larger velvet glove than any revolutionary since his time. The *Nouvelle Héloïse* is a work of excruciating sentiment ; a Bolshevist bomb very cunningly concealed. Had such a bombshell attempted to enter England without the words " Honey : This Side Up" stamped on it, it would have been stopped at the Customs. John Morley remarked that the danger lay in " the mischievous intellectual direction which Rousseau imparted to the effusion "—which is rather obviously true.

The Noble Savage, who was thus introduced, immediately became one of the ruling class in fiction. At first he was merely a foil to throw up the vices of the civilised. By our time he has become a foil to throw up their virtues. The Noble Savage has given place to the Strong Silent Man ; both of them beings with the innocent moral ruthlessness of purpose of a steam-roller. Indeed, it has by now become a convention that the Strong Silent Man shall have either no morals or bad ones.

But though his actions may have changed from those of Adam in his simplicity to those of Casanova in his guile, outwardly he has remained immediately recognisable : " He was pretty tall. . . . His eyes were the most awful that could be seen, and very piercing. . . . His nose was rising and Roman." So might a modern novelist sketch the elemental man. So, in point of fact, did Mrs. Aphra Behn sketch him in 1689 in *Oroonoko*. And with the exception of the point of morals, the only outstanding difference between Mrs. Behn's hero and one of Miss Dell's was that Mrs. Behn's was suffering from the disability of the colour bar. The essential virility is the same.

In such a typically modern piece of fiction as Miss Ethel Mannin's *Ragged Banners* we see the return of the noble savage in his crudest form. The particular scene is so set that the reader's laughter all but destroys its significance. A woman novelist is shown mooning over her boudoir balcony, while below her the jobbing gardener sweats primitively at his labour.

> When she made her breakfast tea she took a cup out to the man. He straightened himself as she approached, and when she stood beside him the pungent smell of his sweating body came to her, sharply, acrid, and she was aware of the dark mat of hair on his chest. That and something she could not define, but it was as though life burned in him like a slow fire and the warmth and glow of it communicating itself to her, so that she was not Mary Thane, the novelist, handing a cup of tea to a jobbing gardener she had hired, but primordial woman in the presence of primordial man listening with her blood to the surge of life in him. She had this sudden blood consciousness of him, and because of it a shyness swept her. . . .

Disgusting and ridiculous? But it is not intended disgustingly, of that I am sure. The scene is intended rather to show how shocking it is that women who could glow like ingots in the furnace of passion (or some such phrase) should be left as cold and shapeless as the original ore.

It is the old story : The Savage showing the Civilised their defects. And the only difference is that our idea of the defects has changed.

With those novels in which the seeds and flowers of

revolution entered the country in disguise came a string of novels which even the most short-sighted policeman should have recognised for what they were. Yet somehow what slipped past the policeman contrived to enter the nursery.

We find such a handbook of gentle Bolshevism as *Sandford and Merton* becoming the infants' Bible. Thomas Day, in the ingratiating form of the parable, preached the exact spirit, if not the text, of Mr. Lloyd George's Limehouse Speech. A reader of the flowing passage who could not see that Mr. Barlow must have been in the pay of Moscow has been misled by the gossiping charm of the style.

The next morning Tommy was up almost as soon as it was light, and went to work in a corner of the garden, where he dug with great perseverance till breakfast : when he came in, he could not help telling Mr. Barlow what he had done, and asking him, whether he was not a very good boy, for working so hard to raise corn ? " That," said Mr. Barlow, " depends upon the use you intend to make of it when you have raised it. What is it that you intend doing with it ? " " Why," said Tommy, " I intend to send it to the mill that we saw, and have it ground into flour ; and then I will get you to show me how to make bread of it ; and then I will eat it, that I may tell my father that I have eaten bread out of corn of my own growing." " That will be very well done," said Mr. Barlow ; " but where will be the great goodness, that you sow corn for your own eating ? That is no more than all the people round continually do ; and if they did not do it, they would be obliged to fast ! " " But then," said Tommy, " they are not gentlemen, as I am." " What then," answered

Mr. Barlow, " must not gentlemen eat as well as others, and therefore is it not for their interest to know how to procure food as well as other people ? " " Yes, sir," answered Tommy, " but they can have other people to raise it for them, so that they are not obliged to work themselves." " How does that happen ? " said Mr. Barlow. T. " Why, sir, they pay other people to work for them, or buy bread when it is made, as much as they want." Mr. B. " Then they pay for it with money." T. " Yes, sir." Mr. B. " Then they must have money before they can buy corn." T. " Certainly, sir." Mr. B. " But have all gentlemen money ? " Tommy hesitated some time at this question ; at last he said, " I believe, not always, sir." Mr. B. " Why then, if they have not money, they will find it rather difficult to procure corn, unless they raise it for themselves." " Indeed," said Tommy, " I believe they will ; for perhaps they may not find anybody good-natured enough to give it them. . . ."

All very much like a child's manual of Communism, complete with leading questions and misleading answers.

At the same time, works not only of revolutionary purpose but of open propaganda were appearing. There was, for instance, William Godwin's *Things as They Are ; or the Adventures of Caleb Williams*, a positively Tolstoyan tract on the " corrupt wilderness of human society." Like Fielding's *Amelia*, it was directed against the grosser injustices of this world. There is an over-emphasised humanitarianism about certain of the passages that set the reader, with his heavy ballast of modern authors in his head, in mind of Mr. John Galsworthy weeping for the sins of society. In short, it comprehends most of the modern sympathies because it is parent of them.

There is, for example, the character of the felon committed for highway robbery.

The character of the prisoner (" a common soldier ") was such as has seldom been equalled. He had been ardent in the search of intellectual cultivation, and was accustomed to draw his favourite amusement from the works of Virgil and Horace. The humbleness of his situation, combined with his ardour for literature, only served to give an inexpensive heightening to the interestingness of his character. He was capable, when occasion demanded, of firmness, but, in his ordinary deportment, he seemed unarmed and unresisting, unsuspicious of guile in others, as he was totally free from guile himself. . . . His habits of thinking were strictly his own, full of justice, simplicity and wisdom. He from time to time earned money of his officers, by his peculiar excellence in furbishing arms ; but he declined offers that had been made him to become a sergeant or corporal, saying that he did not want money, and that in a new situation he should have less leisure for study. He was equally constant in refusing presents that were offered him by persons who had been struck with his merit ; not that he was under the influence of false delicacy and pride, but that he had no inclination to accept that, the want of which he did not feel to be an evil. This man died while I was in prison. I received his last breath.

All this piling up of perfection is intended to move the reader into a rage against the blind cruelty of the law, just as in the masterly ironic sentence in *Joseph Andrews*, which describes how " a lad who hath since been transported for robbing a Hen-roost " was the only person to

IF

play the Good Samaritan to poor, naked, half-dead Joseph ; and how while he stripped off his only garment he swore " a good Oath (for which he was rebuked by the Passengers) that he would rather ride in his Shirt all his Life, than suffer a Fellow-Creature to lie in so miserable a condition."

The Preface to the first edition of *Caleb Williams* contained the statement that the object of the work was to make " a general review of the modes of domestic and unrecorded despotism by which man became the all destroyer of man." Sheer anarchy : in other words, an attack on arbitrary government.

But it would have been easier to get a camel through the eye of a needle than so open a political libel through the bookshops. And the Preface was withdrawn from the original edition. When it was published, the author adds this sweet, brief note of explanation to it :

" Caleb Williams " made his first appearance in the world in the same month in which the sanguinary plot broke out against the liberties of Englishmen, which was happily terminated by the acquittal of its first intended victims in the close of that year. Terror was the order of the day : and it was feared that even a humble novelist might be shown to be constructively a traitor.

Godwin, the indignant anarchist, existing towards the end of his life on eleemosynary titbits from a tainted table, the man of genius, whose work drew the word " masterpiece" from Hazlitt, extracts what life he still has in our minds not so much from his fame, won by this and his later novels, which has declined, as from the part he played in one of the by-comedies of literature.

It was Godwin, after a lifetime spent in preaching

against the institution of marriage, who flew into a passion when he heard that Shelley, applying Godwin's principles, wanted to take Mary Godwin for his wife, while poor Harriet was still living.

Godwin called Shelley " licentious," while he meant merely " consistent," stowed Mary away, told her disagreeable stepmother to sit on her, and drove Shelley from the house. It is a little scene that has greatly comforted the orthodox at heart, this episode of the anarchist turning into the Christian father.

In the few years round the turn of the century, the novel began to throw out its arms, octopuswise, in some of the directions which are now familiar.

Thomas Holcroft, who was always the second-best man in whatever company he was in, played second-best to Godwin. Holcroft, whose novels *Anna St. Ives* and *Hugh Trevor* were simply the old didactic stories of the nursery, the good-boy-and-the-bad-boy sort of thing promoted into terms of political economy, has since been swallowed by his pupil.

SIR WALTER SCOTT

Booby critics have always loved taking a shy at Sir Walter Scott. Because he is by so much the biggest figure that had appeared in the whole field of fiction up to his time, he presents so huge a butt that all except the very wildest arrows of criticism are sure to hit.

Thus Carlyle fired a load of bolts at him in the famous review of the first six volumes of Lockhart's biography. Carlyle tried Scott on the serious charge of not having wanted to write like Carlyle. And he convicted him. It was Carlyle who said : " Your Shakespeare fashions his characters from the heart outward. Your Scott fashions them from the skin inwards, never getting near the heart of them." And we have to admit that at least as regards the principal characters it is something like the truth.

Scott is not even exciting to modern minds. To the historian he is a source of annoyance because he is disdainful of dates, and a thousand ages in his sight are like a moment gone. Judged by the standards of current psychological fiction he is so superficial as to appear silly. He is often too Scottish for the English reader. He was too romantic for Borrow ; and many readers used to the browns and greys of this century unhesitatingly reject the purples and scarlets of his.

Scott's heroines also are poverty-stricken creations : they are the mannequins of fiction, magnificent creatures that never come near to being the female of Man. Amy Robsart stands out among her sisters, a mournful mannequin.

Perhaps, however, we are suffering from one of the

temporary tyrannies of prejudice in imagining that because Scott's women are too uniformly handsome and virtuous they must therefore be a race of glowing cretins. In the romantic conception beauty did not come unprotected by brains.

Scott's heroes again, are often too much like handsome scout-masters to be entirely agreeable. All his characters, indeed, are conceived in the simple terms in which a child understands men and women. Scott knew passion only in its respectable form romantic love, and that so respectably that he has often been accused of not knowing it all. In *St. Ronan's Well* he wrote of incest but drained the passion of all its poison by making it simply a mistake of ignorance. Altogether his mind was a solid unemotional mind : it never soared and it never delved. To expect him to speak rapturously and convincingly of love would be like asking a delicate catlike modern novelist to describe a Border battle.

Scott's faults and short-comings are revealed every time an iconoclastic critic gets busy on him. Even Scott's prose, the mainstay of the narrative novelist, can be shown to be awkward, stubborn stuff judged by Southern standards. And a great deal that he wrote seems rather less than adult in its appeal :

To snatch a mace from the pavement, on which it lay beside one whose dying grasp had just relinquished it— to rush on the Templar's band, and to strike in quick succession to the right and left, levelling a warrior at each blow, was for Athelstane's great strength, now animated with unusual fury, but the work of a single moment ; he was soon within two yards of Bois-Guilbert, whom he defied in his loudest tone.

" Turn false-hearted Templar ! let go her whom

thou art unworthy to touch—turn, limb of a band of murdering and hypocritical robbers ! "

" Dog ! " said the Templar grinding his teeth, " I will teach thee to blaspheme the holy Order of the Temple of Zion " ; and with these words, half-wheeling his steed, he made a demi-courbette towards the Saxon, and rising in the stirrups, so as to take full advantage of the descent of the horse, he discharged a fearful blow upon the head of Athelstane.

This then in short was the Titanic incompetent who in 1814 made the first successful invasion of England from the North. This victorious crusade was the more remarkable since 1814 and 1815 saw the purple close of one of the most alarming cataclysms of European history. For anything to attempt to compete in the mind of an ordinarily intelligent man with the downfall of Napoleon must have seemed as patently absurd as presenting a debtor's letter at the Derby.

Book-selling, indeed, had a poor time in those years when Fact was leading Fiction by a length. But what were the books ? *Mansfield Park*, Wordsworth's poems, Southey's *Don Roderick* ; obviously none of them books to snatch up in the spirit of victory. The only author whose pulse was habitually above the normal was Byron ; and his *Lara* and *The Corsair* beat level with the public's heart.

Then in this exhilarating and military world along came an author who had wanted to be a soldier. And the public heart found itself keeping time to a fresh and more pounding rhythm.

It is wrong to think of Scott as one of nature's novelists turning up to fill one of nature's vacuums. He was not a novelist in an age of poets, but a poet in an age of novelists.

He had refused the Laureateship before *Waverley* had appeared.

In fiction, true, unlike poetry, it was the Golden Age of the Great Forgotten. Figures like " Monk " Lewis, Mrs. Radcliffe and Mrs. A. M. Bennett (who sold ten thousand copies of her six-volume novel *Vicissitudes Abroad* ; *or The Ghost of My Father*, at 36*s.*, on the day of publication) appear, and fade away again immediately like figures in a fog. The novel had spread with the popularity of the cross-word and the variety of human conversation. A critic in the *Edinburgh Review* remarked :

> This is truly a novel-writing age ! . . . Persons of all ranks and professions, who feel that they can wield a pen successfully, now strive to embody the fruits of their observations in a work of fiction. . . . It has been discovered that the novel is a very flexible and comprehensive form of composition, applicable to many purposes. There is scarcely any subject, not either repulsive or of a very abstruse nature, which must be of necessity excluded from it.

It was an age in which moralists were already growing alarmed at the amount of time that the fashion of novel reading consumed. And remembering the novels we may unhesitatingly place ourselves on the side of the moralists.

The commonest character in early nineteenth century fiction was the ghost, just as the commonest character in early twentieth century fiction is the corpse. But whereas detective fiction has never become quite the whole of fiction, the supernatural romance was the whole of fiction then. Scott rescued it. Among the orchestra of squeaks and shrieks and whistles and groans that comprised the contemporary novel Scott sounds like an entire organ in full blast with everything from the sixty-four-foot stop to the *vox humana*.

Scott himself was educated in the horrific ecstasy of German phantasy. It affected his heart, and all but affected his head. There is a record of young Scott, a child of his age, intoxicated with the vapours of hobgoblinry, staring into the fire and suddenly exclaiming, " I wish to Heaven I could get a skull and two cross-bones."

But Scott had a measure and a half of ordinary common sense. And though his romances were bright with the afterglow of the supernatural, he was never at the mercy of his own apparitions as most of his contemporaries were.

Scott indeed was at the mercy of nothing save his inexhaustible and consuming energy. He went through life as if he had hitched his wagon to a shooting-star. His strength even in his idle moments was always fully concentrated. When he walked out across the countryside for pleasure his appetite for fatigue was not satisfied until he had covered thirty miles. As a young man when he needed money he made it by copying legal documents at the rate of 3*d.* a folio, and could write one hundred and twenty folios without a break for food or rest.

The same driving restlessness within him drove him from bed by 5 o'clock, and Lockhart, on whose nerves the habit must have told, writes that :

He rose by five o'clock, lit his own fire when the season required one, and shaved and dressed with great deliberation, for he was a very martinet as to all but the mere coxcombries of the toilet, not abhorring effiminate dandyism itself so cordially as the slightest approach to personal slovenliness, or even those " bedgown and slipper tricks," as he called them, in which literary men are so apt to indulge. Arrayed in his shooting jacket or whatever dress he meant to use till dinner time, he was seated at his desk by six o'clock, all his papers arranged before him in the most accurate order, and his books of reference marshalled around him on the floor, while at least one favourite dog lay watching his eye, just beyond the line of circumvallation. Thus by the time the family assembled for breakfast between nine and ten, he had done enough (in his own language) " to break the neck of the day's work."

So it was that in those mornings, with night unregretfully forgotten, and day a revel of exercise eagerly anticipated, the novels were written, profuse with disorders that a lesser mind would have remembered and corrected. Scott's capacity for work is less described by saying that it was superhuman than by saying that it was inhuman. There is a glimpse of its inhumanity in the episode of a neighbour who looked into Scott's rooms and complained :

There is a confounded hand in sight of me here, which has often bothered me before, and now it won't let me fill my glass with a good will. . . . Since we sat down . . . I have been watching it—it fascinates my eyes —it never stops—page after page is finished and thrown on that heap of MS. and still it goes on unwearied— and so it will be till candles are brought in, and God knows how long after that.

That hand was writing *Waverley*. It needed to be strong : it was also to write half the fiction of the next fifty years. This ferocious midday to midnight energy gained for Scott the reputation of being a machine : which in an idle world that respects industry is by no means a bad thing.

But it also gained for Scott's works the reputation of being machine-made : which, unfortunately, is simply and invariably the solvent of all art.

There is a picture of Scott as the Celestial Coiner, assiduously minting money to pay off his partner's business debts, that has been thickly painted over the Portrait of the Author of a Young Man. And the later painting obscures exactly half the truth.

That Scott planned his life with the regularity of a tradesman has led many people to disregard all those qualities of mind that would not be appreciated behind a counter. And even when the other illusion of Scott as a Talking Tradesman has been dissolved, and he has been promoted in the imagination to the dignity of a study, there appears a rather suffocating set-piece showing Scott, prosperous and porcine, in a room littered with collie dogs and antiquarian armour, and bristling with bric-à-brac like Balzac's. Byron's vase is on the table, Montrose's sword on the bookcase ; an old Border bugle ; James VII's travelling-flask ; Rob Roy's sporran and long gun ; Claverhouse's pistol ; a brace of Bonaparte's ; and over all a beatific and inscrutable bust of Shakespeare presiding like an immutable Oriental Buddha.

It would be difficult to imagine anything lively taking place in such a room. One sees the ghosts of those qualities whose absence people deplore—the abstract, the passionate, the realistic—in retreat from an environment so overpowering. Yet the quality which was to be found in that museum of curios was that rare and obscure quality of common sense. Perhaps it was that Scott was thus constantly reminded that even the relics of the great had their price.

German romantic fiction had been a parody of just those qualities in man—courage, love, faithfulness and so forth—that have given life its nobility. And the early years of the nineteenth century saw the return of a life of true nobility into fiction by the circuitous route of a parody of parody. Just as *Northanger Abbey* opened in the manner of a schoolboy's going to Maskelyne's with the memory of his own conjuring-set at home in his mind, so *Waverley* begins with a sneer at the conventions of romance, even though the sneer soon gives place to a full-throated cheer.

Except for the humorous sanity of the interjections, the retrospective chapters of *Waverley*, that were written earlier than the rest, might be the opening chapters of any black-letter romance. There is the same Gothic Library ; the Great Park with its mouldered Gothic monuments ; the solitary island tower ; an upper atmosphere crowded with griffins, moldwarps and wyverns ; the grim uncle moping about the palace, like a family basilisk ; and Youth, aloof, supercilious and not unlike a valetudinarian Byron, already distinguished by his habits of abstraction and love of solitude.

Readers of Mrs. Radcliffe probably felt themselves perfectly at home in such surroundings ; as they did later in *The Bride of Lammermoor* and *Redgauntlet*. That may even have been why so many of them went on with it.

Yet it cannot have been that the capacity for doubt was entirely suspended in the public mind during the years of the black-letter. It has become customary to regard this period not as one of fancy, as it was, but as one of a kind of literary insanity. Probably nine-tenths of the novel readers of the day were only too thankful to the author who gave them the midnight delights of romance without calling upon them to surrender their daytime incredulity. For, with Scott, always through the mists of romantic material marched the facts of history—

and usually of recent history—hard, indisputable, and in continuous connection with the real business of human life ; like solid, tangible telegraph poles stretching across a mountain mist.

The modern sympathy in fiction is not so much with the spectacle of life as with the more delicate sensation of living. Indeed, the author as spectator was never less honoured than he is to-day. Scott's " big bow-wow " manner, and his habit of seeing life as a perpetual Military Tournament, jar on minds that know life only as a sort of Berkeleyan tree that does not exist except when someone is thinking about it. But when Scott was writing, English readers were slowly recovering from a surfeit of psychology. For Gothic romance, with its superficial encumbrance of physical ghostly gimcrackery was in reality a highly developed psychological literature, in which unfortunately all the major characters were a trifle mawkish, and all the minor characters a little mad. But, psychological it was ; and the success or failure of such a novel depended on whether or not the shivering along the spine was strong enough to reach the brain.

Scott lived to offer an escape from the psychological. John Murray, the publisher, in sending a copy of *Waverley* to his wife wrote, " It is excellent. No dark passages, no secret chambers, no wind howling in long galleries." And from that remark it is to be inferred that there was a movement afoot among readers, if not yet among novelists, for the better illumination of the darker and more dangerous corners of Gothic architecture, the throwing open of monk's holes, and the final exclusion of ghostly draughts.

From the moment when *Waverley* appeared English prose fiction was divided into those novels that were by Scott and those that were not. Scott's anonymity was merely a red-herring drawn along the trail. People followed it up with the nose of curiosity, and arrived one after another at—Walter Scott. When Maria Edgeworth received the three volumes of *Waverley* she replied promptly with a letter of thanks headed " Aut Scotus, aut Diabolus."

Why Scott chose to write anonymously is one of the minor mysteries of literary history. There is a hint in the Preface to *Waverley* when he explains that he was " too diffident " of his merit to place it in opposition to preconceived notions. And he goes on to refer to the " pages of inanity " of the last half century.

Scott, big, bland and a little awkward, was probably rather like an adult at a children's party, not wanting to be seen there by anyone unless it was certain that he was a success.

And he was a success. No other author, unless perhaps it was Dickens, has ever taken so much of the public's time to himself. His success was such that it became just as much a part of the mental picture of him as Goldsmith's poverty was of him.

There is an entire gallery of pictures of Scott in the circumstances of success ; the Prince Regent toasting him as the author of *Waverley* and, when Scott denied it, catching him on the toast of the author of *Marmion* ; the Duke of Wellington receiving him in Paris ; Blücher being polite to him ; Byron limping in and out of time with him down Murray's staircase in Albemarle Street.

Carlyle in the long quarrel with the shade of Scott that appeared as a review of Lockhart's *Life*, sickened at the sight of so great a measure of success. He searched the powder-magazine of his mind for suitable grenades, and slung out the remark that " Scott spent his life writing impromptu novels to buy farms with," and added the little squib that " with respect to the literary character of the *Waverley* novels the great fact is that they were faster written and better paid for than any other books in the world." The truth, of course, remains that such is not the great fact about them. It is no more than a conspicuous incidental, as Carlyle must have known.

Carlyle's real grievance against Scott was that he was a writer without a message. And Carlyle could not really appreciate a writer unless he behaved like a Parnassian postman. But Carlyle had a habit of talking sense even while in a temper. And in denying Scott the title of " great " (which he agrees is largely a matter of words) he gives us perhaps the best summary of essentials that can be made.

> He was, if no great man, then something much pleasanter to be, a robust, thoroughly healthy and withal a very prosperous and victorious man. An eminently well-conditioned man, healthy in body, healthy in soul, we will call him one of the healthiest of men.

Since Scott's work itself contains no record of the transit of a soul, which is what Carlyle would have liked, it is more than ever necessary to see the *Waverley* novels against the background of " Waverley " himself. For the novels are really the inessential part of Scott's life. He was never the sublime, inevitable artist. He brought a mature mind to his first novel.

It would not in any way be attacking his granite tenacity of purpose to suggest that if *Waverley* had failed he would never have written another novel. He was already forty-three years of age, life was running out and creditors' letters were pouring in. *Waverley* had more of urgent need in its publication than in its writing. It was a relief to the pocket rather than to the heart. Indeed there never was another man of substance whose diligent mind and industrious body were so at the mercy of his lavish manner. Whatever may be the natural economic standard of living for the author, Scott exceeded it. Unlike Fielding and Smollett, whose standard of life fluctuated with fortune, Scott insisted on conditions of grandeur, and raised an overdraft on his strength and talents, and ultimately on Time, to pay for it.

The spectacle of Scott well dressed and white haired, sweating his way to solvency and immortality, is one which restores faith in the crude possibilities of human nature. There is but a solitary groan that escaped his lips during this time, and that was when he cried out to his partner in business, " For God's sake treat me as a man and not a milch cow." For the most part Scott suffered in silence on £10,000 a year; for ever simultaneously catching sight of a fresh fortune and another farm. Wealth and rank were essential to him. Maria Edgeworth summed the truth up very nicely when she wrote, " Dean Swift said that he had written his books that people might learn to treat him like a great lord. Sir Walter writes his in order that he may be able to treat his people as a great lord ought to do."

The closing years of Scott's life and, indeed, the whole upward rush to senile decay and precipitate decline present a romantic spectacle which has aged, so far as many readers are concerned, much less rapidly than his literary romances have done. Scott's earthly pilgrimage may be plotted in a graph that has Money—and all that goes with it, Power and Pleasure and Independence—for its upright axis, and the one undefeatable factor, Time, for its horizontal. And the line of the graph flattens out as it crosses the paper, to droop alarmingly as it approaches the year 1825.

In that year Scott owed £10,000 worth of work to Constable and was proposing to borrow another £10,000 on his son's marriage contract and so " dispense in a great measure with bank assistance and sleep in spite of thunder." The trouble with Scott becomes evident here : it is not so much that he was in debt and proposing to wade in deeper, as that he had grown to think in units of a banker's magnitude.

There is an entry in his Journal for the 18th of December of that year that in its hopeless finality might be the last paragraph of an essay upon the vanity of human wishes :

> What a life mine has been ! half educated, almost wholly neglected, or left to myself ; stuffing my head with most nonsensical trash, and under-valued by most of my contemporaries for a time ; getting forward, and held a bold clever fellow, contrary to the opinion of all who thought me a mere dreamer ; broken-hearted for two years ; my heart handsomely pieced again, but the crack will remain till my dying day. Rich and poor four or five times ; once on the verge of ruin, yet opened a new source of wealth almost overflowing. Now to be broken in my pitch of pride.

Yet the destructive fire of energy within him was still burning and consuming. He who had been the halest, sanest, healthiest author in Europe was reduced to childish imbecility. Of the old Scott only his energy remained. " I am not sure that I am quite myself in all things," he said, " but I am sure that on one point there is no change, I mean that I foresee distinctly that if I come to be idle, I shall go mad." And before the end, that came with the gentleness of a benediction, he had insisted on being carried on his bed to his desk, given a pen in his hand, and propped up in his chair, a monstrous and pathetic imitation of an author.

There he was left until the unpleasant piece of comedy was over, and he had cried out, " Friends, don't let me expose myself ; get me to bed ; that's the only place."

That is the last appearance upon the stage of life of Sir Walter Scott the novelist. Two months later he died in bed at Abbotsford as peacefully as Queen Victoria in Lytton Strachey's portrait ; an old decayed man of sixty-one with the murmur of the Tweed, in place of the cawing of the rooks, in his ears.

THACKERAY AND THE NEW SNOBBISM

In the middle years of the nineteenth century, the merchant prince, first of his line and good for a hundred thousand, and the English Radical, who worshipped Rousseau in translation and opposed the Corn Laws, grew up side by side. And the English Radical, looking at the merchant prince over the high wall of unequal income, saw, not a commercial suburban sultan but a snob. Immediately a snob-scare started. Everyone was recognised as a snob. Even those born to the Patrician purple were degraded in the public mind to the level of inflated tradesmen who, in some colossal way, had forgotten not only their place but their price. And, naturally enough, the effect on the snob-hunters was deplorable. A new race of snobs, with noses trained to catch the scent of a distant title or the thin whiff of a putative annuity, grew up and overran society. And to these came Thackeray, like Mahomet to the waiting Faithful.

Considering the essentially mean nature of the prevailing public sentiment, the public did remarkably well to get Thackeray to be the author who was to make it articulate. He was, at least, a full-sized man. And he could spot snobs by looking at them from above—which is really a kind of heavenly rebuke ; and not by spying on them from below—which is often a pretty open kind of earthly envy. His Anglo-Indian origin left its mark on him, and he remained throughout his life the blond British *Raj* genially ruling in Pall Mall ; a member of the sacred oligarchy of democratic intolerance. Thackeray, indeed, is that singularly intractable beast, the Whig, with the isolated dignity of manner of the Tory.

It has been suggested that Thackeray was a child of the eighteenth century living a waif's existence in the nine-teenth. The pattern of his life was certainly of the eighteenth century. He squandered a fortune in youth, and spent the rest of his life in putting himself right with God and the bankers.

His aim as a novelist was much the same as Fielding's : to laugh at affectation. Both writers used the bludgeon of burlesque. But Fielding came before the discovery of the tear in fiction ; and Thackeray came after. Thackeray, therefore, wrote with his hand on his handkerchief. There infects his scenes a lachrymose gentleness that is as remote from the eighteenth century as it is from our own. And such a character as Colonel Newcome is indis-putably a figure of the century that was to produce Albert the Good, and not of the century that gave birth to Tom Jones.

Thackeray has often been blamed for his habit of drag-ging in characters out of one pair of covers, or even out of life itself, where they have earned fame and repose, and thrusting them between another pair. And it is not merely in the minor matter of one novel and another, but in the major matter of all his novels in relation to his *Book of Snobs* that this occurs. For, from this early catalogue of social exhibits came the hints of characters from Major Pendennis and Colonel Newcome to Lord Steyne and Miss Quigley, extending in infinite vigour and variety through his pages.

It has been suggested that Thackeray's soul, in the days when he contributed *The Snob Papers* to *Punch*, was being consumed by the worms of pride and envy. The hour now awaits the man who will explain Thackeray in terms of an inferiority complex. Only, unfortunately, when he does so, he will be wrong. For Thackeray was only about as acutely aware of his inferiority as the Lord Mayor on a Show day. The important fact about him was not that he was below, but that he was alone.

There never was a writer more sensitive to levels in society than Thackeray. He was inflexibly the gentleman, but a gentleman whose head was just a little too large to satisfy the fashion-plate ideal of a gentleman. It was Thackeray who first saw the whole chart of society spread out before him ; though, unfortunately, it was spread out in the club reading-room. And there is always a picture in the reader's mind of Thackeray, plump and urbane, crossing to the window to see if common folk were really as he imagined them, and if his map were properly orientated with Westminster in the south-west.

Since Fielding there had not been an author who could see so much of the spectacle of mankind through one glance of his wide open eyes as Thackeray saw. Jane Austen with her microscope and Scott with his telescope, saw far less. And so it was that the novel that had Society for its hero came into being. *Vanity Fair* was even called by the hero's name. This method of writing, however, has the almost insuperable disadvantage of growing more and more vaguely uniform as it proceeds. And it was to give the novel the variety that usually comes from individual human character closely observed that Thackeray had to bring out the comic noses and big moustaches of carica-ture.

One of the clues to Thackeray's genius, in fact, is to be found in those grotesque little boxes which he designed himself to decorate the uncials of his chapters. The frames are filled with gnomish little grotesques with noses that overhang their chests like bananas, or stick out in front like the superb and stately nose of the narwhal. They are the sort of drawings that would be punished if they appeared within the covers of a school exercise book. But Thackeray escaped punishment and even contrived to get paid for them.

Whenever he had the portrait of a character in his mind he began to decorate it with those ridiculous appendages, until it very soon ceased to be a man and became a fantastic little mandarin.

Half his characters have been christened on the altar of burlesque. Fat chuckles gurgle up from this innocent-hearted author when he thinks of a name of the sort that once seemed funny in the schoolroom. One can excuse Becky a good deal of her temper if she had to mix freely with people of the names of :

The Duchess Dowager of Stilton, Duc de la Gruyère, Marchioness of Cheshire, Marchese Alessandro Strachino, Comte de Brie, Baron Schapsuger and Chevalier Tosti.

No wonder that Thackeray has been accused—notably by Professor Saintsbury—of hating Becky !

The strange thing is that Thackeray's contemporaries, looking at the delicious shadowgraphs which were the animation of his books said " cynic " when they should have said " clown." In his own day Thackeray got a reputation for being a ferocious cynic and satirist. That was perhaps because he frequently called his characters " puppets "—with the suggestion, of course, that the rest of mankind were no more—and often dragged them aside to make room for the fat, pink face and sad, beaming eyes of their author.

Unfortunately, whenever the big, benevolent head

filled the scene it began to say foolish things. Thackeray
at times was no better than a pompous schoolmaster, who
would interrupt a football match to tell the boys that the
harder they strive to win, the sadder it will be if they
lose.

Indeed, if these were the things that Thackeray was
really wanting to say, and his air of seriousness at the
moment of saying them suggests that his works are little
more than elaborate theses designed to illustrate the
point that the preacher in Ecclesiastes was trying to make,
the reader cannot help wondering why he did not find
some simpler and more satisfactory way of making himself heard.

For Thackeray, within the somewhat strangling limitations of an unreliable vocabulary, a complete lack of any
sense of what to omit, and no unique depth of thought,
was a natural essayist. He had a mind in which the past
was always on tap ; a jolt which set it off on full sentimental gush.

Mr. Chesterton has said that : " Thackeray is everybody's past, is everybody's youth." The truth probably is
that the past always simplifies itself into a very simple
pattern. And it is because the remembered past of most
of us is much the same—a view over the shoulder of things
we have done that we ought not to have done, and things
left undone that we ought to have done, that Thackeray
has come to rule a larger corner of fiction than that to
which his intelligence alone would naturally have entitled him.

Thackeray was little of a thinker himself, and he perpetually wrote for readers who were less. He possessed in
remarkable degree the *style coulant*, a style which seemed
to say " *mots justes* may come, *mots justes* may go, but I go
on for ever." He left nothing unsaid in two or three easy

pages that could be said in a single difficult sentence. And anyone, who would follow, could follow.

About one-half of Thackeray's charm as a novelist, indeed, is due to the perfect gossiping ease with which he writes. His novels might have been told to us over the everlasting port at some eternal dinner-table. He is perpetually interesting. The mind of the listener, if not profoundly occupied, is at least always completely absorbed. Thackeray's pressure of invention is so great that every sentence has its own excuse for being. Every chapter, on the other hand, is twice as long as need be. And the action of the story is often reduced to a precarious competition with the story itself.

Anthony Trollope was immensely impressed by Thackeray's realism. " Whoever it is that speaks in his pages," he wrote, " does it not seem that such a person would certainly have used such words on such an occasion ? " The answer, of course, is that such persons do not exist anywhere save in the bright sunlight of Thackeray's imagination, where every wrinkle is visible and shadows fall more darkly than in life. Thackeray's characters speak truly to their types, in just the way in which Charley's Aunt is more perfectly herself every time she opens her mouth. Thackeray's are not perfect characters drawn from life, but perfect characters drawn from the stage complete with heighteners, padding and make-up. But when he made the remark Trollope was really comparing Thackeray's characters with those of Bulwer Lytton, who all talked as though they were descended in direct succession from a champagne bottle.

If Jane Austen is the novelist of the polite tea-table, Thackeray is the novelist of the polite dinner-table. The difference is approximately the difference between the two centuries. The early nineteenth century was the age of gastronomy. It was the age that made indulgence respectable by making it dignified.

In the generation which bridged Bulwer Lytton, Disraeli and Thackeray, the cook entered the novel in glory, and remained to preside as an Epicurean deity over fiction, with Brillat-Savarin as his prophet.

Lord Lytton rapturously devoted a chapter of *Pelham* to the adoration of the cook Guloseton. Disraeli, the Jew, showed his national taste for good cooking in *Tancred*, in his chapter on Lattimer. And Thackeray in *Pendennis*, produces the burlesque "Alcide Mirobolant," who made love as only an artist, and an artist sure of his public, could :

Her lovely name is Blanche. The veil of the maiden is white ; the wreath of roses which she wears is white. I determined that my dinner should be as spotless as the snow. At her accustomed hour, and instead of the rude *gigot à l'eau*, which was ordinarily served at her too simple table, I sent her up a little *potage à la Reine—à la Reine Blanche* I called it—white as her own tint and confectioned with the most fragrant cream and almonds. I then offered up at her shrine a *filet de merlan à l'Agnès* and a delicate *plat*, which I have designated as *Éperlan à la Sainte-Thérèse*, and of which my charming Miss partook with pleasure. I followed this with two little *entrées* of sweetbread and chicken ; and the only brown thing which I permitted myself in the entertainment was a little roast of lamb, which I laid in a meadow of spinaches, surrounded with croustillons, representing sheep, and ornamented with daisies and other savage flowers. After this came my second service : a pudding *à la Reine Elizabeth* (who Madame

Fribsbi knows was a maiden princess) ; a dish of opal-coloured plover's eggs, which I called *Nid de Tour-teraux à la Roucoule ;* placing in the midst of them two of those tender volatiles, billing each other, and con-fectioned with butter ; a basket containing little *gâteaux* of apricots, which I know all ladies adore ; and a jelly of marasquin, bland, insinuating, intoxi-cating, as the glance of beauty. This I designated *Ambrosie de Calypso à la Souveraine de mon Cœur.* And when the ice was brought in—an ice of plombière and cherries—how do you think I shape them, Madame Fribsbi ? In the form of two hearts united with an arrow, on which I had laid, before it entered, a bridal veil in cut paper, surmounted by a wreath of virginal orange flowers. I stood at the door to watch the effect of this entry. It was but one cry of admiration. The three young ladies filled their glasses with the sparkling Aÿ, and carried me in a toast. I heard it—I heard Miss speak of me—I heard her say, " Tell Monsieur Miro-bolant that we thank him—we admire him—we love him." My feet almost failed me as she spoke.

Thackeray's comic brilliance in such a passage strangely enough gives us a clue to his great limitation as a novelist. He knew as much about dining as Lord Lytton, and as little about eating as Disraeli. Life when it came to meet him wore a white tie, or an exceedingly dirty one. For Thackeray did know the taverns also. And they gave him such a shocking impression of debauchery—his *Cave of Harmony* is more like a temperance advocate's picture of a tavern than a novelist's—that he receded deeper and yet deeper into his shell in Pall Mall.

Perhaps it was his slight uneasiness in the modern world that sent him on his voyage of delightful discovery to the world of the Virginians. He did not approach it as a historical novelist would have done, with his nose to the ground for battlefields and the trails of marching men, but in very much the spirit in which a poet might return to Atlantis. There was a formality about life in Old Virginia, a discipline of dignity, that attracted Thackeray. In his mellow, melancholy masterpiece *Esmond* he was completely at his ease, as none but the great writers have been at ease with their subjects : and that despite the stilts of rigidly observed history upon which his language walked.

The one thing that Thackeray really wanted was home life. This he could never have. His young wife had fallen ill and lost her reason. After that, a meaner man might have continued his career with a perpetual grudge against life. But with Thackeray it was different. To the end he remained bruised, a trifle wounded, but on excellent if subdued terms with existence.

He became the man of clubs, the man of society, the man of letters. Success was placarded over him ; and it did not improve him. He grew to look more and more like a fat, pink Sphinx, always just on the point of saying something cleverer than he had ever yet said.

But even without ever actually saying it, he remains one of the talking giants of his century.

CHARLES DICKENS

To pass from Walter Scott to Charles Dickens is to pass from the real founder of the trade of fiction to the first journeyman of genius of modern times.

Praise of Charles Dickens passed saturation point a generation ago. Most of what has been said since has simply and inevitably sunk to the bottom, till the whole bottle of Dickens criticism needs shaking before using. And to find something to say about Dickens that is at once new enough to be interesting, and true enough to be worth being interested in, has exhausted more critics, perhaps, than the criticism of any other writer in the language, save Shakespeare.

It would be easy enough to shock people into curiosity by redrawing Dickens's portraits to show him as a specious and spiteful cynic (who after all is usually only a sentimentalist that has been rather badly snubbed) enjoying the sight of the cracks in the universe. Or to explain him in terms of social sadism, and call up the Smikes and the Little Nells, and the Olivers and the Davids as witnesses for the Crown.

But some subtler method will have to be found if we are to lead readers up the garden. Even though it is only a bouquet that is to be presented at the end of the path.

Strangely enough the true secret of Dickens's genius, to say nothing of his popularity, is to be found, not in any piece of remarkably profound criticism, but in a piece of sheer critical folly.

I refer to the remark commonly made by those who do not like Dickens, that he was writing down to the public. Such a remark would have astonished Charles Dickens. The wild irony of the little ten-year-old boy sticking labels on pots of blacking and solemnly patronising the great English nation would have delighted Dickens. For, as *David Copperfield* shows, young Charles Dickens, the baby on the treadmill, was a figure that remained in his imagination throughout his life. And Dickens, the golden, successful author, would take periodical dives out of prosperity back into poverty to look at life again through the eyes of fatigue and failure.

That memory of worse things, indeed, is about half the secret of his huge and human sympathy.

But to defend anyone against the charge of " writing down " is difficult. In the first place, it is not a charge at all ; it is a kind of grudging compliment. It implies a consciousness of the supreme importance of one's words, together with complete unscrupulousness about the use of them. The Parables are examples of the same kind of thing : heavenly truths designed for the consumption of earthly blockheads.

But Dickens did not speak from a point of isolation. When he emerged, he emerged among the blockheads. Dickens was the product, not of an act of God, but of an Act of Education. There was nothing airy about him : he was of the earth, earthy. He was quite simply and satisfactorily a member of the great British public.

Dickens has been heralded so long and so loudly as the author of the people that the truth that he never wrote about real people at all has been lost in the general din. If he had written about the poor as they really were, ninetenths of his contemporaries would have been merely annoyed ; and historians, not novel-readers, would have been grateful to-day.

He wrote, instead, about the poor as they manifestly

were not. He condensed the characteristics of eccentricity of a dozen men into a single man, so that if you met any one of the dozen you would declare that Dickens had hit him off. He made his characters entirely entertaining by making them only partly lifelike. He created a world like, even ludicrously like, our own, but with startling differences. It was about as near to the world of real life as the world of Harlequinade is.

Santayana, in a single sentence, has expressed this by saying that " the secret of this new world of Dickens lies . . . in the combination of the strictest realism of detail with a fairy tale unrealism of general atmosphere."

Mr. E. M. Forster has found nearly all the people in Dickens " flat characters " ; characters who, like a notice-board, have one obvious purpose, and are meaningless when looked at from anywhere but in front. They are characters, he argues, of remarkable singleness of motive ; and singular simplicity of obligation so far as the novel is concerned.

" Nearly every one of them," Mr. Forster writes, "can be summed up in a sentence, and yet there is this wonderful feeling of human depth. Probably the immense vitality of Dickens causes his characters to vibrate a little, so that they borrow his life and appear to lead a life of their own. It is a conjuring trick ; at any moment we may look at Mr. Pickwick edgeways and find him no thicker than a gramophone record. But we never get the sideway view." That is quite true. We do not. And for the very reason, that no good actor talks over his shoulder to the audience.

For Dickens, it should be remembered, was a novelist with all the instincts of a dramatist. And he fitted all his characters with little tags that they could pull out as soon as they came on the stage he built for them. Polonius,

Mr. Pickwick, Falstaff, Mr. Micawber, Mr. Surface, Mr. Squeers, are all characters that could exist perhaps better on the stage than in a novel. They have all the qualifications for a good dramatic career. They are instantaneously recognisable, and they are masters of mannerism. They are always splendidly and isolatedly themselves. And because of some obscure vagary of the human intelligence their habit of saying the same thing, or the same sort of thing, with the remorseless iteration of a parrot, further endears them to their audience every time they say it.

To some extent they are the wastrels of prose fiction, these flat characters. I qualify the extent of their failure because, though it is easy enough to explain their charms away, their remarkable success obstinately remains. It is the flattest characters that often have the fattest reputations.

But the novel offers possibilities, carrying responsibilities with them, that do not exist in drama. The dramatist, with the supreme advantage of being able to put his characters—or, at least, flesh and blood people that, for a weekly arrangement with the manager, are willing for some hours every day to swear that they *are* the dramatist's characters—before his audience, also has to pay the supreme penalty. The field of life that is open before him is no larger than that illumined by an old-fashioned spyglass. He can exhibit everything material about his characters with incomparable ease of conviction. But in reality only a fraction of what happens to a man is capable or necessary of exhibition.

Indeed, when it comes to understanding the mind, it is a mere distraction to see the body—five feet six inches of it—and a face like someone's we know. Like a priest in a confessional we need to erect a filter between ourselves and the body of the other soul, so that nothing irrelevant and distracting can penetrate.

And here the novelist is more fortunate than the dramatist. He can describe. He can remove the mind, by a piece of surgery that is almost invariably fatal in drama, and concern himself and his readers with it alone. He could keep Hamlet in soliloquy for a chapter, or two, or three, or for an entire novel if he wanted, instead of for a mere sixty-six lines. In short, the novelist has incomparable opportunities for providing his characters with a complete armoury of conflicting emotions and fears and ecstasies and sentiments, in addition to their primal literary motive ; of making them real men, capable of failure—even of failure within the limits and intentions of the book ; like the characters in a Russian novel that drift, aimless yet accurate, across the pages, and finally swerve right out of sight executing the broad curve of the question mark.

But with Dickens, as with Scott, his popularity is not so much a matter of present taste as of historic fact. To follow the small boy in the blacking warehouse, merging into the solicitor's clerk, becoming a parliamentary reporter whose voracious appetite for knowledge drove him into that huge, dull, circular eating-house, the British Museum Reading Room, contributing first his paper, " A Dinner in Poplar Walk " to the *Monthly Magazine*, and then his " Sketches by Boz " to the *Evening Chronicle*, and finally receiving one hundred and fifty pounds for them on republication, is to follow a young man on a prosperously ascending curve.

And to continue the curve so far as the publication of the *Pickwick Papers* is to arrive at a point that establishes Dickens on a unique pedestal of public good favour. The popularity of the *Pickwick Papers* grew with them.

Of the first part 400 copies were bound : of the last 40,000.

To call the *Pickwick Papers* an example of the slip-shod, shambling work that Dickens produced is to waste criticism. It never was a novel. It was a great bundle of comic sketches published month by month, that comes no nearer to being a novel than a convivial evening's songs, bound between covers, would come to being a cantata.

But even if it was not a novel, it anticipated all that was to be characteristic of Dickens's novels. There was the same verbosity : the same rush of little inventions that go branching off the main stem like the tails on a monkey tree ; the dismal clichés ; the innocent and irrepressible vulgarity of the comedy.

That it was the work of a sentimentalist may be seen from the way in which Dickens puts the hands of his clock back to yesterday, the day in which all sentimentalists live. The background of his novels, indeed, was always the background of his own childhood. Coaching was as much out of date in Dickens's time as hansom cabs are now. The inn of escapades and adventures had already given place to the railway hotel of time-tables and propriety. But Dickens, like Smollett and Fielding, set out to erect a memorial to an age that was rapidly slipping out of sight.

Most of Dickens's novels, in fact, were out of date within his lifetime. To-day, when they are definitely antique, it does not worry us that they should once have been old-fashioned. But at the time it did.

One of the earliest critical commentators, Adolphus William Ward, writing in 1882, remarked, with the date stamped large on every word : " It would, of course, be against all experience to suppose that to future generations Dickens, as a writer, will be all that he was to his own. Much that constitutes the subject, or at least furnishes the background, of his pictures of English life, like the Fleet Prison and the Marshalsea, has vanished, or is being improved off the face of the land." But without drawing out the old tag, that human nature remains constant from age to age, we may say that farcical humour remains constant. Dogberry and the watch, and Fielding's watchman and Mr. Samuel Weller and Mr. W. W. Jacobs's nightwatchman are all members of an immutable brotherhood. And it does not matter that the Reform Act has made impossible a second election of Eatanswill. With farcical comedy it is enough that such things should have happened once.

After the *Pickwick Papers*, Dickens's genius split into two halves : art and energy. The first increased : the second diminished.

If *Pickwick* had been written with only as much vivacity and invention as went into *Little Dorrit*, it would have sagged throughout its artless length. If *Little Dorrit* had been as clumsy in construction as *Pickwick*, it would have nothing to commend it. As it is, each has something, and each has enough. For Dickens even in dilution remains unmistakably Dickens. And though *Our Mutual Friend* is poorish Dickens compared with, say, *David Copperfield*, and *The Mystery of Edwin Drood* is quite good Wilkie Collins, both are plainly stamped with the signature of " the Inimitable."

That his invention wore thin is hardly surprising; he was writing with the printer at his elbow : not once was he a number ahead in the whole course of the periodical publication of *Nicholas Nickleby*.

Dickens has won a false reputation as a social reformer. He was something quite distinct. He was the warm-hearted, hot-headed, sentimental humanitarian, with

LF

nerves permanently on edge at the callousness of the rest of the world. His sort are a fair barometer of the feelings of the best ; they are never anything to the worst.

Charles Reade, the good Samaritan, stuffed with facts from Blue Books as well as with indignation, was the true reformer; the kind of man to convince an M.P. Dickens's heart was always bleeding for someone ; always rebelling against injustice.

This gallant anger was a substitute for much else in his life. His youth had left him insensible to those subtle things that are appreciated most by those who have known them when young. The world of formal beauty was undiscovered by him. Religion was a country that he saw only in passing through, and disliked. Ecstasy in any form was unknown to him. And in his novels he gives as much thought to love between the sexes as a healthy boy of twelve does. He enjoyed the comic gaucheries and pink-and-white tenderness of love-making without appearing even to understand what lay behind it all.

Yet Dickens himself was an exquisite and beautiful lover. It is true that he married the wrong woman. But the right one—his own sister-in-law—was so much to him that perhaps he left any hint of passionate devotion out of his books for the sincere and human reason that he disliked talking about it.

The girl was only seventeen when she died in 1837. " If she were with us now," Dickens wrote in his Diary, " the same willing, happy, amiable companion, sympathising with all my thoughts and feelings more than anyone I knew ever did or will, I think I should have nothing to wish for but a continuance of such happiness." And, in a letter to her mother, he wrote : " After she died, I dreamed of her every night for many weeks, and always with a kind of quiet happiness, which became so pleasant to me that I never lay down at night without a hope of the vision coming back in one shape or another. And so it did."

Sooner or later some sublimely confident writer will assess the mystic contribution of Mary Hogarth to the genius of Charles Dickens. Possibly we have assessed it already in saying that he excluded real love from his novels with more than merely a casual disregard for it. For Mary was always in his mind. In his fifty-seventh year he wrote : " She is so much in my thoughts at all times, especially when I am successful, and have greatly prospered in anything, that the recollection of her is an essential part of my being, and is inseparable from my existence as the beating of my heart is."

Those last years had a sad influence on Dickens. Like Scott, he was trapped in the pit of his own energy. He was impelled through all the exhausting business of daily work, though the excuse for it was entirely absent. Like Scott, again, he rested his mind by walking great distances to tire his body.

But he was consuming his own frame by his restlessness. Even his handwriting shows how cruelly his body was being overdriven. He was naturally a whole platoon of men : but he tried to do the work of an army. To those that met him the essential concentration of vigour, of life even, was at once apparent. Leigh Hunt declared : " What a face is his to meet in a drawing-room ! He has the life and soul in it of fifty human beings."

And in the end, his face of steel—as Mrs. Carlyle called it—led to his destruction. It was such a magnificent headpiece that he could not be persuaded to cease displaying it. Dickens was an actor who had been suffered to escape from the stage. But the love of having all eyes fixed upon him remained.

Up to middle-age he commanded all the attention that he could desire simply by letting the perpetual fountain of his imagination send up its clouds and rainbows across the crowd. But as the fountain began to choke in its depths he adopted other means of attracting notice.

He became like a little god stepped down from his altar and gone off to canvass for new worshippers in the streets. He was as much a national figure as the Great Duke. People would break from the crowd to press his hand and thank him for having been himself: all of which was so gratifying that it led Dickens into giving that tragic series of readings, throughout the length and breadth of the country, that ultimately killed him.

There is something rather chilling to the spirit in the notion of the ageing author abandoning the quietude of his study to become a sort of giant performing flea.

Had it been a lecture tour that ended in tragic failure it would have been easier to approve than was this reading tour that closed in colossal success. The records that Dickens had been making all his life might simply have been gramophone records for the use he made of them. For with nothing new to say—only supreme art in knowing how to say it, how to perform, how to move, how to impress—he was content with proving and re-proving to himself and others that he was a great popular attraction.

With the delicacy of feeling of a box-office manager he records how " Eleven bank-notes were thrust into the pay-box . . . for eleven stalls," and boasts that " Neither Grisi nor Jenny Lind, nor anything nor anybody seems to make the least effect on the draw of the readings."

He gave eighty-seven readings in under four months and declared : " I seem to be always either in a railway-carriage, or reading, or going to bed. I get so knocked-up, whenever I have a minute to remember it, that then I go to bed as a matter of course "—just as though he were an overworked actor in a provincial stock company. And the extraordinary thing is that Dickens could not see that he was degrading himself.

When the strain of being Dickens finally killed him, there came one of those undignified but well-intentioned competitions for the remains, that mar the decent burial of the great. Dickens had wished to be interred at Gad's Hill, and once had felt a passing desire to be disposed of in a disused graveyard beneath the walls of Rochester Castle.

And because he was a man whose singular cogency of thought had startled the whole world, as soon as he was dead, his wishes were overridden and he was treated as though in life he had not known his own mind.

First, the Dean and Chapter of Rochester Cathedral petitioned for the remains. Then, Arthur Stanley, the Dean of Westminster, applied. And Dean Stanley won. Dickens, against his wishes, was buried with all possible decorum in the circumstances, in the Poet's Corner.

It is no profit to say that a brain of the singular brightness of Dickens's is a national property. Dickens directed his entire life on the assumption that it was not, and that he was his own indisputable master; and the whole circumstances of the funeral show that sometimes only those who work in the brightest colours of the comic and fantastic get near to portraying accurately the world of fact.

THE BEST OF THE SECOND-BEST

Imagine the rocket of true genius bursting in the night sky of Victorian prose fiction and you will see the two durable and brilliant suns of Dickens and Thackeray drifting away in opposite directions ; an iridescent twin-star that is the Brontës soaring to sudden and magnificent extinction ; and a nebula of smaller stars—for this was the golden age of the second-best—glittering and glowing, half of them being blotted out in the moment of their conception.

Attach names to them and you have among the bright glittering ones Bulwer Lytton and Disraeli ; among the red-hot, glowing ones, Kingsley, George Eliot and Charles Reade ; and among those neither bright nor burning, Anthony Trollope, Wilkie Collins, Mrs. Gaskell—though in *Ruth* she burned as brightly as any of them—and those two untiring and unenterprising historians who posed as novelists, G. P. R. James and Harrison Ainsworth.

Leaving the hair-oil and damask group, and the pamphlet-and-platform party, for a moment, the most considerable artists we meet are George Eliot and Anthony Trollope, the best of the second-best.

George Eliot, *née* Mary Ann Evans, is conspicuous as the novelist of sanity and common sense. If you like the manner of the female preacher and continuation-school teacher you will like George Eliot. She is religious and confident and independent.

Adam Bede, for instance, is the best protest in all fiction against the Chadband type of Dickens caricature of Nonconformity. Dinah Morris, despite her permanent,

unblinking, Salvationist smile is a living woman, the first
of a long line. Indeed, George Eliot's heroines, such as
Dorothea from *Middlemarch*, are better drawn than those
of any other woman novelist. That was because George
Eliot was perfectly unsentimental ; she was masculine in
mind as well as in the name she assumed. That George
Eliot's mind was such a calm, moderate mind, Leslie
Stephen has suggested, was due to the calm, moderate
Warwickshire countryside in which she was brought up.
It may have been. I am doubtful of these geographical
explanations. What we can safely say is that the differ-
ences between George Eliot and the Brontës are as the
differences in their native landscapes.

So far as the present generation is concerned, George
Eliot's clerics have aged more rapidly than those of Anthony Trollope. He has come in as she has gone out.

Trollope nearly became a second Jane Austen ; but not
knowing, only imagining, the world of which he wrote,
he was kinder, and so lost the opportunity.

The coral structure of life within the bright glass-case
of the novels is the same ; and within the limitations of
the circumscribing rim their measure of success is very
much the same.

Trollope, like his friend Thackeray, faced middle-age
with his soul in good, charitable working condition, but
slightly battered from ill-usage in youth. And it was not
until after middle-age that he wrote his best. Unlike the
scream-till-someone-hears-us band of social reformers,
who invaded fiction about this time, he used his novels
not as a protest against persecution but as a precaution
against poverty. And to his unromantic and logical mind
the one *was* the other.

He simply wrote the best novels that he could write,
and sold them as Scott did his for the highest figure that

he could get. But once the truth got about that he had the acumen of a tradesman as well as the art of an author, everyone forgot the latter in utter disgust at the former. His contemporaries could never quite forgive the penniless, dirty-faced little boy who contrived to make £70,000 by his pen.

Trollope's *Autobiography* is the kind of reminiscent volume that a successful butcher might have written had he suddenly grown perfectly and persuasively articulate. I suppose without doubt it is vulgar, supremely vulgar, this record of a huge horseman riding roughshod over other people's heads.

It is a strangely stunted production : from it is excluded even a glimpse of the worlds of beauty, or passion, or anything higher than ambition. It is the story of a man's backing himself heavily in the race of life and winning. It reminds one of the dream that is embodied in Smiles's *Self-Help*, pleasantly and plentifully come true.

> My marriage was like the marriage of other people, and of no special interest to anyone except my wife and me. It took place at Rotherham in Yorkshire, where her father was the manager of a bank. We were not rich, having about £400 a year on which to live. Many people would say that we were two fools to encounter such poverty together. I can only reply that since that day I have never been without money in my pocket, and that I soon acquired the means of paying what I owed.

The marriage " was like the marriage of other people " —that is the remark of a verger not of a bridegroom. And the rest of the quotation shows a mind as little affected by the sentimentalities of marriage as Jane Austen's, and

THE BEST OF THE SECOND-BEST   169

as fully aware of the economics. But throughout the *Autobiography* there is one quality even more apparent than its vulgarity. And that is its honesty. Trollope's *Autobiography* says all those things that one suspects other authors of having felt, and left unsaid.

Trollope extracted as much pleasure from the business of success as Arnold Bennett did. Both men were impressed by themselves, and both men loved conveying the impression. There was always a look-first-at-this-picture-and-then-on-that invitation in Trollope's personal writing. This is the diptych :

> I remember well, when I was still the junior boy in the school, Dr. Butler, the headmaster, stopping me in the street, and asking me, with all the clouds of Jove upon his brow and all the thunder in his voice, whether it was possible that Harrow School was disgraced by so disreputably dirty a little boy as I.

That was when he was seven, the helpless child of ruined parents. And this is when he was sixty-three; fat, defiant and captain of his fate.

> It may interest some if I state that during the last twenty years I have made by literature something near £70,000. As I have said before in these pages, I look upon the result as comfortable, but not splendid. . . . If the rustle of a woman's petticoat has ever stirred my blood ; if a cup of wine has been a joy to me ; if I have thought tobacco at midnight in pleasant company to be one of the elements of an early paradise ; if now and again I have somewhat recklessly fluttered a £5 note over a card-table—of what matter is that to any reader ? I have betrayed no woman. Wine has brought me to

no sorrow. It has been the companionship of smoking that I have loved, rather than the habit. I have never desired to win money, and I have lost none. To enjoy the excitement of pleasure, but to be free from its vices and ill effects—to have the sweet and leave the bitter untasted—that has been my study. The preachers tell us that this is impossible. It seems to me that hitherto I have succeeded fairly well.

There is about that passage and, indeed, about the whole of the *Autobiography* the self-satisfied glee of the schoolboy who has managed to break all the rules without being punished.

Trollope, cheating his father's bailiffs at fifteen and living within his income at fifty like a squire, is truly and typically the pattern of a Victorian author, as Fielding or Smollett, tracing the reverse course through life, is of the eighteenth century.

When Trollope left school his contemporaries went to the University and he went into the Post Office. His contemporaries are all forgotten by now, partly no doubt because the life they found there fitted them like a glove and they wanted to do nothing but wear it. The Post Office fitted Trollope like a thumbscrew and he spent years trying to fling it off. He regarded the years spent at St. Martin's-le-Grand merely as a particularly barren patch of the great Sahara that spread across his early life. The truth probably is that they comprised his imaginative Garden of Eden, out of which a river flowed. It must have been there, as inescapably surrounded by the society of his fellows as a monk, that Trollope learned with tears of boredom the comic littleness of man.

It may seem puzzling why Trollope did not write the supreme novel of the Civil Service. And the puzzle is perhaps most satisfactorily solved by saying that he could not because he disliked it too much. If he had attempted it he would have been looking round the whole time for faces to punch instead of for noses to pull. And pulling clerical noses was what he did to perfection in the Barchester novels. When he tried in *The Three Clerks* to write the novel of the Civil Service he failed as unmistakably as he succeeded in *The Warden.*

Indeed, Trollope, after he left the Post Office, may be regarded as the complete novelist, his mind driven back into itself by unhappiness, and with a digested store of humorous observation ready for delivery. All that he needed to begin his writing was a similar restricted scene of society in which to let his little comedy be played. And he found it in Salisbury.

When Trollope took the train to Salisbury, Fortune drove the engine and Mischief rode in the van. " I visited Salisbury," he wrote, " and whilst wandering there one midsummer evening round the purlieus of the cathedral, I conceived the story of *The Warden*, from whence came that series of novels of which Barchester with its bishops, deans and archdeacons was the central site "; and he added, " I never lived in any cathedral city except London, never knew anything of any Close, and at that time had enjoyed no peculiar intimacy with any clergyman."

Of course he had not : " peculiar intimacy " is one of the easiest ways of destroying the capacity for humorous observation. Trollope's real strength lay in the fact that he knew—he was one of those men who can acquire instinct at a glance—the life of clergymen without suffering from the hobbling restriction of knowing the clergymen themselves. In consequence he could openly laugh in their faces, which they enjoyed, and not behind their backs, which no one would have liked. If Trollope had really lived in a real Barchester he would have been simply the Cathedral Untouchable. As it is he is the greatest layman of ecclesiastical letters. And so it is that Barchester and Barsetshire, the one really convincing rural Ruritania out of many, came into existence out of the imagination and not out of experience. That Barchester *is* convincing, is despite rather than because of Trollope's art as a story-teller. For he *would* adopt the maddening habit of assuring his readers that they were merely fiddling about with fiction, instead of allowing them the illusion that they were being given some miraculous opportunity for handling life : which is the object of every intelligent novelist.

There is, for instance, the heart-breaking opening to *The Warden :*

> The Rev. Septimus Harding was, a few years since, a beneficed clergyman residing in the cathedral town of—let us call it Barchester. . . .

That is very much like bursting the bubble before it is blown. And Trollope's activities with a pin are some of the most regrettable pieces of destructive work in fiction. Henry James said of them :

> These little slaps at credulity are very discouraging, but they are even more inexplicable, for they are deliberately inartistic, even judged from the point of view of the rather vague consideration of form, which is the only canon we have the right to impose upon Trollope . . . when Trollope suddenly winks at us and reminds us that he is telling us an arbitrary thing, we are startled and shocked in quite the same way as if Macaulay or Motley were to drop the historic mask and

intimate that William of Orange was a myth or the Duke of Alva an invention.

Trollope had other faults. His plots were like haddock lines with rows of hooks on which to hang things—usually comedy—and nothing more. His mind recognised nothing stranger than a curate with a funny face like Mr. Slope. But as a story-teller Trollope can hold up his head and his reader's time with any.

There are other Trollopes than the Puck in the Cathedral Close. In all, Trollope wrote fifty-one novels as well as travel books and biographies. The last years of his life were like those of a smaller and unworried Scott, spent in feverishly paying off debts that did not exist.

Trollope wrote quickly and often badly. *Dr. Wortle's School* is a sudden bright spot of real Trollope amid works that satisfied their purpose the moment they were paid for. Towards the end of his years, Anthony Trollope was merely the vulgarly successful literary merchant taking his revenge out of Life for having kept him short of pocket-money when at school.

THE INDEPENDENT BRONTËS

Haworth Parsonage in 1840 was absurdly overcrowded with female genius. That bleak house set in a barren landscape was the kindling point of one of the celestial burning-glasses of the imagination. Indeed, so intense is the imaginative quality in the work of Emily and Charlotte that *Wuthering Heights* and *Jane Eyre* might serve better as the theme for a sonnet than as a subject for criticism. Not only did the novels of the Brontë sisters handle those thoughts that poetry can handle better than prose, but their own lives were planned in the pattern of poetic tragedies. And Charlotte, whose life spanned the abrupt, glowing fragments of the lives of Emily and Anne, was both spectator and actor in the play.

The Brontës mixed life and work so much in one that it is hard to say where the one stops and the other begins. There are few authors for whom the critic has to wait so often and so patiently on the biographer : Mrs. Gaskell is not an incidental luxury but a critical necessity.

Because the Brontës are so manifestly inexplicable, new explanations of their unique genius succeed each other in rapid succession. One of the most common of these is to explain the Brontës in terms of local geography, and attribute the wildness of their minds to the wildness of their native scenery. It is a good explanation, except that it fails to explain how it is that Brontës are not born in every wild and lonely corner of Great Britain.

Haworth Parsonage has undergone that distortion in our minds which occurs when we look at anything too long and too hard. We have come to see it only as the cold mortuary where the bodies of the Brontës rested briefly in their quick passage to the churchyard, and not as the home where a family of children enjoyed all the ordinary juvenile freedoms of body and imagination.

It is true that Fate in that household seems to have been both hard and in a hurry. There was a door—one would almost say *the* door, for symbolists have set it so large in the foreground of the picture—between the house and the graveyard. And the door opened and shut too often and too soon. In 1821 Mrs. Brontë died and was carried through. In May, 1828, Maria followed her, and a month later her sister, Elizabeth. Then Fate stood off for a space—for twenty years, letting two of this family declare their worth and the third his worthlessness—and then it struck them down, one, two and three.

First there was Branwell Brontë, drunken and drugged, who yet retained sufficient of that almost fanatical independence of mind which distinguished all the Brontës to carry out his old, defiant resolve of dying standing upright.

Then, less than three months later, Emily's body withered into death. Charlotte wrote of her :

Never in all her life had she lingered over any task that lay before her, and she did not linger now. She sank rapidly. She made haste to leave us. . . . Day by day, when I saw with what a front she met suffering, I looked on her with an anguish of wonder and love. I have seen nothing like it ; but, indeed, I have never seen her parallel in anything. Stronger than a man, simpler than a child, her nature stood alone. The awful point was, that, while full of ruth for others, on herself she had no pity ; the spirit was inexorable to the flesh ; from the trembling hand, the unnerved limbs, the fading eyes, the same service was exacted as they had rendered in health. To stand by and witness this, and not dare to remonstrate, was a pain no words can render.

That passage is as memorable a monument to Charlotte as it is to Emily. And in that single brave, bright phrase, Biblical in its brevity, broad in its comprehension, " stronger than a man, simpler than a child," there is a hint of the difficulty that has beset the commentators of Charlotte Brontë. For Charlotte Brontë not only lived life in its largest terms but had also the natural eloquence to describe such existence. The company of those who have written about her has not yet produced one with the swift sweep of language of the original. And all reports of the emotional intensity of the alpine moments of her novels, as for instance, of that lonely drifting cry of Rochester in *Jane Eyre*, come down flat and stale, like text-book versions of the passions of Sappho.

Mr. Chesterton once rolled up his sleeves and wrote that *Wuthering Heights* was " written by an eagle." And some phrase of like idiotic and courageous emphasis will have to be found to describe the mystery of Charlotte's writing. " Thou hadst all Passion's splendour," recorded Robert Bridges of Emily, " Thou hadst abounding store of Heaven's eternal jewels," and the description might be appropriated and be shared with her sister.

The only Brontë not carried through that door from the Parsonage to the churchyard was Anne. She died in that absolute placidity of heart which was Emily's and Charlotte's too, extracting the truth that she had only four hours to live from the doctor, and saying as her last words : " Take courage, Charlotte ; take courage." It was the death of Anne Brontë, the brilliant baby, the author of *Agnes Gray*, yet almost the duffer of the family, that broke down the battered defences of heroism with which Charlotte's nature was surrounded. When she returned home she wrote :

> I shut the door—I tried to be glad that I was come home. I have always been glad before—except once— even then I was cheered. But this time joy was not to be the sensation. I felt that the house was all silent—the rooms were all empty. I remembered where the three were laid—in what narrow dark dwellings—never more to reappear on earth. So the sense of desolation and bitterness took possession of me. The agony that was to be undergone, and was not to be avoided, came on.

Whether the deaths of the Brontë sisters would have remained set out so clearly as scenes on the stage of our imagination, if they had not been recorded by Charlotte, is improbable. It is as improbable, in fact, as whether Charlotte would have become one of the lifelong heroines of romance without Mrs. Gaskell. In each instance it is as though Destiny had been aware of the responsibilities of the occasion, and had sent first Charlotte and then Mrs. Gaskell as recorders, as Boswell and Lockhart were sent to record Johnson and Scott.

There never was a family that spent so much of its time in making records of itself as the Brontës. From the cradle to the early grave each member scribbled unforgettable words about itself, and then handed the pencil over to the one that was left, to carry on. The whole history of the Brontës is like a relay race run against Death.

To have gone into Haworth Parsonage in the year 1830 would have been like stepping into a world where children

MF

had miraculously grown as articulate as their elders, and
where genius was announcing itself on odd scraps of paper,
on old book covers : anywhere and everywhere that presented itself to a family of children without any of the
ordinary indolences of youth. Any attempt at explaining
the Brontë's books in the light of the Brontës themselves
is ridiculously incomplete unless the explanation makes
clear that the Brontës were children who drifted tragically through life without growing up and without ever
having been really young.

The Rev. Patrick Brontë describes how he put questions to his children and how their answers confounded
him :

> I began with Anne, and asked what a child like her
> most wanted ; she answered, " Age and experience."
> I asked the next, Emily, what I had best do with her
> brother Branwell, who was sometimes a naughty boy ;
> she answered, " Reason with him, and when he won't
> listen to reason, whip him." I asked Branwell what was
> the best way of knowing the difference between the
> intellects of men and women ; he answered, " By con-
> sidering the difference between them as to their bodies."
> I then asked Charlotte what was the best book in the
> world ; she answered, " The Bible." And what was the
> next best ; she answered, " *The Book of Nature.*" I then
> asked her next what was the best mode of education
> for a woman ; she answered, " That which would make
> her rule her house well." Lastly I asked the oldest what
> was the best mode of spending time ; she answered,
> " By laying it out in preparation for a happy eternity."

It might be argued that the real comedian of that scene
was the Rev. Patrick Brontë putting such questions to his

babies. But there is also the rather awe-inspiring comedy of premature sagacity on the part of the children. For at the time Anne was four and Charlotte ten. And in that nursery of prodigies, invention was a continuous industry.

There is a library of Brontë manuscripts, ranging from *The Young Men's Magazine*, in six numbers, dated 1829, and *Characters of Great Men of the Present Age*, to romances, fairy tales and poems, to the number of thirty—that much from Charlotte ; of Emily's work there has been preserved three manuscript collections of poems together with two compositions in French ; Anne has left us seven manuscript volumes of poems ; and the idle Branwell, twenty-five manuscripts, from *The Battle of Washington*, written when he was ten, to *Lord Nelson and other Poems*, written when he was twenty-seven.

There never was a schoolroom of children to whom composition was so easy and natural ; children whose *juvenilia* were less juvenile. The only child whose mentality is comparable was Walter Scott ; so that if young Charlotte had met young Walter and conquered her shyness, the two infants would have had a large portion of literature and whole continents of adult life to discuss together.

" We had very early cherished the dream of one day becoming authors," wrote Charlotte Brontë of their dream when it had become reality. " This dream, never relinquished even when distance divided and absorbing tasks occupied us, now suddenly acquired strength and consistency : and took the character of a resolve."

But before the dream had grown in strength, Charlotte, Emily and Anne had been scattered about the countryside first as schoolgirls and then as governesses. The year 1845 was a late and misleading date for the publication of their volume of poems. Everyone now knows that it appeared as the work of Currer, Ellis and Acton Bell. The reason, Charlotte tells us, was that : " We did not like to declare ourselves women, because—without at that time suspecting that our mode of writing and thinking was not what is called ' feminine '—we had a vague impression that authoresses were liable to be looked on with prejudice ; we had noticed how critics sometimes use for their chastisement the weapon of personality, and for this reason, a flattery, which is not true praise."

That sentence about authoresses being looked on with prejudice has for modern ears the hollow boom of antiquity. It fixes the date of its composition as definitely as if it had been written on the page of a calendar.

Charlotte Brontë was a womanly anarchist. And she moved in a society in which the extreme of feminine independence was to be a governess. When one remembers the straining forces that were at work within her, Charlotte's placid life takes on the new and deeper beauty of restraint.

How far she was really revolutionary and dangerous may be seen from *Jane Eyre*. Again, it was by Currer Bell ; only this time Currer Bell pushed a blazing bundle of propaganda beneath the noses of the reviewers. It seems incredible to us that anyone could ever have imagined *Jane Eyre* to be the work of other than a woman. It is valiantly, even violently, an epistle sent forth by Eve to all mankind. It was *Jane Eyre* that for the first time established one of the great Rights of Women, the Right of Passionate Love, even though it was in *Villette* that she crowned it. Charlotte Brontë almost made passion respectable : she certainly made it respected. The freedom of women, as reflected in fiction has shown some revealing changes, none more revealing than those seen in *Jane Eyre*.

Independence had hitherto been obtained at the cost of all those things for which it is worth being independent. Freedom was in the hands of the Molls and the Miss Williamses. Orthodox heroines, from Pamela Andrews to Sophia Weston, were about as free as a parrot chained by one leg ; they could look pretty and flutter and squawk, but the chain was always there ; and so was Mr. B. or Tom Jones, or whoever was the unheavenly husband, looming in the background. There were also the wifely heroines, the red-eyed, red-elbowed creatures, the Amelias, Mrs. Primroses and Mrs. Micawbers, born to suffer for the follies of their husbands. No freedom there. And no freedom either in the fainting, flopping heroines of romance. Jane Austen's characters suffered from too many colds in the head to be really independent women, though a certain snappish spinsterishness gave them some of the appearance of the dignity of separate existence. It was left for Charlotte Brontë to establish the first Independent Woman in fiction.

It was, I believe, no sudden overflow of charity that made Charlotte give Jane Eyre a surprise legacy of £20,000. It was not so much a sentimental liking for wives as a most unsentimental dislike of husbands that prompted her to do this thing. That cry of Jane's, " I am an independent woman now," has set up a whole orchestra of echoes.

Charlotte Brontë was not, of course, the first to draw a heroine happy and proud of having a dowry as large as her husband's fortune. She was merely the first to draw a heroine conscious of the significance of it. She established the new line of wives who were partners and not wealthy dependents. When Jane Eyre said to Rochester, " If you won't let me live with you, I can build a house of my own close up to your door, and you may come and sit in

my parlour when you want company of an evening,"
Charlotte Brontë was quietly and humorously announcing
a piece of feminism that even to-day is startling in its
implications.

There is something in Charlotte's propaganda for her
sex that recalls that exquisite modern artist, Mrs. Virginia
Woolf, who has seen the connection as clearly as Charlotte
saw it, between independent means and an independent
mind. In point of fact, this underwriting of female genius
is one of the heresies of literature. The very women who
most wanted liberty and seclusion did their best work
without it. And perhaps it is better not to contribute freely
to the doctrine of the locked room and the separate
cheque-book, so much as to observe that a century of
progress in the liberation of woman has left them in one
particular exactly where they were.

But, at the time, people did not see that the dangerous
character was Jane Eyre. They concentrated on the unspeakable Mr. Rochester. "Bigamy!" they cried. "This is
bigamy!" Even to-day the reader cannot feel the rush of
affection for Rochester that Jane Eyre and Charlotte felt.
And that is due to the fact that all the virtues in the
Brontë novels are the virtues, not of life but of the imagination. They are so much the products of the burning
brain that at times it seems as if the eyes of the author
are casting out living beams like searchlights and not
merely receiving sights like normal eyes. Search for reality,
for strict fidelity to fact, and you will never find it in the
novels of the Brontës.

What you will find in its place is imaginative reality ;
something that stuns you by being bigger and brighter
than the thing for which it is a substitute.

Thus, Charlotte saw the flaming Rochester as a man
dragging himself painfully and slowly out of the flames

of Hell. Jane, cool and helpful, was needed to pull him over the brink and extinguish the fire. And—because it was all a purely imaginative conception—the thought of bigamy did not deter Charlotte for one moment, for that was an irrelevant interruption from the unimaginative world of fact.

There is something often a little disconcerting about the imagination of the Brontës. For, though their *juvenilia* were often astonishingly unjuvenile, works of their maturity have thick streaks of what for want of a better name we will call childishness, running through them.

Jane Eyre, for instance, is intended by the author to be the study of an unhappy little girl ; and Charlotte strenuously proceeds to do what is popularly and picturesquely known as piling on the agony. Lowood Institution soon ceases to be the Lowood Institution of reality, and becomes a kind of nightmarish prison house where little girls have their hair cut off if it curls in defiance of evangelical regulations. And this sort of under-the-bedclothes atmosphere of excitement and alarm is present throughout the book.

Mr. Rochester is in plan the Byronic hero of romantic schoolgirlhood ; the man with a murky past and a maddeningly mysterious present. The *Church Quarterly Review* at the time, but in different words, made the entirely sensible suggestion that he would have to undergo a complete change of heart before his contrition would deceive a milkmaid. And so, of course, it would, if Rochester had been other than one of those half-nursery inventions who go through the storms of life in a perpetual moral mackintosh, and are as dry when they have taken it off as though it had been fine weather all the way.

Poor St. John, the missionary, too, is one of those

characters that rush into the brain from the side that is remote from life. This habit of creating a new world from within herself naturally made her unpopular with a great deal of the old world that was already outside.

One of the unpopularities that soon reached the giant size of hatred came over Charlotte's religious unorthodoxy. Charlotte was of those intensely exasperating and impossible people, who have a true mystic's vision that does not by any means coincide with the religious vision of the time. Whenever convention went one way Charlotte went the other. And whenever convention called on Religion, Charlotte called twice as loud on True Religion. And Charlotte, the tame governess turned rebel, had a very emphatic and dogmatic way with her.

There is that famous preface to the second edition of *Jane Eyre*, in which she wrote : " Having thus acknowledged what I owe those that have aided and approved me, I turn to another class ; a small one, so far as I know, but not therefore to be overlooked, I mean the timorous or carping few who doubt the tendency of such books as *Jane Eyre* : in whose eyes whatever is unusual is wrong ; whose ears detect in each insult against bigotry—that parent of crime—an insult to piety, that regent of God on earth. I would suggest to such doubters certain obvious distinctions : I would remind them of certain simple truths. Conventionality is not morality. Self-righteousness is not religion. To attack the first is not to assail the last. To pluck the smirk from the face of the Pharisee, is not to lift an impious hand to the Crown of Thorns."

A woman who talks like that is clearly impossible ! Charlotte was as sure that she was right as St. Joan. And she was nearly as provocative in her manner of saying so. For the real trouble lies in the fact that conventionality *is* morality, so far as the world is concerned. And Charlotte, in making it possible for people to live better by throwing over convention was making it in the eyes of the world probable that they would live worse ; at least that was how her contemporaries saw it.

That catch-phrase, " Conventionality is not morality," savours not only of the Red Prophet, but of the red herring. Certainly since Charlotte's time it has been used, not by those who care nothing for the first and a great deal for the second, but by those who care nothing for either. The whole sentence has degenerated into one of those blunt, vulgar weapons of controversy that deflect a charge without defeating it. But Charlotte had a natural manner that both challenged contradiction and punished it. She remained a governess long after she ascended Parnassus.

Emily is the only one of the trinity who was free from the habit of going after the public's knuckles as well as going after its heart or head. Anne, indeed, remained a governess without ever ascending Parnassus. But Emily sat in the high places of the mind all her life. She would have been a poor enough hand at drawing diagrams on a schoolroom blackboard, but she could paint patterns in lightning across the night sky of the imagination so bright that they bewilder when they do not blind.

Wuthering Heights is all imagination ; which is what Charlotte meant when she said that it was the product of " Fate or Inspiration."

Literary discipline makes as little show in *Wuthering Heights* as a cavalry formation among Exmoor ponies. As a piece of construction, it is one of the worst novels in the language. The tale leaps about from narrative to narrative like a frog, and flashes across the generations like a dragon fly. Beside it *Tristram Shandy* seems to advance as regularly as a multiplication table. *Wuthering Heights* succeeds, as perhaps no other novel is successful, by force of those things that are left when everything that usually goes to the making of a good novel has been taken away.

That is not to say that its success could not be greater —or, at least, that it could not be successful for more readers—if some of the more common qualities of fiction were there as well. Again and again we feel the old conviction that we are reading the work, not of a mature mind but of a marvellous child. Imagination steps forth in a naked glory that is positively indecent outside poetry. And often it remains as naked as when it was born : which is contrary to the whole idea of art. For instance :

> . . . I heard distinctly the gusty winds, and the driving of the snow ; I heard, also, the fir-bough repeat its teasing sound, and ascribed it to the right cause ; but it annoyed me so much, that I resolved to silence it, if possible ; and, I thought, I resolved to endeavour to unhasp the casement. The hook was soldered into the staple : a circumstance observed by me when awake, but forgotten. " I must stop it nevertheless ! " I muttered, knocking my knuckles through the glass, and stretching an arm out to seize the importunate branch ; instead of which, my fingers closed on the fingers of a little, ice-cold hand ! The intense horror of nightmare came over me : I tried to draw back my arm, but the hand clung to it, and a most melancholy voice sobbed, " Let me in—let me in ! " . . . Terror made me cruel ; and, finding it useless to attempt shaking the creature off, I pulled its wrist on to the broken pane, and rubbed it to and fro till the blood ran down and soaked the bedclothes : still it wailed . . .

Except as an imaginative canter, the sort of canter that we take on the back of the nightmare, the notion of a child's having its wrist sawn through on a broken window pane is intolerable. And even then it remains essentially the nightmare terror of a child.

Indeed, the childishness of the Brontë imagination is nowhere seen so clearly as in *Wuthering Heights*, in which bad men can do nothing but growl, disgruntled princesses nursing their beauty in a lonely tower can only complain, the dogs would be accounted savage even among wolves, and the weather glass is set permanently stormy. Everyone in *Wuthering Heights* appears to have raw nerves and too many of them. There is a bleakness about their souls which is terrifying ; even the house is like a Greenland meteorological station.

The question has often been asked : How did these sisters in a parsonage learn so much about the sort of life that never comes near a parsonage ? And the answer probably is that it was Branwell who played Apollo, and went down into the world to mix with mortals and bring back news of them.

That he went down too far for recovery is Branwell's part of the tragedy. So far as the sisters were concerned, they were receiving in each burst of their brother's intoxicated loquacity glimpses of a life that had all the fascination of strangeness. What came through the dirty filter of Branwell's brain, they boiled to purity in the heat of their minds. Nothing that got past Charlotte or Emily on to paper had even a minute smear of impurity.

When Miss Martineau archly said, " You know you and I, Miss Brontë, have both written naughty books," Charlotte writhed in disgust and at once began writing letters to see if it were she or Miss Martineau who was mistaken.

For Charlotte was a woman of that hopeless purity of mind that could never see through the grimy eyes of other people. When she set out to display weakness or vice she distorted it because she did not know it, and gave the world her Blanches and Mr. Reeds and Elizas and Georgianas.

THE DAUGHTERS OF PUBLICITY

The anti-Victorians have always pointed to the novelists-with-a-purpose, Charles Kingsley and Reade and the virtuous, vociferous others in that age, as ample evidence of the corruption of Victorian society. The pro-Victorians have always pointed to them as equally ample evidence of the birth of a national conscience. Probably the trouble lies in a misconception as to the real nature of the purpose, and hence as to the real nature of the novel.

It was a remarkable feature of Victorian authorship that so many writers were also rich, respectable men of the world. As men of the world they needed an excuse for writing. And one of the excuses for writing was that they were as serious, not to say as solemn, in their intentions as the politicans or bishops.

Once the excuse was accepted, they could write twenty-four hours a day without sacrificing their status as gentlemen. And the true purpose of many novels-with-a-purpose was nothing more, indeed, than the novel itself.

Novels of this kind inevitably recede farther and farther from the normal world of fiction, and approach continually nearer to a world of exaggerated fact, in which the novelist is half social-historian and half church-missionary. The novelist deliberately renounces the freedom that is the first child of fancy, and has to strike a bargain with a strict and inartistic discipline that is the uncompromising heir to fact. He has to collect his material like a Kelly's Directory clerk and test it with the patience of a chemist.

For, once a single detail is proved false, the fattest novel-founded-on-fact subsides like a concertina, in a dying wail.

Of all the Victorian novelists-with-a-purpose Charles Reade is the most formidable. He is the fiercest and the best-documented. He looms over the fiction of his day like a gigantic, angry barrister, crying out to the heavens for justice, and holding every shred of evidence up his sleeve.

There was a great deal of the catfish in his nature. Wherever he was there was trouble. Despite his sales, publishers grew to dread him. To extract profit from Charles Reade by publishing him was like trying to extract a gold tooth from a lion's jaws. The profit was there. But so were the jaws.

The trouble was that Reade in his youth at Oxford, too impatient with form and formula to become a priest, and too squeamish to become a doctor, had taken up the study of the law. And from that moment he was on the look-out for abuses.

When I say that he found them, I am not referring only to his legal action with his publishers to restrain them from publishing a cheap edition of *It's Never Too Late to Mend*, or to his injunction against the theatre-manager for pirating one of Reade's adaptations from the French, or to this or to that bitter personal episode. That much was natural. To tell Reade to live peacefully would have been like telling a baby to live without breathing. Reade took his policeman's lantern and his policeman's baton and went out exposing evil and hitting at it and making notes on it.

I am not, however, comparing Charles Reade's novels with the stumbling reports written by thick fingers in a police notebook. For Reade was a novelist of urgent and impetuous power. True, he never acquired any grace but that of competence. But supremely competent he was, and never dull.

Yet it is not for such excellent novels as *Peg Woffington* or *Christie Johnstone* that Reade is remembered. It is for those novels, intended foremost if not exclusively for their own time, and successful then within the measure of their intention, that he is read and remembered.

With our prisons now humanely conducted (up to a point), and our lunatic asylums as gently disciplined as a children's nursery (presumably), we can still rouse ourselves to a fierce and frantic anger over the wickedness revealed in *It's Never Too Late to Mend* and *Hard Cash.*

For, once Reade was emotionally affected—which was for about twelve hours in every day—he grew to twice his normal stature. He was a reformer who swelled like a cobra before striking. And a born reformer he was. Anyone who doubts it has only to turn to his magnificent historical novel that Sir Walter Besant thought " the greatest historical novel in the language," *The Cloister and the Hearth*, to see him bravely and busily reforming something that could now never be reformed—the law of celibacy for priests, as laid down and practised in the mediæval Church.

Reade prepared his novels with the thoroughness of a prosecuting counsel. Thus he records :

In the year 1835 I began to make notes with a view to writing fiction, but, fixing my mind on its masterpieces in all languages and all recorded letters, I thought so highly of that great and difficult art, that for fourteen years I never ventured to offer my crude sketches to the public.

His notebooks accumulated, until even the indexes of the notebooks themselves had to be indexed in a "fat folio ledger entitled ' Index and Indices.' "

Before Reade wrote *The Cloister and the Hearth* he searched and researched in ecclesiastical history as assiduously as though he were preparing a standard work on the subject, and not a novel. This unique capacity for taking himself seriously was what carried him to success. He shut himself up to fight the Devil, formulated the doctrine of infallibility, pronounced a commination of God's anger against any sinner who disagreed with him, and issued encyclical after encyclical.

Reade always wrote in terms of melodrama. He had to do so. His intention was to conduct democratic commissions into a half-a-dozen abuses and publish the reports in such a fashion that the most unlettered would want to read them. But melodrama is a solvent of good judgment, and occasionally he made a scene intellectually feeble by making it melodramatically emphatic. Thus in *Hard Cash* the reformer in him wanted to show how a sane man could be confined, with the full concurrence of an iniquitous system, in a madhouse. That was all. What actually happened according to the book, was this :

At eight, four keepers came into his room, undressed him, compelled him to make his toilette, etc., before them, which put him to shame—being a gentleman— almost as much as it would a woman ; then they hobbled him, and fastened his ankles to the bed, and put his hands into muffles, but did not confine his body ; because they had lost a lucrative lodger only a month ago, throttled at night in a strait-waistcoat.

Alfred lay in this plight, and compared with anguish

unspeakable his joyful anticipations of this night with the strange and cruel reality. " *My wedding night ! My wedding night !*" *he cried aloud, and burst into a passion of grief.*

That melodramatic flourish at the end of the passage (I have punished it by putting it into italics) simply destroys the chapter : it degrades the whole affair from the level of the general—the affair of all mankind—to the particular—the affair of young Alf.

And almost on the last page Reade committed the howling blunder of making Alfred's wicked persecutor himself not merely bad but mad. The only evidence Reade adduces of the old man's monomania is a perfectly justifiable outbreak of anger, and the fact that "Alfred saw the truth and wondered at his past obtuseness."

There is no more striking example of the dangers of teaching a moral lesson by sensational methods. After reading such a passage one feels almost like advising the author to read *Hard Cash*, as a terrible example of the effects of miscertification of madness.

But to accuse Reade of inconsistency (though he would never have admitted his inconsistency himself) is rather like accusing a Hyde Park orator of a sore throat. In such media there is no time to think about such things. Reade did successfully what he set out to do. He raised a storm with himself in the centre of it. He wrote a vast, historic, historical novel in which the view and the thought, and not merely the language, as is usually the case, were really archaic. He improved the position of the author—if he had stuck by his early trade of violin-trading he would doubtless have secured legislation for the protection of violin-traders. He linked arms with Justice, and for half

Nf

a century paraded up and down, showing her off to a world that knew nothing nobler than equity.

And he coined one wonderful phrase which all novelists-with-a-purpose should know and carry on their shields as well as on their sleeves alongside their hearts : " Justice is the daughter of Publicity."

THE ARISTOCRATIC NOVEL

"Like all civilised societies we give due weight to rank and wealth "—thus Edward George Earle Lytton Bulwer, first Lord Lytton, to the assembled youth of a great public school. If Lytton had been elected out of all England to be the oracle of the upper classes, and the mouthpiece of every headmaster in the country, he could not have made a more orthodox and inspiring remark. Earlier ages might have found something vulgarly displeasing in this casual levelling of prosperous tradesman and impoverished peer. And since his day, the peer has definitely failed in his attempt to preserve even a precarious equality with the tradesman. But in the middle years of the nineteenth century, those words must have carried across the School Hall as irresistible and irrefutable as a muezzin's.

Unfortunately they are foolish, inflated words : they do not explain how large the due weight that we give to rank and wealth is. They merely leave a feeling in the mind that it is not the sort of due that you give the Devil, and that the speaker sees God as a Plantagenet Rothschild.

So far as Bulwer Lytton himself was concerned, the words are justified. A needy member of the untitled aristocracy of England, by his industry and intellect he got the matter both of need and title set right before he died.

He preserved an attitude of contemptuous, golden indifference towards the rest of the world. His energy, like his pride and ability, was colossal. The first led him to write some of the most patiently and laboriously detailed and romantic historical novels in the language : the second and third caused him to produce some of the brightest gilding in fiction.

Lytton saw the whole of life as a perpetual Ascot Week : all tall hats and quick smiles. And in *Pelham* he said that that was how he saw it. *Pelham*, in consequence, is a great sweep of aristocratic cynicism ; a sneer out of the ermine. It is remorselessly witty ; even though the wit seems to have turned a little rancid in places. The hero is more Byronic than Byron, and more agreeable than Alcibiades. He is so ravishingly himself that he blows about the book like a piece of social blight, scattering the germs of inward rot.

The book is founded on the assumption that with Youth at the prow and Pleasure at the helm, Youth will pretty soon be on the rocks. It is a moral lesson smuggled to the reader under the guise of amusement.

As a novel, *Pelham* is constantly amusing, at least in its early portions, by the ceaseless vivacity of malicious incident.

Mr. Conway had just caused two divorces ; and of course all the women in London were dying for him— judge then of the pride which Lady Frances felt at his addresses. The end of the season was unusually dull, and my mother, after having looked over her list of engagements, and ascertaining that she had none remaining worth staying for, agreed to elope with her new lover.

The carriage was at the end of the square. My mother, for the first time in her life, got up at six o'clock. Her foot was on the step, and her hand next to Mr. Conway's heart, when she remembered that her favourite china monster, and her French dog, were left behind. She insisted on returning—re-entered the house, and was coming downstairs with one under each arm, when she was met by my father and two servants. My father's valet had discovered the flight (I forget how), and awakened his master.

When my father was convinced of his loss, he called for his dressing-gown—searched the garret and the kitchen—looked in the maids' drawers and the cellaret—and finally declared he was distracted. I have heard that the servants were quite melted by his grief, and I do not doubt it in the least, for he was always celebrated for his skill in private theatricals.

Or :

I think at this moment I see my mother before me, reclining on the sofa, repeating to me some story about Queen Elizabeth and Lord Essex ; then telling me, in a languid voice, as she sank back with the exertion, of the blessings of a literary taste, and admonishing me never to read above half an hour at a time for fear of losing my health.

The charm of this method of writing lies in the lively heartlessness that infects it. Unfortunately, it infected Lytton, too, in places. And his spiteful pleasantries sometimes lose their pleasantness in a sweating attack of comic disillusion :

I was in her boudoir one evening, when her *femme de chambre* came to tell us that the duc was in the passage. Notwithstanding the innocence of our attachment, the duchesse was in a violent fright ; a small door was

at the left of the ottoman on which we were sitting.
" Oh, no, no, not there," cried the lady ; but I saw
no other refuge, entered it forthwith, and before she
could ferret me out, the duc was in the room.

In the meanwhile, I amused myself by examining the
wonders of the new world into which I had so abruptly
immerged : on a small table before me, was deposited
a remarkably constructed night-cap ; I examined it as
a curiosity ; on each side was placed *une petite côtelette
de veau cru*, sewed on with green-coloured silk (I remember even the smallest minutiæ) ; a beautiful golden
wig (the duchesse never liked me to play with her hair)
was on a block close by, and on another table was a set
of teeth *d'une blancheur éblouissante.*

A passage like that explains why it was that Lytton
was never able to draw the romantic portraits of heroines
that his historical novels, *The Last Days of Pompeii* ; *Harold,
Last of the Saxon Kings* ; *Rienzi,* and the rest of the yearning
and magnificent tributes to vanished greatness, demanded.
He became *the* historical novelist of his age, wonderfully
well-read, pompously perfect in every line and paragraph,
when he should have become rather a kind of dignified
and disinfected Oscar Wilde ; a poseur ridiculing all poses
but his own.

He took himself, naturally, as seriously as a judge. He
moved in the best circles of Paris and London with a
supreme sense of his own talents and importance. He
lived in an age when it was fashionable to be clever ;
and Lytton was a leader of fashion. He wrote fiction in
much the manner in which an Elizabethan youth of the
same distinction of intellect would have written poetry ;
because his mind was both alive with thoughts and re-
spectful of the prevailing conventions.

A few years earlier, and he would have written elegant and expert Don Juanish verses. As it was, he came into a world that was growing tired of Don Juans. So he dressed his Pelhams and Clintons in the complete uniform of Byronism, and then just carted them about in his books like Guys ready for the burning. There is an opulent tawdriness about Lytton's world in which the mad, bad characters of an earlier age move in a new serious world of virtue.

Lytton, indeed, stands midway between the age of the libertine and the era of the evangelical Liberal ; between the Byronic open shirt and the Gladstone collar.

There was, however, another reason than convention for Lytton's writing novels ; and that was marriage. Lytton, with the remarkable misguidance of heart which has distinguished most of the English novelists, married the wrong woman. He broke with his mother—who was also his banker—to marry a tragic wife, who after the birth of two children separated from him and with insane perseverance tried to ruin his life. His mother disapproved of the match from the start, and stopped his allowance. Thus, in the early years, it was necessary for him to write to support a home. And in the later years he wrote, just as he flung himself into politics, because, with no home life to provide the normal comforts of a man's life, he needed some distraction for his mind.

He was a man isolated by his own cleverness ; and further removed from the ordinary conduct of life by his unexceptionable breeding. He was a man of too good manners ; and, too many of them. And after middle-age he became rather like an expensive, polished lectern ; golden, standing alone, and magnificently glittering.

Bulwer Lytton was just a little too clever to surrender

his mind to the common business of life long enough to write a novel of ordinary human sincerity and, therefore, of ordinary human appeal and endurance.

Benjamin Disraeli, throughout his life was another who was the victim of a morbidly enlarged intelligence. But he was a Jew ; and a Jew is naturally more comfortable in his own cleverness.

His intelligence would never have been an embarrassment to him if he had not chosen to ally himself to the one political party that distrusts cleverness. He was, it should be remembered, born in an age when the qualifications for a successful political career were strikingly unlike those of to-day. It would be a parody of a perfectly serious and sincere politician to suggest that Disraeli was simply a Lyttonesque exquisite from some unmentioned, unmentionable ghetto, gloriously declaiming with more than Christian cleverness and less than English reserve. Indeed, in *Sybil* Disraeli flings facts, of the unpleasant kind that have to be faced, at us as though he were a novelist-with-a-purpose who cared less for literary form than for the formula of his convictions.

But to say that Disraeli invented the political novel is to mean something very different from what the same words would imply to-day. In *Coningsby* Disraeli approached the political world in the spirit of carnival. Balls, breakfasts, steeplechases, hunt-suppers, salons— such was the political laboratory in which he and Coningsby worked. There is always a smattering of the ambassador—braid, white gloves, wit, and an expression of Chinese wisdom—about the writer of Disraeli's novels. The mind of the reader moves perpetually on thick carpets and smooth floors. The clarets and champagnes make poets of politicians. The natural eloquence, the fatal, fulsome eloquence, of the author adds excess to the luxury of the scene. Even breakfast tables look as though furnished by Drage.

The breakfast room at Brentham was very bright. It opened on a garden of its own, which at this season was so glowing, and cultured into patterns so fanciful and finished, that it had the resemblance of a vast mosaic. The walls of the chamber were covered with bright drawings and sketches of our modern masters and frames of interesting miniatures. . . .

It is a pity, indeed, that so much of Disraeli's fiction should support the Gladstonian view of the inspired flunkey. But, undeniably, it does so. Half the descriptions of characters are like those of a man who knows people intimately by appearance but has never met them on terms of even casual acquaintance. All the pageantry of the social scene is there and it is soon obvious that the author has not even begun to be interested in his characters as they exist off the stage. Thus :

The guests reassembled in the great saloon before they repaired to the theatre. A lady on the arm of a Russian prince bestowed on Coningsby a haughty, but not ungracious, bow ; which he returned, unconscious of the person to whom he bent. She was, however, a very striking person : not beautiful ; her face indeed at the first glance was almost repulsive, yet it ever attracted a second gaze. A remarkable pallor distinguished her ; her features had neither regularity nor expression ; neither were her eyes fine ; but her brow impressed you with an idea of power of no ordinary character or capacity. Her figure was as fine and commanding as her face was void of charm. Juno, in the full bloom of her

immortality could have presented nothing more ma-
jestic. Coningsby watched her as she swept along like
a resistless fate.

All that character and pallor (and padding) and not
a hint of the implications until we arrive at the last sentence ! And that is not all. Such a sentence as that about
Juno gives a hint of the worst of Disraeli's weaknesses ;
his fatal tendency to gush.

There is a kind of facile fatuity about Disraeli's method
of opening a chapter that is fatal to anything that follows
on it. " What wonderful things are events ! The least are
of greater importance than the most sublime and comprehensive speculations ! "—a remark that should be
decorated in acknowledgment of its mature idiocy—or,
" There are few things more full of delight and splendour,
than to travel during the heat of a refulgent summer in
the green district of some ancient forest," such are the
too lavishly lubricated Disraelian openings.

There probably never was a generation that has found
it harder to take Disraeli's fashion of prose seriously than
our own. As we see him in his novels he is like a small
thinking fly ever getting caught in a tangled web of
extravagant description. Sir Arthur Quiller-Couch has
compared this glamour with the magic of the *Arabian
Nights* ; a legacy of the world that lies east of England.
But I am not sure that it is the luxury of sensation in the
picturesque metaphors that affect us unfavourably, so
much as their incredible ineptness. For example :

Farther on the fruit trees caught the splendour of the
night ; and looked like a troop of sultanas taking their
garden air, where the eye of man could not profane
them. There were apples that rivalled rubies ; pears of

topaz tint ; a whole paraphernalia of plums, some purple as the amethyst, others blue and brilliant as the sapphire ; an emerald here, and now a yellow drop that gleamed like the yellow diamond of Gengis Khan.

A man who pretends that he cannot tell the difference between an orchard and a harem is either a fool or a fraud. It is not to be wondered at that the rural electors of Bucks rejected Disraeli at his first attempt if he spoke about their farms and holdings in such terms. To an English mind there is something pathetically silly in the notion of an expatriated Jew trying to make the sight of an English orchard by moonlight presentable to his own imagination by putting a jeweller's price on every pear and apple ; by dangling a carat before his long, donkey's nose.

But when all the stuffing has been knocked out of this over-stuffed book, *Sybil* remains a powerful and intelligent novel. In intention, it is considerably larger than most of the novels of that day or of ours. Its object was to unite the lives of men with the events of the time ; it was the Chartists' Charter.

Where it came nearest to failure was on the human side, not on the historic. Sybil herself is simply a china statuette with streaming eyes. The march of the Chartists is described with the full impetuous sweep of urgent and excited narrative. In the alarm of the moment the author finds his head and his feet, forgets that he is Dizzy, and makes straight at his goal.

The march of Bishop Hatton at the head of the Hellcats into the mining districts was perhaps the most strikingly popular movement since the Pilgrimage of Grace. Mounted on a white mule, wall-eyed and of hideous form, the Bishop brandished a huge hammer with which he had announced that he would destroy the enemies of the people : all butties, doggies, dealers in truck and tommy, middle masters and main masters. Some thousand Hell-cats followed him, brandishing bludgeons, or armed with bars of iron, pick-handles, and hammers. On each side of the Bishop, on a donkey, was one of his little sons, as demure and earnest as if he were handling his file. A flowing standard of silk, inscribed with the Charter, and which had been presented to him by the delegate, was borne before him like the oriflamme. Never was such a gaunt, grim crew. As they advanced, their numbers continually increased, for they arrested all labour in their progress. Every engine was stopped, the plug was driven out of every boiler, every fire was extinguished, every man was turned out. The decree went forth that labour was to cease until the Charter was the law of the land : the mine and the mill, the foundry and the loomshop were, until the consummation, to be idle : nor was the mighty pause to be confined to these great enterprises. Every trade of every kind and description was to be stopped : tailor and cobbler, brushmaker and sweep, tinker and carter, mason and builder, all, all ; for all an enormous Sabbath, that was to compensate for any incidental suffering which it induced by the increased means and the elevated condition that it ultimately would insure ; that paradise of artisans, that Utopia of Toil, embalmed in those ringing words, sounds cheerful to the Saxon race : " A fair day's wage for a fair day's work."

If Disraeli could always have written like that, he would have taken his place alongside the virile novelists of the language. But the trouble is that an interest in events, without an equal interest in the individual actors, makes poor fiction. And Disraeli never invented a character sufficiently satisfying to convince even himself.

In his most nearly successful novel, *Coningsby*, he simply pinned new names on well-known backs, and stood to one side to watch the fun. The weakness of the method is obvious : once the well-known men are dead and forgotten the reader has to go through the book with a key to the characters at his elbow to ensure that he is getting all of portraiture, all of scandal and all of impudence that the book has to offer.

Politics was the Disraelian substitute for philosophy. He saw the whole of life in terms of governments and downfalls of governments. Those of his books that do not point towards Westminster are completely forgotten. In the collected edition of his works, he describes how as a child " born in a library and trained from early childhood by learned men," he grew to survey the political scene from a scholar's perch. And he remarks that " what most attracted my musing, even as a boy, was the elements of our political parties, and the strange mystification by which that which was natural in its constitution had become odious, and that which was exclusive was presented as popular."

We can disregard the two obvious facts that compared with Gladstone, who really was a scholar, Disraeli, so far as learning went, was simply an undergraduate with a flower in his buttonhole, and that to say that Whigs were odious and Tories popular was either a purely temporary or else a prejudiced opinion. But prejudiced or ephemeral it was Disraeli's political faith.

Coningsby, *Sybil* and *Tancred* form an imposing philosophic trilogy, which Disraeli really believed presented a picture of the whole of English society. They presented the picture as seen through the eyes of an alert foreigner. Actually they presented a far better picture of Disraeli, cunning, inspired and anxiously trying to dig a hole in which to take root in English soil.

MEREDITH AND HARDY

We now come upon a pair of novelists, men of the first rank, Meredith and Hardy, who had much in common, yet whose resemblances serve merely to throw their dissimilarity into sharper relief.

They were like two men travelling along the same road at the same time, one on the way to an everlasting wedding feast, the other on the way to bury the baby. They were both writers who saw life in the large terms of poetry. But one was lyrical, the other epical. One was radiantly cheerful. The other unremittingly tragic ; we might almost say inevitably tragic, for extend a lyric and you generally find a tragedy.

One was on good terms with the universe ; the other as soured in his writing as though God had trodden on him and not apologised. Meredith would have said that creation was on his side ; or at least, that he was on the side of creation. Hardy suffered grave doubts as to whether creation were not actually cruel in creating anyone.

Both writers were unchristian, or anti-christian ; though remembering the age in which they lived, it is something—like measles in an epidemic—that one would hesitate to adduce as evidence of any fundamental originality. A violently anti-christian, or atheistic novelist, nowadays, would be worth any amount of individual notice ; like an industriously enthusiastic Israelite uselessly making an eighth round of the walls of Jericho.

That Meredith was a novelist at all is astonishing. There is so much that is commonplace in the greatest of novels—indeed a novel scarcely can be great without a lot of the ordinary business of life in its pages—that to see Meredith turn novelist is rather like seeing a tight-rope walker earning his living by carrying hods of bricks across a builder's plank.

Meredith was a poet of remarkable lambency of emotion. And a philosopher of quite inchoate philosophy. He had in him the makings of a far more uniformly successful poet than novelist. But there were fewer interested in that kind of success, and Meredith shrank from neglect with a most unphilosophic instinctiveness.

Meredith, indeed, is one of the most unnatural novelists in the language. He had—at least in his early years—an impetuous load of things to say, but the manner he adopted of saying them was anything but the novelist's. Wilde remarked that " as a novelist he can do everything, except tell a story." And Meredith certainly seems in places to keep up a running fight between his philosophy and his fiction, between himself and his characters.

He became a novelist for quite the wrong reason. It was not because he even *wanted* to tell a story, or to paint a picture of human affairs, that he wrote. It was simply that he had evolved a theory of Life. And since it was one of those theories that fit life only about as well as the Procrustean bed fitted its occupant, he had to invent a world in which he could perform his choppings and loppings to his, and his theory's, satisfaction.

Mercifully, he was an optimist ; and he was that far rarer thing, an intellectual optimist. He believed in Nature as ardently as men an age or two before him had believed in God, and he evoked Man where they had called upon the Son of Man. In other words, he was a passionately, even fanatically, religious man, though in a fierce, free, irreligious fashion. His theory, however, was always getting under his feet. It was a theory of comedy, and therefore of laughter. The one illogical thing that remains in a natural world is laughter. And to theorise about it is perhaps the most dangerous thing that a humorist can do.

Mankind is one, said Meredith, and anyone acting selfishly, is a subject for huge and brooding merriment. Looked at through such a pair of philosopher's spectacles, life is a perpetual contortion in which the nose is being cut off to spite the face. It is a theoretical, spiritless laughter that Meredith's high comedy provokes ; but once a mind has enjoyed the amusement that his books offer, the rest of fiction, for a time, at least, seems a little sodden to the taste.

The unique thing about Meredith is the way in which he contained within himself the vital parts of both a propagandist and a poet. At that very moment when his theory seems to drag his comedy down from the level of Olympian laughter, there is the beat of wings in the air ; and Meredith, the poet and the lover, is there doing his djinn's work, and carrying his creation back into the clouds where it belongs.

It may seem a perfectly fruitless occupation discovering what it is that destroys Meredith's novels, when they are there before us glittering with competence. But with Meredith we have always a feeling that his brilliance is consuming him ; that his speaking voice might be more pleasant if he had not sung so much.

If Meredith's genius (to change the metaphor) could have been fitted with some anti-dazzle device before it set

O F

out, he would have had twice as many admirers to-day, and there would not have been one hundredth of those casualties that he left strewed behind him in the ditch. He did not even have the sense, or the modesty, to start dimly. He had the headlights of his mind blazing before he had left the drive. Thus, *The Egoist* opens with a Prelude, good enough in its way as a piece of pranked-out philosophy that is about as inviting to the timid reader as the notice to tramps that there are man-traps set. It is not even as though the author were content with drawing a moral from his story. He is at the other game of writing a parable to fit a moral.

Meredith is an example of the dangers of longevity in literature. Charles Reade said that a writer of any magnitude would become great merely by growing old. But Meredith shrank with age. He accumulated a big, rambling reputation at the cost of himself. He became simply a wan crusader, wrapped in perpetual evening, dreaming war.

To understand the real Meredith, it is necessary to re-inflate the Sage of Box Hill, and restore him to the original size of the Surrey Strong Man, tossing iron bars about for pleasure like a navvy at a country fair, hirsute and heroic like a buccaneering Christ. He was a man with the storm-wind behind him ; a man in a rage with the rest of the world. He was a far greater figure than the attenuated philosopher, the stiffened athlete, acidly complaining that the reviewers had been against him all his life.

The conviction that the small world of men was on its own side and not on his, led to that quite unnatural tautening of muscle and arching of neck that Meredith adopted to shoulder his way through the crowd. If a reason has to be found for every peculiarity of a writer, we can lay our fingers on the exposed nerve of Meredith without undue hesitation.

Meredith was born the son of a naval outfitter in Southampton—Marryat mentions the firm—and he had an almost morbid sensitiveness about his parenthood. His family moved in that uncertain social twilight between the petty tradesman and the petty gentry. Probably he was never quite sure whether an advance of his would be met by a salute, or a snub. His aloofness earned him the name of " Gentleman Georgie." And the whole early years of his life—the death of his mother, his father's dislike of him, the distaste for his fellows—are the period of painful transformation of the obscure tradesman into the famous writer.

Mr. Priestley has suggested that in later years Meredith was " ashamed not of the tailor's shop, but of his shame of the tailor's shop." Certainly the figure of a tailor's son feverishly trying to escape the abhorrèd shears is one on which the spirit of comedy could play to advantage. It would have been very difficult for the sage to confess the snob. And once he ascended the public pedestal he left the snob behind for the literary historian to discover. Thus in *Evan Harrington* he laughed at the colossal accident of his birth. And in *Henry Richmond* he obscured the fact that there had been any accident at all.

This manipulation of things in his mind, his habit of flicking a fact about like a ball in a fives court, is like that of no other writer so much as it is like that of Laurence Sterne. Both writers had their theory of comedy. And both writers took a mischievous delight in arriving at the comic situation by the roundabout route of letting their comic spirit bounce from the four sides of their mind on its way.

In ornament as well as in structure there is a great

deal of Laurence Sterne in George Meredith. That fantastic passage about a leg in *The Egoist* could have been written only by one of two writers :

Mrs. Mountstuart touched a thrilling cord. " In spite of men's hateful modern costume, you see he has a leg."

That is, the leg of the born cavalier is before you : and obscure it as you will, dress degenerately, there it is for ladies who have eyes. You *see* it : or, you see *he* has it. Miss Isabel and Miss Eleanor disputed the incidence of the emphasis, but surely, though a slight difference of meaning may be heard, either will do : many, with a good show of reason, throw the accent upon *leg*. And the ladies knew for a fact that Willoughby's leg was exquisite ; he had a cavalier court-suit in his wardrobe. Mrs. Mountstuart signified that the leg was to be seen because it was a burning leg. There it is, and it *will* shine through ! He has the leg of Rochester, Buckingham, Dorset, Suckling ; the leg that smiles, that winks, is obsequious to you, yet perforce of beauty self-satisfied ; that twinkles to a tender midway between imperiousness and seductiveness, audacity and discretion ; between " you shall worship me," and " I am devoted to you " ; is your lord, your slave, alternately, and in one. It is a leg of ebb and flow and high-tide ripples. Such a leg, when it has done with pretending to retire, will walk straight into the hearts of women. Nothing so fatal to them . . .

Indeed, the more one reads about that remarkable leg the more one expects to find that it is attached to the same body as that which sprouted the amazing nose in *Tristram Shandy.*

In both writers there is the habit of stopping the clock of narrative when their mind becomes more than usually interested in anything ; though before the end of the passage it is usually apparent that they have ceased to be interested in the thing and have merely become fixedly, even fatally, interested in their own interest.

But Meredith did not grow great because of his reckless originalities of style. He grew great despite them. His greatness came from the beautiful optimism of his mind. There is a passage in *The Egoist* in which Sir Willoughby Patterne describes a girl by saying that, " she has now what was missing before, a ripe intelligence in addition to her happy disposition—romantic, you would say." That phrase glows with all the peculiar lamps of Meredith's brain. If a reader understands it he is more than half way to understanding the whole of Meredith. It is one of those sudden phrases in which an author sets out merely to direct his lens upon a sympathetic character, and ends by photographing himself. Ripe Intelligence and Happy Disposition are the two rarest bedfellows in literature. It is one of the shortcomings of modern fiction that the ripest intelligences seem all to have been wedded to atrabilious dispositions.

Before Meredith there had been no author who had combined them as the two partners of his mind ; and there was certainly no author who would have thought of suggesting that the first child of intelligence and optimism was romance.

Meredith was romantic from intellectual conviction. Rapture of the heart is common enough ; rapture of the head is a far rarer thing. And being of the head it can survive criticism more easily. This rapturous, romantic vision of Meredith had most important effects on fiction.

In the first place, it gave birth to a new heroine, mother

of a new line of heroines. In an age that was being shocked
to its foundations by the theory, incorrectly reported, that
men were descended from monkeys, Meredith was on the
other side making his heroines more like angels than they
ever had been before.

Of course, there had been angelic-looking heroines already; creatures whose beauty left all men, and apparently
themselves as well, dumb with wonder. And there had
been heroines like Fielding's Amelia who had grown wise
with sorrow. But to Meredith was left the creation, or
rather the re-creation, of the heroine in fiction whose
beauty dwelt not so much in her face as in the mind of
those—including the reader—who met her. Diana War-
wick was a heroine whose brain balanced her beauty. She
would have been charming even by letter. There is never
the least doubt that Meredith was in love with her mind
and not with her body. All Meredith's heroines, indeed,
are starry souls that tread on the peaks of this world knowing sex only as a kind of warm sunrise flush across the
pale snows of the mind.

It may have been this habit of dwelling within the minds
of his Dianas and Lucys that led Meredith on to his habit
of flitting from one mind to another as he wrote. It was
a bad habit inasmuch as it meant that the narrative had
to plunge about like a game of follow-my-leader after
a butterfly. But it meant also that every incident in the
story glowed with the light of emotion. That there was
nothing on which someone was not shedding rays of
feeling.

This subjective method of story-telling is so well known
to-day that it may now seem almost to be the natural and
eternal method of the narrator. In reality there is the
same chasm of difference between the method of, say,
Richard Feverel and *Robinson Crusoe* as there is between a

parliamentary report in *Hansard* and the sketch from a
special correspondent in the Gallery. *Hansard* will certainly contain more facts : they will proceed in a perfectly
logical and natural sequence and they appear to present
the entire essentials of the scene. Yet to the average reader
the words in *Hansard* are as unsatisfying as an echo of
which the original is missing. The special correspondent,
on the other hand, will inevitably lose nine-tenths of the
facts ; all the essentials may be missing and only the
luxuries of the scene may be left. Yet the account
bears the signature of humanity.

Robinson Crusoe, for instance, is as enchanting as a magic-
carpet simply because desert islands in themselves are
enchanting and Defoe wrote as though he believed in this
one. The figure of the solitary man on a desert island is
a fascinating object, for the simple and adequate reason
that he is the figure of a solitary man on a desert island.
If the island became fully inhabited no one would give
him a second thought. In short, *Robinson Crusoe* interests
us ; and Robinson Crusoe does not. But Richard Feverel
is as great a creation as *Richard Feverel*. Every character
in Meredith's novels is infused with a lot of life and a little
of Meredith. And dull scenes become delightful when
viewed through eyes that are alight with other interests.

The " Diversion Played on a Penny Whistle " in
Richard Feverel is one of the happiest of all the scenes
in fiction. In it Meredith did perfectly a thing that had
never been done so well before, and has never been done
so well since. Love-scenes are in the province of poetry
rather than of prose and Meredith brought to literature
a mind that moved in the moods of a poet.

> " *Lucy ! my beloved !* "
> " *O Richard !* "

Out in the world there, in the skirts of the woodland a shepherd boy pipes to meditative eve on a penny whistle.

Love's musical instrument is so old, and so poor : it has but two stops ; and yet, you see the cunning musician does so much with it !

One has only to compare that with the stupid, clumsy antics of Fielding's Tom and Sophia and Smollett's Roderick and Narcissa and Thackeray's Pendennis and Laura and Dickens's Copperfield and Dora, or for that matter anyone else's someone and somebody else, to realise that Meredith, like an Olympian was looking on love from above.

Like an Olympian, with winds and lightnings perpetually about his head and his feet caught in a long trailing jumble of words, epithets, ellipses.

*   *   *

Thomas Hardy was considerably less kind to Fate in his books than Fate was to him in his life. It was a piece of irony that none would have appreciated better than Hardy himself. But irony it remained. And before kicking God, with Hardy's compliments, for being cruel, it is well to remember the penniless, studious architect's apprentice who enjoyed as sensational a measure of success as though Providence had been reading the novelettes.

Hardy like Meredith is a writer who lingered on, an intelligent, shrinking shell of himself, too long after he had done the work that made him precious.

To understand him it is necessary to forget the closely guarded Grand Old Man in the old house of Max Gate,

and extend all our lines of thought backwards until we
arrive at the Wild Young Man in the new house of Max
Gate.

Once that is done his proverbial pessimism ceases to
be a kind of individual melancholia, and becomes merely
one of the most interesting cases in an historic epidemic
of doubt. For Hardy was living and working in the world
of Darwin and Huxley, and he accepted the defeat of
Protestantism with equanimity.

It was another of those little ironies of which he was
so fond—feeling that clumsy and chance creation had
produced them and that he had spotted them—that Hardy
should have spent his early life building and rebuild-
ing churches and his more mature life in emptying
them.

Hardy, I said intentionally, accepted the defeat of
Protestantism. Apostates from the Roman Catholic Faith
are usually men of a more militant and pugnacious heresy.
Hardy merely accepted the new theory that life was without a benevolent supervision from above. But in his first
plunge of enthusiasm he plunged too far and began to
believe that life was planned by a Euripidean malevolent
supervisor. Which is as religious as the other view, even
though it happens to be Satanism and not Christianity.

To understand Hardy's agnosticism it is necessary to see
him not merely as an independent member recording a
solitary note against the President of the Immortals, but
rather as one of the official Opposition passing into a
rigidly prepared division. It was an opposition with John
Stuart Mill and Matthew Arnold and Meredith in its
shadow Cabinet. The Prime Minister in power was Newman. Meanwhile God had pulled his robes around him
and retired into Brompton.

When Hardy came to London as a young man he

treated religion as a sort of subsidiary subject in the examination of life ; something in which he could get honours by eagerness and application. Thus he solemnly recorded in his notebook : " Worked at J. H. Newman's *Apologia*, which we have all been talking about lately. A great desire to be convinced by him . . . style charming, and his logic really human, being based not on syllogisms but on converging probabilities. Only—and here comes the fatal catastrophe—there is no first link to his excellent chain of reasoning, and down you came headlong. . . ."

Those notebooks which Hardy kept between the ages of twenty-one and twenty-seven reveal a mind already morbidly mature. In the entries there is a great deal of dismal Dorset turned melancholy Dane. " The world does not despise us ; it only neglects us," he wrote on the eve of a career during which people were very soon to stop neglecting him—he was talked about by the time he was thirty-three—and shortly after was to cease despising him.

The remark, no matter how regarded, is some comfort. Probably it was written in one of those false flashes of optimism that strike across the placid world of the pessimist, like a shooting star in a thick mist. When Hardy wrote those words he was doubtless feeling more conscious of the world's contempt than usual. Few men, indeed, who have any depth of belief in themselves, have ever been left neglected for long without searching for a cause outside themselves.

Hardy's bleak belief was certainly not that Providence sometimes failed to help human beings but that it actually hindered. He saw Fate as something that was as remorseless as a steam-roller, and as dogged as a bloodhound ; as something that would flatten and follow. Thus if you were innocent and impetuous, like Tess, you suffered. If you were deliberate and resolved, like Jude, you suffered just as badly. His epic novels, indeed, are a kind of prose *Hound of Heaven* in which " the strong feet that followed, followed after," are the feet of diabolical Fate and not of divine friendship.

The division of Hardy's fiction into dramatic novels and epic novels is an obvious and, if there are examiners about, a useful separation. Between 1871, when Hardy published *Desperate Remedies*, and 1891 when *Tess of the D'Urbervilles* appeared, he had written thirteen novels of which not more than four are really important. These are the dramatic novels, *Far From the Madding Crowd*, *The Return of the Native*, *The Mayor of Casterbridge* and *The Woodlanders*. During that period he had risen from grey anxiousness about the future to a roseate serenity in his own affairs. Yet during the same length of time he had changed from a suspicious uncertainty as to the future of the lives of human beings to a calm certainty of failure. Fate might have anything from a farmyard to a church-yard in store for Elfrida or Bathsheba, or any of the earlier heroines. But nothing but tragedy could be the lot of Tess.

In 1893 Hardy moved into a new study facing east. Thereafter the east wind blew about his soul. He was naturally a man who could not have lived for a moment in the warm, boisterous Meredithian south-west wind. He was always re-orientalising himself towards the east— after sunrise. In that bleak study Hardy wrote *Jude the Obscure*. And turning his back on the sun was a gesture that was repeated in his book. He set Jude on a hopeful pilgrimage across the earth, and followed him, snuffing out the stars one by one over his head as he went.

There is a common misconception that a pessimist is a

man who looks at things with the distorting eyes of a melancholic imbecile. He is, of course, nothing of the sort. He is merely a man who makes less than the usual allowance for the general and genial habit of wearing pink spectacles for flooding a dull world with cheerful light. He is not a man who calls black white, as confirmed optimists are thought to do ; he does not even call white black, which is what he is accused of doing. He merely calls everything universal grey. Hardy himself once defined pessimism as " a reasoned view of effects and probable causes deduced from facts unflinchingly observed." And, true to the type of the pessimist who sees himself the one sane man in a world of foolish faces, wreathed in perpetual grins, he described optimists as wearing " too much the strained look of the smile on a skull."

Hardy was a perfectly complacent pessimist. Indeed, there is reason to believe that the word " pessimistic " should be reserved for the *intention* of his books and the word " humorous " both for their manner and for him.

For some reason the word " pessimist "—especially in the last century when it was taken simply to be a mishearing of the word "atheist"—exercises an infectious fascination over the mind. People talk of Hardy as though he were merely a lugubrious guide to the gloomier parts of Wessex, continuously weeping because a piece of local colour had become lodged in his eye. They forget how much he enjoyed the Oaks and Leafs and Poorgrasses and Worms, and all the buffoons who travel across Wessex in his novels, making it into a circus. If *Jude* and *Tess* had never been written, and the public had not been given something new to think about, there would still have been that sequence of novels extending backwards from *The Mayor of Casterbridge* to *Far From the Madding Crowd*, which would have earned Hardy a reputation for the immense sympathy that was the fount of everything he wrote.

Within his mind Hardy was philosophic with a painful tenderness that is remote from the grey half-hatred of the pessimist. It was in the world outside that he saw those things that saddened and sickened him. If he had stayed within the four walls of his study he would have remained all his life the shy architect contentedly drawing. " So far as my experience goes," he once wrote, " conclusions about the universe do not affect the spirits, which are a result of temperament. What does depress me is the sight of so much pain in the world, constant pain ; and it did just as much when I was an orthodox churchman as now ; for no future happiness can remove from the past sufferings that have been endured."

Both *Tess* and *Jude* were written as though cruelty to others were a raging tooth set in the writer's head. They were written when despair at the world's pain had mounted within Hardy's mind to a desperate defiance ; at a moment when he had the invalid's instinctive hatred of the robust.

In calling Tess " a pure woman " Hardy displayed a rather aggressive broad-mindedness. Nowadays, when the word " pure " is almost an archaism, we should suffer no special incredulity in hearing Hardy call her such a thing. But those who objected at the time really had a quite good case. Her mind may have been white as freshly driven snow—such was obviously Hardy's view—but it was one of the innocent minds that led its owner on a devil's dance through life. A bastard and a murder are awkward entries to appear on the credit side of purity. And it did not help either Hardy or Tess that Hardy should have adopted the attitude : " Don't blame me, or Tess. If you must blame anyone, for this ghastly mess, blame God. He arranged it—I didn't." That sentence at the end of *Tess* in which " the President of the Immortals " " ended his sport with Tess," put Hardy definitely on the other side of conventional morality. And his ingenuous defence of the sentence by citing Shakespeare's words in Gloster's mouth in *Lear*, " As flies to wanton boys are we to the gods ; they kill us for their sport," does suggest that perhaps Hardy was a little deaf in the orthodox ear, that he did not realise that it was the startling and stimulating blasphemy of the sentiments that had attracted orthodox Christians so irresistibly.

Actually the blame on God in *Tess of the D'Urbervilles* was more than a little unfair. The truth is that Hardy had got into the habit of hurting Tess, and apparently could not get out of it. It was Hardy, who wanted to sear our hearts by showing us a woman hanged, who made Tess stick the knife into D'Urberville. God would probably have been content with something less sensational than that ironic bright blob of blood that leaked through the floor, and printed itself like a gigantic ace of hearts on the landlady's ceiling beneath.

The drip, drip, drip which the landlady heard when she applied her ear to the keyhole of the room in which Tess had been so demonstrably asserting her purity is an historic sound, like the report with which Ibsen's Nora slammed the front-door on the home behind her, and made the whole world her prison.

Both were a part of the work of the New Spirit in Woman ; the work of wives who had thrown-over, or overthrown, their husbands. Tess paid the penalty on the gallows for being a New Woman without the New Education. She was, indeed, about midway between the New

Woman and the Noble Savage. It was Jude's cousin Sue, the girl who could say " Don't you dread the attitude that insensibly arises out of legal obligation ? Don't you think it is destructive to the profession whose essence is its gratuitousness," who was the complete New Woman with the New Education, even though she had been unable to throw off all the instinct of the older Eve.

Strangely enough, to mention the legal obligation in marriage is one of the easiest ways of annoying the very people who see salvation for the world through the sacrament of marriage and the office of the law. And annoy them Hardy did. His obstinate way of showing marriage both in *Tess* and *Jude* as hallowed, but unholy, and illicit love as holy but unhallowed, naturally enraged the orthodox.

A Scottish reviewer wrote that " Swinburne planteth, Hardy watereth and Satan giveth increase," a reader in the Antipodes posted Hardy a packet purporting to contain the ashes of *Jude the Obscure*, and an American reviewer intending to admonish Hardy, unintentionally insulted three other writers of genius :

> When I finished the story I opened the windows and let in the fresh air, and I turned to my bookshelves and said : " Thank God for Kipling and Stevenson, Barrie and Mrs. Humphry Ward."

It was in a sudden anger against criticism of that sort that Hardy exclaimed :

> If this sort of thing continues no more novel writing for me. A man must be a fool to deliberately stand up to be shot at.

And in his Diary Hardy describes how he and Swinburne condoled with each other on having been the two most abused of living writers, Swinburne for *Poems and Ballads* and Hardy for *Jude the Obscure*.

The last years of the last century will be regarded by future historians as one of the Ages of Abuse. Huge issues have always meant high voices; and when Hardy raised great questions, voices on both sides were raised as well. By the time he had published *Jude*, Hardy had managed to direct half the stream of abusive public criticism from Ibsen to himself. Without searching for resemblances like a forewarned passport officer, and certainly without indulging in the popular and pernicious habit of rechristening, by giving Hardy some such title as the Dorchester Ibsen, it remains for us to comment on some notable and obvious common aims and methods and qualities and deficiencies common to Hardy and Ibsen.

Both preached a new morality ; a morality founded not only on having seen the orthodox God, but on having seen through him. Both wrapped up their gospel of " facing life unflinchingly " in a covering about as comfortable to the average touch as a porcupine's. Both regarded the denial of love as the ultimate crime of Life. Both saw Society built on Deceit as Venice is built on piles, ready to collapse at a shake. Both saw Religion as a deceit ; a promise of dividends without reasonable security. And both saw that man willingly and wilfully deceives himself long after the first innocent deceit of ignorance is past. Both, therefore, set upon the demolition of the soul of society with the energy of housebreakers, just as Lassalle and Karl Marx had already started to demolish its body. In their method of work Hardy and Ibsen were both bold with the broad bravery of the man to whom boldness is not itself an end, but a means of arriving. Both achieved a mastery of form that only the remarkable nature of the material itself concealed. And both—but here it is necessary to invoke the aid of Genius as an explanation—managed to invest mean individual occurrences with a noble universal significance ; to promote the small hardships of men into the whole tragedy of Man. Thus when Tess stabbed D'Urberville it was not merely a sordid George Gissing kind of lodging-house affair in which the first-floor front happens to be a bad lot. It was a huge event in which all Womankind rose against its male oppressor, and did mad deeds for love. It was not *News of the World* but news of the World. Jude is not the prematurely wrinkled President of the Union of a correspondence college, but is the divine spirit weighed down by the whole human weight of the flesh. Like Ibsen's Nora and Hedda Gabler and Rosmersholm, Jude and Tess are creatures not so slavish as to be patently symbolic, yet who cast a shadow of symbolic size.

Hardy was a " regional " novelist who kept to his boundaries with the scrupulousness of an ordnance survey map. Yet confining the implications of Hardy's novels to Wessex, by saying that at this point and at that the map ends, would be as futile as the erection of the wall with which the Wise Men sought to imprison the cuckoo and preserve eternal Spring. Egdon Heath somehow spreads out until it is hard to say where the Great World begins and where the Heath stops ; the woods of *The Woodlanders* stretch across half England, appearing in odd, idyllic hollows in strange places many miles from Wessex ; and though Hardy's characters talk with a local burr they speak with the large voice of mankind.

The scenery in Hardy's novels is one of the strangest things in fiction ; it is well painted but not apparently

PF

well beloved. Often it seems as though Hardy were unhappy in it ; certainly less happy than Meredith among the shrubs of Surrey. There is something in Hardy of the man who is irresistibly attracted yet more than a little miserable in his attraction ; like a man who goes to the Lakes each year grumbling about the rain.

So much for the qualities in common between Ibsen and Hardy. If there are defects in Ibsen and Hardy to be looked for, they will be found I think in the tags of contemporary philosophy and thought they carry with them; such as a rather pathetic confidence in heredity. Indeed there would at least be a precedent for an idiotic line of inquiry into Darwin's authorship of Hardy.

Again in a labouring of points such as " the coming universal wish not to live," as the " outcome of new views of life," which is how the doctor explained the baby butchery in which Jude's son indulged when he murdered his brother and sister, the philosophy bears its date brightly upon it. Little Jude is a victim of just that same death which carried off little Bertha in the attic menagerie where the wild duck lodged : both were helpless children with a load of more than adult cares. And both Ibsen and Hardy were writers of an immortal genius that was the immediate and inevitable product of nineteenth century Protestantism. They were children who happened to dislike their parent, but who nevertheless bore a strong family resemblance to him. They were black sheep in a white flock ; but undeniably and recognisably sheep all the same.

Hardy remained artistically agnostic to the end. He died to a verse from 'Omar Khayyám read to him before an open window listening to bells his ears were too drowsed to catch :

Oh Thou, who Man of baser Earth didst make,
And ev'n in Paradise devise the Snake ;
*   For all the Sin wherewith the Face of Men*
Is blackened—Man's forgiveness give—and take !

Thus did Thomas Hardy salute the President of the Immortals—impolitely.

HENRY JAMES

Within the last generation the novel has tended to change from being a record of events into being a record of the causes of events. The name psychological has been applied to it, and it has become conscious, even self-conscious, of its new duties and responsibilities. For the new duties of the novel have demanded a new form, and when novelists spend their time talking about a New Form, as Conrad did, it is a miracle when they produce anything finer than a freak.

Certainly the old novel was about as well adapted to its new duties as a cart-horse for steeplechasing, and the work of a notably important section of writers during these years was that of breeding a new and volatile creature which could clear the ditches and hedges that divide the physical world from the mental.

No author better illustrates what the psychological novelists were trying to do than Henry James. Joseph Conrad might seem an equally good example. But in his case the mind of the critic cannot help straying into wondering how it was that Joseph Conrad Kurzeniowski, the Pole, wrote such nearly perfect French novels in English. And it is Henry James, the naturalised American who ends by becoming more nearly the typical new English novelist.

Henry James, at first, inevitably puts one in mind of those parties of American tourists, with pale, flat, child-like faces, who stand in groups about the Temple during the summer months pondering profoundly on Art, Architecture and Antiquity. But he is like the one member of the party who not only knows where Elia was born, but even knows Elia, having read him in some far Western university. And possibly—quite probably, in fact—has published an immense volume of detailed and minute Elian criticism.

Henry James came to Europe from the wrong side of the Atlantic, and spent thirty-seven close, painful years in showing those born on the right side how crude, barbaric and colonial they were. He was driven out of the United States, as remorselessly as if he had been deported, by the sheer material pressure of ambitious, immature life. And he was as miserable in consequence as a gigolo in a farmyard. His mind moved always as though it were in the thinnest of dancing-shoes. It drew back appalled when it found that a single step would carry it clean off the narrow pavement of culture. There was something rather ridiculous in his having been born in an unfinished country. And he realised it. It was as artistically absurd as the thought of Fenimore Cooper in a *salon*.

Europe glittered on the horizon of his imagination, stately with age, strangely alluring with the euphonious names of the south, and with plenty of pavement everywhere. Henry James visited it with that sleep-defying thoroughness of intention that is the unconcealed secret of his work. In paradoxical inversion of the natural law, Henry James came to Europe as the emigrant from America because Europe seemed the more promising land. And in becoming the perfect European he showed himself the born American; the man who is at home anywhere outside his own house, the true pioneering Colonial.

That the United States should have produced so physically useless a creature as Henry James is due to the fact that strange lands have always meant strange religions, and that strange religions have always occupied men's minds to exclusion. Henry James the elder was a Sweden-borgian whose mind walked naturally with ease amid the abstract and mysterious. His son, William James, was the founder of the philosophy of Pragmatism, that theory of life which in its combination of psychological and physical elements satisfies no one completely, and reminds the European mind of philosophy at play.

It has often been remarked that William and Henry seemed to share a common genius for the subtle and the psychological ; that they wrote their books—William his *Pragmatism : A New Name for Old Ways of Thinking*, Henry his *Wings of the Dove*—as two brothers who do their school homework together, without any clean dividing line be-tween the results.

A legend has grown up around Henry James that he is, if not actually unreadable, at least readable only in a quiet room, with the aid of ice-packs, grammars and a reverent nature. In that, James is simply a victim of himself. He is like a man who gets a reputation for an ass simply because he has deliberately cultivated an extreme mannerism in youth, and cannot throw it off in age ; there is about him a suggestion of grey hairs and corsets. The trouble is that Henry James's later books have obscured his life's work.

He is judged by *The Golden Bowl* and not by *Roderick Hudson* or *Daisy Miller* ; which is as patently unfair as judging a supreme talker like Coleridge by what he said on his death-bed.

Henry James's was a mind of remarkable lucidity. He had a tight-rope walker's nerve, and could keep his head in traversing the thinnest threads of narrative suspended over vertiginous deeps of psychology. Unfortunately for his success, he did not realise that other people simply lacked the nerve, and that after a few steps they halted and turned back to try again—or fell floundering right out of the bottom of the tale.

Consider a typical passage from *The Wings of the Dove*.

It was to the honour of her sincerity that she made the surrender on the spot, though it was not perhaps altogether to that of her logic. She had wanted, very consciously, from the first, to give something up for her new acquaintance, but she had now no doubt that she was practically giving up all. What settled this was the fulness of a particular impression, the impression that had throughout more and more supported her and which she would have uttered so far as she might by saying that the charm of the creature was positively in the creature's greatness. She would have been content so to leave it ; unless indeed she had said, more familiarly, that Mildred was the biggest impression of her life. That was at all events the biggest account of her, and none but a big clearly would do.

That short explanation of the conduct of a soul contains both what is typical of Henry James's qualities and shortcomings. Even raped from its context the thought remains perfectly intelligible ; it proceeds elaborately and usefully.

The grammar on the other hand, is moderately baffling. It is clearly that of a very clever man—or of a man who works at his prose like a child practising scales on a piano, going over it again and again, so that he meets the reader on unfair terms, having prepared all the difficult bits beforehand. There is that awkward ellipsis in the opening sentence, clumsily repaired by the insertion of the words

" that of " ; there is the doubt in the mind as to whether " consciously " should, or indeed can, be modified by " very," and the further doubt as to whether " practically " should come before or after " giving up " ; and at the end there is that horrible murder of words, by poison drawn from metaphysical text-books, " none but a big clearly would do." To complete some of the ellipses the mind must hop like a frog, and to appreciate the method of speaking in terms of philosophic abstractions the mind must also be able to hover over certain words and phrases like a hawk. At times, and in such a sentence as, " To be the heir of all the ages only to know yourself, as that consciousness should deepen, balked of your inheritance, would be to play the part, it struck me, or at least to arrive at the type, in the light on the whole most becoming," the syntax and the punctuation are bad to wickedness.

In short, Henry James's style is only moderately successful even for its own delicate purpose. For, save to a few clever, persistent minds, it defeats itself for all time when it first defeats the reader. About the quality of the thought itself, no one who has read, for instance, *The Ambassadors* (which James considered his best book) can remain in doubt. For here was an author who knew more reasons why his characters should not do the things they did, than most authors seem to know for their actually doing. But anyone who has read *The Golden Bowl* will inevitably have all kinds of doubt about his grammar.

Henry James was like a trick-dancer walking on eggs. Nine times out of ten he is marvellously successful. But on the tenth time we feel as though we have been present at a rehearsal.

The reason for Henry James's unique style is not perhaps so consciously artistic as has generally been imagined.

He dictated the later books in which his style is at its most
perverse. And no man living has any real command of
his mannerisms in *speech*. Those jostling second thoughts,
and the recurrent " as-it-weres "—even the slang said
self-consciously with rounded lips like a clergyman
deliberately and decently swearing—probably have their
origin in the air and not on paper. We seem even to see
the gestures that accompanied the mannerisms.

That is not, of course, to suggest that Henry James ever
let his novels go out into the world as a busy business man
sends out his letters, " dictated but not read." But from
the moment when he began to dictate his books his mannerisms began to run away with him. And his revisions
then became merely the crystallising into prose of the
loquacity of an elaborate and diffuse speaker.

There is a phrase somewhere in *The Wings of the Dove*
that exactly describes a Henry James novel. There are,
indeed, many such phrases : it seems that something in
the quality of Henry James's thoughts does not lend itself
comfortably to the ordinary apparatus of description. The
phrase to which I am referring is the one that describes
a girl as having " stature without height, grace without
motion, presence without mass " : a veritable ghost of a
girl. And, indeed, Henry James's novels often seem to be
merely splendid ghosts of real novels, needing just height,
motion and mass to bring them into the full, fat life of
fiction. As it is there is an intangible tenuousness about
them that frequently makes the reader wish that he had
read more carefully when nearer the beginning.

With Henry James the novel becomes more consciously
literary than ever before ; and not with entire success.
Henry James was an experimentalist who wrote fiction
in the manner of a chemist in a laboratory. He was
laboriously and lovingly trying to evolve a formula of

fiction ; and more of his professional life than a novelist should be able to spare was occupied with mixtures and messes.

The prefaces to the Collected Edition of Henry James's novels form a prose " Prelude or Growth of a Novelist's Mind." They are the most nearly complete declaration of a novelist's policy that we have in the language. Every novelist must more or less plan a novel, must have within his mind at one moment or another a sudden bright shaft in which the whole pattern of the book is illumined. Yet, such is the weakness of the human brain, that detail and form can rarely be seen at the same instant. With Henry James they could.

The preface to *The Wings of the Dove*, for example, opens with the explicit announcement that : " The idea, reduced to its essence, is that of a young person conscious of a great capacity for life, but early stricken and doomed, condemned to die under short respite, while also enamoured of the world . . ." And the rest of the preface contains an outline in the exact terms of a chemical formula of how the author is going to achieve the fulfilment of his idea. It is as though James had emptied his brain of the plan, in outline and detail, as it existed within him. And to what extent that meticulous brain of his concerned itself with detail may be seen from the way in which he describes how he is going to build up the novel scene by scene, character by character, value by value, with the awesome competence of a small child building a whole cathedral out of toy bricks.

There was the " fun " to begin with, of establishing one's successive centres—of fixing them so exactly that the portions of the subject commanded by them as by happy points of view, and accordingly treated from them, would constitute so to speak, sufficiently solid blocks of wrought material, squared to the sharp edge as to have weight and mass and carrying power ; to make for construction, that is, to conduce to effect and provide for beauty. . . .

It would almost be true to say that if a Henry James novel fails, it fails because Henry James has intended it to fail in just that particular way. Certainly when it succeeds, the manner of its success has been exactly predetermined.

In scope Henry James had a mind of remarkable narrowness of range ; most " psychological " novelists have. Once he had rid himself of the desire to be eerie, once he had disentangled himself from the Hawthorne tree that he had climbed in youth, he settled down to observing not only social comedy, but Society comedy ; a comedy of manners in which all the manners were good ones.

The only point at which life, crude and irresistible, scattered the bric-à-brac and orchids of his mind was when his beautiful cousin, Mary Temple, who was to Henry James through life as Agnes was to Dickens, a fixed, immutable, marvellous star among women, died at the age of twenty-three. Hers was a death in just those conditions of desperate vitality that were framed in *The Wings of the Dove.*

If Henry James's contribution to the novel could be described in a phrase it is thus : he gave the novel new nerves of sensitiveness, he taught it to explore the mind for the little half resolutions and misgivings as well as for the decisions and rejections that ultimately make for action.

He was a man fascinated by the unexpectedness of the

human mind. In that he resembled most of the post-Freudian novelists of to-day. But he was interested primarily in the normal mind ; or at the most in the normally abnormal mind. And in that he differed from the novelists of to-day.

THE CASE AGAINST
D. H. LAWRENCE

It was only to be expected that the novel which had become a supplement to the *Universal Dictionary of Psychology* (the modern counterpart of Fielding's " vast authentic doomsday book of nature ") should now become a supplement to the *Universal Dictionary of Abnormal Psychology* : for connoisseurs always finally go after the few and the freakish. And the writer whose frantic intensity of expression and fantastic conception of mankind promote him above all his kindred is D. H. Lawrence.

Lawrence was so sensitive to the rest of life that he was like a man born without his skin ; impressions and emotions everywhere struck him full on raw, naked nerves. Having none of those useful barriers that ordinary thick-skinned men have between themselves and experience, he seemed to be a part of experience itself—which is really what is meant by people who take Lawrence to pieces and reconstruct him in the Middleton Murry manner to show that he is a huge symbolic figure ; not a man but Man himself.

Lawrence was never greater than any situation in which he found himself. He strove hard to be equal. But he remained always inferior to circumstances. And his books are essentially the expression of the rat in the trap.

Mr. Murry, whose eloquent volume *Son of Woman : The Story of D. H. Lawrence* has all but become the Bible of Lawrence's faithful, has been responsible for a thin and rather tiresome comparison between Lawrence and Christ.

In a slight, superficial sense it is just. In neither case can we understand the works without the life. But the works of Lawrence grew steadily and inevitably out of the life, and not the life necessarily and remorselessly out of the works as in the more important case.

The details of the dark and distressing childhood of Lawrence are now better known to a great many people than the details of the fresher and more fragrant childhood of Christ. But just as Matthew, Mark, Luke and John must be forgiven a somewhat trying reiteration of one well-known theme, so must any commentator on D. H. Lawrence be forgiven the repetition of the open secrets of Lawrence's life.

Lawrence was the fourth child of a drunken collier, and a woman who should never have made the blunder of becoming a collier's wife. David Herbert was not wanted. But once he was born his mother sent wave upon wave of love crashing over him. This is his infancy reflected in his fiction :

> In her arms lay the delicate baby . . . A wave of hot love went over her to the infant. She held it close to her face and breast. With all her force, with all her soul she would make up to it for having brought it into the world unloved. She would love it all the more now it was here ; carry it in her love. Its clear, knowing eyes gave her pain and fear. Did it know all about her ? When it lay under her heart, had it been listening then ? Was there a reproach in the look ? She felt the marrow melt in her bones, with fear and pain.

Paul Morel's life in *Sons and Lovers* is more like Lawrence than a good many portraits-of-the-artist are like the original. He was the first of a band of characters who stretch through the novels in tormented profusion, whose difficulties have been their author's.

Lawrence's love for his mother would seem exquisitely beautiful in a world in which sons could remain sons and not have to grow into husbands. In the world as it is, the beauty of that love is too thickly streaked with what is morbid for the whole to remain beautiful.

Just as we can see a child's being spoiled by being given too much toffee so we can see Lawrence's life being spoiled by being given too much womanly love. Lawrence's mother would have been considerably more kind to him if she had continued in her dislike. As it was, she concentrated on him all the love she had once directed on her husband. And the son, made too delicate for the task by too much loving, was called upon to give an unhappy woman the assurance that should have come from her husband.

If the emotion could have stopped short at that deep, though possibly destructive, devotion that Ruskin felt for his mother, and had not steered towards darker waters, the mind of the reader who sees the events from a distance would be lighter. But in the shape that events took we cannot view this relationship with anything but a mounting nausea. For Lawrence tragically grew ; and in a passage in *Sons and Lovers*, that sends a moan of anguish up from the page into a reader of any sensitiveness, he describes how a mother went to the very Hell Gates of sex with her son :

Paul was very ill. His mother lay in bed at nights with him ; they could not afford a nurse. He grew worse, and the crisis approached. One night he tossed into consciousness in the ghastly, sickly feeling of dissolution, when all the cells in the body seem in intense irritability to be breaking down, and consciousness makes a last flare of struggle, like madness.

"I s'll die, mother!" he cried, heaving for breath on the pillow.

She lifted him up, crying in a small voice :

"Oh, my son—my son!"

That brought him to. He realised her. His whole will rose up and arrested him. He put his head on her breast, and took ease of her for love.

Mercifully Lawrence was romantic and not realistic. That passage otherwise would have been intolerable.

And so this son grew to worship his mother like a god, and to have adopted her like the slave of his bosom ; which is bad theology. And Lawrence's strangely beautiful funeral poem to his mother, beginning :

> *My little love, my darling,*

and running on to :

> *I kiss you good-bye, my dearest,*
> *It is finished between us here.*
> *Oh, if I were as calm as you are,*
> *Sweet and still on your bier !*
> *Oh God, if I had not to leave you*
> *Alone, my dear.*

is a poem in which even the language has changed from that of the son to that of the lover. Anyone who is not aware of a rare beauty in these passages must be insensitive to the facts of writing. But anyone who is not aware also of a strange ugliness must be blind to the facts of life.

If Lawrence's love for his mother is full of shadows there

is a corner of his mind that already by the time he was sixteen is midnight black. In *Sons and Lovers* he is as frank about Paul Morel's fornications as about his affections. At sixteen Lawrence was pestering a girl of his own age to have sexual intercourse with him. This is the fictional account :

> I held forth with rapture to her, positively with rapture. I simply went up in smoke. And she adored me. The serpent in the grass was sex. She somehow didn't have any ; at least, not where it's supposed to be. I got thinner and crazier. Then I said we'd got to be lovers. I talked her into it. So she let me.

She let him. But it was not enough. She did not encourage Lawrence in his persuasive rape. And Lawrence left her in the first of those disgusts that were to sweep through his soul like a whirlwind scattering and destroying all that was good, all that was beautiful, in his mind.

Mr. Middleton Murry has penetratingly and exactly explained Lawrence's desertion of the passive partner in this adolescent escapade by saying that while Lawrence's mother still lived, " he was incapable of giving to another woman the love without which sexual possession must be a kind of violence done ; done not to the woman only, but also and equally to the man : above all to a man like Lawrence." And not only while his mother lived. After her death Lawrence could still look back to that embracing love, the only utterly satisfying love that he had known in his life, with regret heightened by his present awful hunger. A Freudian might explain the whole thing by saying that what Lawrence was really longing for, with an insatiable desire, was the blissful twilight of the womb, where perfect union was the natural state of life.

Q F

Lawrence's books, in one important particular are by no means the mirror of his life. There was only one woman—a passionate school-teacher, a tempting Sue Bridehead—who came between the incident of the farmer's obliging daughter and the woman who became Lawrence's wife. " Now, why "—the reader must inevitably ask—" did Lawrence, the liver of this comparatively placid life, write novels which were simply proud and protracted phallic hymns ? With Lawrence, as with St. Augustine did the strength of the Devil lurk, roaring in his loins ? " The answer apparently, is, " no." On Mr. Murry's authority, founded on intimacy, we are assured that Lawrence was " almost a sexual-weakling." All those colossal strainings of which his novels are full, which seem to shake and shatter the very foundations of sex, are obviously not the emotions of a man to whom accomplishment brings rest. There is always a hint, rising in some places to an articulate suggestion, and in others— *The Rainbow* is one of them—to a shout, that Lawrence's novels are the work not so much of a potent novelist as of an impotent man.

If we compare the work of a novelist whose manhood *was* an affliction, Tolstoy, with that of Lawrence, I think we might guess that Lawrence was not the great husband but the small lover; a physically bankrupt man, ashamed of living on a woman's charity.

Tolstoy begat a family, and ploughed the fields of Yasnaya Polyana, and danced Cossack dances, and defied the Church and the State, and wrote *War and Peace*. Life roared through his veins like a stream in flood. His sexual pleasures and remorses were as great as Lawrence's. But sex to him was simply a sudden and usually uncontrollable outburst of his tremendous vitality. With Lawrence, it was sex for which he lived and sex which kept him alive. Sex with him is not only a means but an end. It was an inescapable circle ; a vicious circle which he blindly saw as a magic circle.

It is not possible to write of Lawrence merely as an urgent and intense story-teller, though there is some strangely emotional compulsion within all his best work that drives the reader irresistibly onwards. Neither is it possible to think of him merely as one of the supremely imaginative writers whose language (when he could forget the dismal jargon of psychology with its hyphens, like stiles that have to be climbed) could soar without effort and remain aloft without fatigue.

True, both these qualities do occur within his good work, and even break through in his bad like a pure note in the voice of a platform speaker. But the story is always a story with a moral, even though the moral may happen to be a bad one. And the prose at its most persuasive is never without a purpose, usually a dark purpose, in its persuasion. The moral and the purpose are that man has ceased to worship sex as it should be worshipped, that only through sex can man arrive at the true understanding of life, and that it is the duty of man to repair the great rent in the cloth of nature that Christ had made in tearing body and soul apart ; in dividing the body by a girdle of chastity.

And so it is that the critic of Lawrence is driven away from such works as *Sons and Lovers* and *Women in Love*, which really established Lawrence as a novelist, to the *Fantasia of the Unconscious*, in which he could teach his lessons about sex without the accidental interruption of having to write fiction ; lessons which would have startled the Serpent—who probably had not even thought of the sharper daggers of impotence at the time of the original temptation.

And from the *Fantasia* the critic is driven onwards to *Lady Chatterley's Lover*, in which Lawrence returned to the form of fiction without ever allowing it to interfere with the propaganda.

Consider one of the typical passages in which the imaginative mind of Lawrence endeavours to describe the supreme act of sex. One is inevitably rather appalled at the writer's courage in trying to describe such a thing at all. Even the vocabulary of description is missing and he must make his own. It is all curiously unrealistic. For Lawrence had the fastidious man's natural dislike of real flesh, no matter how much he worshipped it in his imagination. And it is all strangely unconvincing, like the prose description of a piece of music.

But what is the experience? Untellable. Only, we know something. We know that in the act of coition the *blood* of the individual man, acutely surcharged, with intense vital electricity—we know no word, so say " electricity," by analogy—rises to a culmination, in a tremendous magnetic urge towards the magnetic blood of the female. The whole of the living blood in the two individuals forms a field of intense, prolonged magnetic attraction. So, the two poles must be brought into contact. In the act of coition, the two seas of blood in the two individuals, rocking and surging towards contact, as near as possible clash into a oneness. A great flash of interchange occurs, like an electric spark when two currents meet or like lightning out of the densely surcharged clouds. There is a lightning flash which passes through the blood of both individuals, there is a thunder of sensation which rolls in diminishing crashes down the nerves of each—and then the tension passes.

Such was Lawrence's method of recollecting emotion, not in tranquillity but in a mood of remembered ecstasy. He was like a man taking a stiff whisky-and-soda to bring himself to the point of remembering exactly how it feels to be drunk.

Exactly what Lawrence's real lesson was in all this has never become quite clear. At least it became as clear as daylight. But like the daylight it was constantly changing. At the time of writing *Women in Love*, it was that the sexual act had been performed perfectly only when there had been " mingling and intimacy." But by the time he wrote *Kangaroo* he was searching for something that could not come by nakedness alone.

All through his life Lawrence had not liked the flesh. He had merely been educating it to become a worthy servant of the soul. He had coached and instructed it in its athletics so that it might run level with the mind. And by the end of his life when, in writing *The Man Who Died*, he took the body of Christ down from the cross and put it into a woman's warm arms, he was still trying to make the body as rich in experience as the mind.

It made Lawrence furious to see anyone so startlingly and intelligently alive as Christ having developed so naturally without the assistance of Woman. Christ was the supreme example in history that exploded Lawrence's theory. That was why Lawrence hated him.

The Man Who Died contains a lot of Lawrence that was his best. The description of the resurrection of Christ within the tomb is the writing of a man to whom sorrow and pain do not come as strangers to the mind :

Slowly, slowly he crept down from the cell of rock with the caution of the bitterly wounded. Bandages and linen and perfume fell away, and he crouched on the ground against the wall of rock to recover oblivion. But he saw his hurt feet touching the earth again, the earth they had meant to touch no more, and he saw his thin legs that had died, and pain unknowable, pain like utter bodily disillusion, filled him so full that he stood up, with one torn hand on the ledge of the tomb.

To be back ! To be back again, after all that ! He saw the linen swathing bands fallen round dead feet, and stooping, he picked them up, folded them, and laid them back in the rocky cavity from which he had emerged. Then he took the perfumed linen sheet, wrapped it round him as a mantle, and turned away to the wanness of the chill dawn.

He was alone ; and having died, was even beyond loneliness.

Lawrence at times could write prose that bleeds with compassion, as the last extract does, when the experience seems to have been drawn into him. And at times, especially when angry, he could write prose that simply explodes along the printed line. This kind of thing :

I would like to be a tree for a while. The great lust of roots. Root-lust. And no mind at all. He towers, and I sit and feel safe. I like to feel him towering round me. I used to be afraid. I used to fear their lust, their rushing black lust. But now I like it, I worship it. I always felt them huge primeval enemies, but now they are only shelter and strength. I losc myself among the trees. I am so glad to be with them in their silent, intent passion, and their great lust. They feed my soul. But I can understand that Jesus was crucified on a tree.

There we have that powerful impulsive prose corroded with sexual images. For Lawrence, despite his contempt for the Freudians, who find a sexual origin for all things as easily as a Bolshevik finds a capitalistic one, saw enough sex in ordinary life to make a Freudian gape.

Whether he was looking at a cat or at catkins he divided them, male and female, according to their kind. There is that passage in *Women in Love* in which Birkin trespasses into a class-room during a nature-study lesson and says to the teacher :

> " Give me some crayons, won't you . . . so that they can make the gynæcious flowers red, and the androgynous yellow. I'd chalk them in plain, chalk and nothing else, merely the red and the yellow. Outline scarcely matters in this case. There is just the one fact to emphasise . . . "

that makes Lawrence appear to have the image of sex printed on the inside of his eyelids : whenever he closed his eyes to think, he saw it.

There are those horrid darknesses which over-cloud his mind from time to time, when Lawrence, like a war-horse, grows stamping and impatient at the smell of blood. As in *The Woman Who Rode Away*, he worships at red, stained altars.

There was also the mounting hatred of the world that would not attend to him, a hatred that changed the great teacher with the words of salvation in his mouth, to the nihilist with a bomb in his pocket. In the words of Birkin :

> Well, if mankind is destroyed, if our race is destroyed like Sodom, and there is this beautiful evening with the luminous land and the trees, I am satisfied. That which

informs it all is there, and can never be lost . . . let
mankind pass away—time it did. The creative utter-
ances will not cease, they will only be there. Humanity
doesn't embody the utterance of the incomprehensible
any more. Humanity is a dead letter. There will be a
new embodiment, in a new way. Let humanity disappear as soon as possible.

Lawrence's contempt for the world accumulated within
his mind until finally he could announce it only in thin,
strident shrieks. His later poems are simply declarations
of anger, often inarticulate in their rage. He had ceased
to be a novelist; and unless something could have restored
sympathy to his heart he would never have become a
novelist again. And to recover his sympathy he would
have needed to recover his sanity. His early books may
seem terribly wrong to us. But they contain the tremendous errors of a man, fully articulate and finely intelligent;
and so are in urgent need of correction. The later work is
not so much in need of correction as of cure.

With all things one must draw a line somewhere. And
the object of a line through Lawrence—if, indeed, the
line is flexible enough not to exclude him altogether—
must be to divide the sane from the insane. Probably it
should be drawn at the point at which *Kangaroo* appears.
Possibly it should be drawn to include *The Fantasia of the
Unconscious* on the debit side. And the position of the line
is not only a matter of prejudice but of period. We shall
draw the dividing line of reason nearer to those last, mad
monodies, *Nettles*, than any age before us would have
drawn it.

MR. GEORGE MOORE

Mr. George Moore belongs to no class in fiction. During most of his long and varied career he has generally been disowned and in the corner.

He has made two large distinct reputations as well as several smaller blurred ones. Back in the 'eighties—Mr. George Moore's seventy-eight years take him back into a world of fiction that was gaslit—he established himself with *A Mummer's Wife* as a realist of startling and defiant frankness.

Now, even his *Esther Waters*, which so notoriously shocked 1894, has been left somewhere in the rear of the race for frankness ; and Mr. George Moore has very wisely not attempted to produce another book that will regain him the first place. Instead of following the French realists —who were his early models—any longer, he adopted the method of the French philosophical novelists. He was a man who, after sampling all France, preferred the manner of Anatole, even though he despised the man. So it was that at the age of sixty-nine he wrote *The Brook Kerith*, on which his reputation, as a writer of some of the most melodious and placid prose in the language, now rests.

As there is the thick, morocco-leather odour of the library about Henry James, so is there the smell of scent and turpentine, of concert hall and studio, about Mr. George Moore. In his liberal understanding of the arts he is unique among the English novelists. It is, I know, usual to say that Mr. George Moore writes in the manner of a painter, that his scenes in fiction have the shape that a graphic artist would have given them. I am doubtful, however, whether long study of painting or music ever contributed anything to a prose writer more tangible than a capacity for taking pains.

The two disciplines of perspective and diatonics if once obeyed *may* leave some sort of orderly impression in the mind. But if they do, examples of that impression are few. And much of the talk about Mr. George Moore's painting in prose is no more than being wise after the event.

Mr. George Moore's mind, one must remember, is not one mind but a multitude. There is the little Irish Catholic boy who attended confession ; and there is the Irish Catholic Apostate who mocked the confessional. There is the Irish Protestant convert ; and there is the Irishman who guyed English Protestantism. There is the sparklingly independent mind that used religion as an Aunt-Sally at which to throw epigrams ; and there is the mind so sensitive to beauty in any form that it was irresistibly drawn back to the mysteriously beautiful story that Protestants and Catholics rather uncomfortably share. There is the disciple of Manet ; and there is the man who gave up painting for writing. There is the scholarly musician ; and there is the man who has had no real connection with music. There is the author of *Parnell and His Island* who spat on his native land until his spittle became exhausted ; and there is the author of *The Untilled Field*, which was adopted as a class-work by the members of the Gaelic League. There is the Parisian art student who kept a pet python, chained to a Louis XV stool and fed on guinea pigs ; and there is the independent Fenian who painted his front door Nationalist colours in the most Unionist quarter of Dublin. There is the author of *Ave, Salve* and *Vale*, who published details about his friends, like an unscrupulous blackmailer who in some unaccountable way failed to call to collect the money ; and there is the author of *The Brook Kerith*, in whose drowsed ears nothing more modern than a Syrian sheepbell seems ever to have sounded. There is the humorist ; and there is the author of *Esther Waters*.

Of course, as the experiences and changes came to him, the mind of George Moore grew complex and compound, until no one thread of thought could be followed and extracted without one's getting tangled up in the whole skein, like a kitten playing with a ball of knitting-wool.

Susan L. Mitchell, the author of a provocatively independent study of George Moore, gives us a description of Moore's being received into the Protestant Church. Before the event, " Æ." gave Moore the sane and salutary advice not to be an ass, and warned him that he would be called upon to " kneel and pray," an exercise which he would find extremely awkward and doubtless extremely silly.

After a week had elapsed, " Æ." met Mr. Moore and asked him about the initiation. " Well," said Moore, " what you said nearly burst up the whole thing. When the clergyman came I did not wish to appear to be taken in too easily and I worked up a few remaining scruples, fenced for a while and finally announced my scruples as conquered, and myself ready to be received into the fold. Then the clergyman said, ' Let us have a prayer,' and I remembered your words and saw your face looking at me, and I burst out laughing. When I saw the horrified look in the clergyman's face I realised it was all up unless I could convince him that it was hysteria ; and I clasped my hands together and said, ' Oh, you don't realise how strange all this appears to me to be. I feel like a little child that has lost its way on a long road and at last sees its father,' and I, folding my hands anew, began ' Our Father.' I took the wind out of his sails that way, for he had to join in, but he got in two little prayers on his own account afterwards and very nice little prayers they were too."

It may be objected that such behaviour was not so much that of a man who was a Protestant and a humorist, as that of a man who was a Catholic and a clown. At least, it is typical of the confusion of character that is George Moore's.

But our chief concern must be with the two books *Esther Waters* and *The Brook Kerith*—two books that might more easily have been written by different men than by the same man—on which his reputation rests. Now is not the moment to deal either with him or with his other works, such as *Evelyn Innes*, in which he spilt his musical and æsthetic knowledge about like a clumsy workman carrying a whitewash pail, or with *Aphrodite in Aulis* in which he wrote of love as a woman thinks of it.

That unfortunate girl, Esther Waters, like Tess, seems to have had Fate slamming doors in her face all through life. *Esther Waters* lacks entirely those moments of exalted emotion which transformed Tess's sordid affair into epic tragedy. But against that loss there is the gain of that observant, and sometimes peeping, naturalism that Balzac practised. In short *Tess* moves, and *Esther Waters* depresses.

George Moore's novels were always getting swamped by those things in which his mind was interested at the moment. In *Evelyn Innes* it was musical criticism ; in *Esther Waters* in was wet-nursing ; in *The Brook Kerith* it was theology. *Evelyn Innes* died to the sound of music ; *Esther Waters* and *The Brook Kerith* survived because the

mechanics of motherhood and the Bible were more nearly
their subjects.

Esther Waters is a novel of magnificent intention. Its
subject is the love of a mother for her child. Unfortunately,
the fulfilment of the intention is marred by the wretched-
ness of the writing. It is of that kind of half naturalism that
is about as much like life as it is known to-day as the faded
photographs, full of big hats and bell-sleeves, that fill old
albums.

" I'm your father," said William.

" No, you ain't. I ain't got no father."

" How do you know, Jackie ? "

" Father died before I was born ; mother told me."

" But mother may have been mistaken."

" If my father hadn't died before I was born he'd've
been to see us before this. Come, mother, come to tea.
Mrs. Lewis 'as got hot cakes, and they'll be burnt if we
stand talking."

" Yes, dear, but what the gentleman says is quite
true ; he is your father."

Jackie made no answer, and Esther said : " I told
you your father was dead, but I was mistaken."

" Won't you come and walk with me ? " said
William.

" No, thank you ; I like to walk with mother."

And it is not only the quality of the writing that is poor.
Mr. George Moore's mind never, as Hardy's does in *Tess*,
gives the impression of rising an inch above the scenes he
describes ; it simply drifts about in the slums on flat feet
like a charity-worker. And the proportion of things in the
mind occasionally seems to be wrong ; in the first half of
the book, for instance, the parturient is considerably larger
than the whole. Esther Waters herself, the loyal, loving,

illiterate savage, is one of the noble figures of fiction ; far finer, in fact, than the novel in which she lives.

Any coldness that we may feel towards Esther may be due to the fact that Jackie was not the only child of sin she bore, and that from her time onwards, fiction has been considerably overcrowded with women to whom the wages of sin has been publicity. *Esther Waters*, in fact, despite the lavish praise that has been paid to it, proves that it was as something larger than an outspoken Gissing that Mr. George Moore was to make a name.

He made that name with *The Brook Kerith*. The subject was one that had to face unnatural competition, and was bound to meet its readers with as heavy a handicap as any story ever carried. The Christian story has been a trap in which faithful and heretics have fallen in hideous confusion. But somehow the perfection of the Gospel version has had a fatal fascination for the courageous of all creeds. If the Gospel version has been done less well already, that is, if it had exercised a less powerful appeal, there would have been fewer competitors. As it is, the sheer hopelessness of the task has released some silly catch in men's minds and set them off. It is bad enough in the public Christian mind when the writer fails clumsily and reverently. But the embarrassment is proportionately greater when a writer, who succeeds exquisitely, suggests that the Gospel version is not so much a masterpiece as a mistake.

The Brook Kerith is really not so astonishing a thing in Mr. Moore's life as it might at first seem. It was written at a moment when a kind of Catholic mushroom left over from childhood broke the adult, sceptical soil. Like Rénan's *Life of Jesus* it is the work of a man to whom the Christian story is a thing of beautiful associations. Mr. Moore was never more nearly Catholic than he was in writing this story of the crucified Saviour who was taken down from the cross and nursed back to health and obscurity. True, from the orthodox point of view Mr. Moore has got the story all wrong. But the important fact remains that he had got it at all.

The deep reverence of the narrative is far more impressive to the unreligious mind than the quick genuflexion of a busy priest. Mr. George Moore's journey to gather local colour for the book was far more in the nature of a pilgrimage, even though it was a pagan pilgrimage, than a pleasure-trip.

Susan Mitchell describes *The Brook Kerith* as " an epilogue to a beautiful story written by a man tired of the theme, yet who cannot invent anything more beautiful than the story he wrecks." That was written by a Protestant. Mr. Moore had been a Catholic ; and Catholics do not regard the Bible—possibly because theirs is a poor one—with the respect shown by Protestants. I do not understand how a man could be called tired of it who was drawn back to a story of his nursery days as dramatically as if a stockbroker had suddenly got down on all fours on the floor and asked his mother to tell him the story of Red Riding Hood. And the fact that Mr. Moore changed the tale as fundamentally as though Red Riding Hood had eaten the wolf, was not because he was tired of it, so much as because he was George Moore.

The Brook Kerith is one of those beautifully written books that defy quotation. To exhibit it in portions would be as silly as picking a bunch of flowers and pretending that they adequately represent Kew Gardens.

The prose is as moderated as though Mr. George Moore were a conductor continually damping down the ardour of his orchestra. It is a work that can be read for the slow beauty of its language, and can be searched for the purple passage without revealing anything like one. It is the work of an old man only in the number of things, the tricks, artifices and devices of writing, for which he no longer cares. If a passage in the whole work can be found for isolated reproduction it is probably this :

> The sunny woods were threaded with little paths, and Joseph cast curious eyes upon them all. The first led him into bracken so deep that he did not venture farther, and the second took him to the verge of a dark hollow so dismal that he came running back to ask if there were crocodiles in the water he had discovered. He did not give his preceptor time to answer the difficult question, but laid his hand upon his arm, and whispered that he was to look between the two rocks, for a jackal was there, slinking away—turning his pointed muzzle to us now and then. To see he isn't followed, Azariah added : and the observation endeared him so to Joseph that the boy walked for a moment pensively in the path they were following. It turned into the forest, and they had not gone very far before they were aware of a strange silence, if silence it could be called, for when they listened the silence was full of sound, innumerable little sounds, some of which they recognised ; but it was not the hum of insects or the chirp of a bird or the snapping of a rotten twig that filled Joseph with awe, but something that he could neither see, nor hear, nor smell, nor touch. The life of the trees—is that it ? he asked himself. A remote mysterious life breathing about him and he regretted that he was without a sense to apprehend this life.

But quotations from *The Brook Kerith* tend to run on from sentence to sentence, and even from chapter to chapter.

The real reason is that, artist as he is, Mr. Moore is primarily a story-teller, and a story is something that lives only in its own completeness.

It is a strange thing that Mr. Moore's art should have so obscured his intention. But it has done so. Most people remember Gosse's description of Moore as " one of the most conscientious and chastened artificers of the written page whom English literature possesses," and forget that Moore is also of the type of the everlasting yarn-spinner.

His industry has magnified itself in the public eye out of all proportion, and his name has shrunk in the public ear, until George Moore has become a sort of mythical, solitary figure, a little shrunk with age and a little out of temper with the world, indefatigably crossing out, and rewriting and amending, in his quiet study in Ebury Street.

THE REGULAR ARMY

With the turn of the century, competent novelists crop up like thistles ; and like thistles spread their seed. In choosing such writers as Henry James and George Moore and D. H. Lawrence in preference to those men who are more generally popular I do not pretend to have chosen men who are necessarily the best novelists, but merely those who are the most novel ; men who found fiction doing one thing and taught it how to do another.

Yet simply because one artistically adventurous man discovers that old bottles can be used not as bottles to hold liquor, but as vases to hold strange flowers, or as ornaments to hold nothing, there is no call to despise the less experimental and curious men who continue to use the bottles for their original purpose of having new wine put into them. And the main stream of the novel was fed not by the experimentalists but by such men as Arnold Bennett and Mr. H. G. Wells and Mr. Galsworthy, and later by Mr. J. B. Priestley.

The English novel was never successfully written by gentlemen since the eighteenth century when gentlemen could live like rakes in the intervals of living like royalty. Thackeray and Disraeli and Lytton were all bothered by their breeding just as Mr. Galsworthy has been by his to-day. In the early twentieth century, the two great novelists who were of the people and for the people, were Bennett and Mr. Wells. It is true that the former organised himself into a syndicate of Bennetts for the writing of novels, short-stories, articles, advice on self-management and the general acquisition of culture, and kept the firm so constantly busy that at times the head of it was doing the work that should have been left to the junior clerk who was turning out any trash. It is true also that the other became the supreme popular newspaper scientist and sociologist, whose facts strangely enough were always scientifically unassailable. But despite the width of their other interests it is these two novelists who have provided the real substance of modern, if not modernistic, fiction.

Arnold Bennett became a novelist in the same irreverent spirit in which he wrote. At the age of twenty he had not even ᵣₑₐd anything of importance. And he wrote nothing until a pᵣ. ᵢncial paper advertised for a story with local interest. Then he wrote a novel designed to illustrate " the evils of marrying a drunken woman." It was not a flattering view of the local interest, and nothing came of it.

But if it had been a design for a new local town hall, the opportunist soul of Arnold Bennett would still have urged him to compete. Instead of precariously apprenticing himself to literature without tools or training, he went into a solicitor's office, where the strict suppression of anything approaching originality drove his mind to some sort of imaginative recreation, a sort of kick of the heels, as soon as he got away.

And so it was that at the age of twenty-six, having read widely meanwhile, he felt near enough to the spirit of the Muses to apply for the post of assistant-editor of a woman's magazine. And the woman's magazine felt him to be near enough to the spirit of the masses to accept him. And under the name of " Gwendolen " he learnt how to be effortlessly and aimlessly entertaining. A lesson that had very much the effect of a music-hall part on an actor, and nearly ruined him for anything else.

It would have ruined him completely if he had not been

so much in love with success, and had not seen that even to be the editor of a woman's magazine was not quite the Alexandrian conquest of life that he had planned. He therefore definitely and deliberately set out to write a great novel and make a great reputation ; a reputation that would enable him to unbend and perform—for higher fees—the sort of work that he had naturally been doing all the time.

The reputation came with the publication in 1908 of *The Old Wives' Tale*, which, being based on French models that were worshipped at the moment, satisfied the critics, and being based also on common sense satisfied the public. Thenceforward Arnold Bennett was his own conception of a great man, and his admiration for himself and his life became immense.

He always remained the Provincial in Piccadilly, agape at the lights and the ladies, and at himself also because he, Enoch Arnold Bennett, who had risen in brilliance from the smoke of the Five Towns, was probably better able to afford the gilt on his gingerbread than any of them. Arnold Bennett was always the huge vulgarian, whose clothes were wrong, whose boots were wrong, whose Bank-Holidayish forelock was wrong, and whose voice was wrong, who had somehow contrived to get himself admitted among the Really Right People.

That, at least, is what it has come to be the custom to say about him. But people are apt to talk as though Bennett, the man who knew at least modern French literature better than most Englishmen know English, who knew the vintages of wines as well as he knew the dates of first editions, the man who collected pictures and adored music, the man who knew the whole delicate business of living daintily, was the one boorish Philistine in a London of fashionable fastidious æsthetes.

The real trouble with Arnold Bennett was that as he cultivated those qualities that usually distinguish a man for his discernment and good taste, he cultivated also his native capacity for enjoyment. And obvious, naked pleasure at being alive has rather sadly never been one of the characteristics of the æsthetic life.

It is perfectly true that Bennett enjoyed the mirrors and marbles of the kind of high life that can be paid for ; which was vulgar. But he also enjoyed enjoying them ; which was merely artistic. And somehow neither of these figures, the provincial or the provincial snob, or the two of them together, quite add up to the conscious and conscientious novelist who produced *The Old Wives' Tale*.

With an air of immense cunning people have long hit on one of Bennett's contributions to the literature of Success, *The Card*, and have thenceforward exhibited Bennett as a living, conquering Denry. But Denry could not have written *The Old Wives' Tale* ; he could not even have written *The Card*. And this view of Bennett as the bourgeois Epicurean simply does not include the whole of the scene. It is perfectly true that the Bennett of *The Old Wives' Tale* is not the whole Bennett that only he and his Maker knew about. But it is equally true that it is the Bennett—the man who won the Success that justified his writing about it—who is respected as the novelist that rejected the machine-made plots of the moment and set out to make a new one by hand.

Admittedly, it might be said that when finished *The Old Wives' Tale* was not only hand-made but second-hand made. For when Arnold Bennett came to write he was as much under the influence of Maupassant as though he had been mesmerised. In *The Old Wives' Tale* Arnold Bennett defied convention, though his manner was so

orderly and conventional that the revolution that he led
was bloodless.

In keeping up with his heroines even into middle-age
and after, he dismissed sentiment from the novel and
sacrificed the spinner-of-dreams type of novelist to the
new type of the omniscient reporter. His achievement is
indisputable, even though at the moment we are beginning to wonder whether Zola, Balzac and Maupassant
are by so much greater than the English novelists as we
used to think.

The Old Wives' Tale was designed in the spirit in which
Hampton Court was designed : to provide England with
something as fine as the finest on the Continent. " In the
'sixties," Bennett wrote, " we used to regard *Une Vie*
with mute awe, as being the summit of achievement . . .
Une Vie relates the entire life history of a woman. I
settled in the privacy of my own head that my book about
the development of a young girl into a stout old lady must
be the English *Une Vie*. I have often been accused of
every fault except lack of self-confidence, and in a few
weeks I settled a further point, namely, that my book
must go one better than *Une Vie*, and that to this end
it must be the life-history of two women instead of one."

Sheer nonsense, of course ! As for going one better by
dealing with two heroines instead of one it might just as
well have been really ambitious and dealt with a family
of a dozen daughters and so automatically have been
twelve times as good. If in the end *The Old Wives' Tale*
did turn out to be the better book, it was simply because
Arnold Bennett's was a sanely informed mind and Maupassant's was not. And Bennett was not going out for the
blood of anything as Maupassant was going out for the
blood of the Catholic Church.

The real contribution of naturalistic novelists such as

Maupassant to the practice of fiction is that they presented
the novelist with a passport of the imagination entitling
the holder to roam freely through all the inner domains
of life, and not merely to coast up and down looking at
marriage through a telescope held politely to the blind
eye. Arnold Bennett used the same passport, but set off
on a totally different tour from Maupassant.

He was not interested in those variations in the human
orbit that arise from sexual attraction half so much as he
was in the whole bright spectacle of human revolution.
And except for the fact that *The Old Wives' Tale* presents
the complete picture of two lives, with a growing interest
in the women who live them as they grow older and richer
in character and personality, there really is very little—
except the suppression of himself—that he learnt from the
French.

There is about all Bennett's novels of the Five Towns
a deliberate, rather impudent search after the raw material of romance that reminds one of the crack detective's
search in fiction for clues in unlikely spots. This appreciation of the surprising little views that suddenly appear
through the chinks in the dullest and most impossible
places was very largely a substitute for other kinds of
beauty with Bennett.

Thus he found a great hotel enthralling whereas most
other people would find it merely expensive. In the matter of hotels, ultimately, he was unfortunate. When he
first invented the Grand Babylon Hotel—which was a
childishly simple device for concentrating a collection of
oddities of character—everyone found it fascinating because it was strange. But by the time he had invented
Imperial Palace—which was a much more finely imagined
structure—the public had grown a little tired of these
mountainous bergs that had so suddenly arisen and

blocked out the old skyline of Park Lane. And his huge attempt to show the human beehive of a great hotel in full buzz failed not because it was superficial, but because it was superfluous.

Apart from *The Old Wives' Tale*, Bennett reached the kind of supremacy that lasts, twice ; and the kind of supremacy that technically and temporarily satisfies, a hundred-and-one times. The first was reached in *Clayhanger*, the second in *Riceyman Steps*, where he was again searching for the finger-prints of romance, this time in the dust and dirt of a miser's frowsty life. One useful result of *Riceyman Steps* was that it showed that Bennett, in writing the literature of the Five Towns, was not simply a local novelist in the way in which Barrie or Blackmore was, but was a cosmopolitan with the sense to write only about what he knew intimately.

Before he knew the life of London with more than provincial penetration he merely extemporised brilliantly on the external scene.

When he got to know the real London he discovered that the Five Towns were not the only place where a shaft of intelligent sunlight striking through gloom could pave a dull street with gold and set the individual lives of passers-by glowing like jewels. And he never tired of talking about his discovery.

* * *

If it is difficult to account for all the Arnold Bennetts whose divided activities together add up to Arnold Bennett, it is wellnigh impossible to make a list of all the H. G. Wellses in Mr. H. G. Wells. To consider Mr. Wells purely as a novelist is rather like considering Mr. Gordon Selfridge purely as a greengrocer, or a sports-outfitter, or a hairdresser, or any other of the small tradesmen he happens to include within his enormous self.

For years now Mr. Wells has been a novelist only in the intervals of being a sociologist, or an international linguist, or a Utopian, or a prophet, or an historian, or a scientist, or a working journalist, or a barn-ball player. One might say that he has been a novelist in the intervals of working his mind ; one might even say that he has been a novelist in the intervals of changing his mind.

Certainly fiction with him has been either a recreation or a last resource. Either he was writing *Kipps* simply to amuse his busy brain, or he was writing *Meanwhile*, or *Mr. Blettsworthy on Rampole Island*, or *The World of William Clissold* because he had a great many things of importance to say, and he had learnt from experience that people would listen to them only if they were disguised to look as though they were really of no importance at all.

Because Mr. Wells can do so many things a rumour has gone out that he must do some of them rather badly. Thus despite the fact—or more probably because of the fact that Mr. Wells's novels such as *Kipps* and *Tono-Bungay* are so perfectly stimulating and satisfying to the mind—it has become the essence of Wellsian criticism to discover why they are not satisfying to the ear and the eye as well, and to refer to the clumsy, bungled sentences, the ungraceful constructions, and the hard, ugly words ; to say in effect that poor Mr. Wells is only an honest workman with a brain and not a cunning artist with a soul.

The truth is that Mr. Wells is a marvellously competent artist who enjoys writing for its own sake and who extracts from his words all that they have to offer. He has the virtuosity of the expert performer—a thing that would have been noticed immediately on a smaller stage—and obviously rather fancies himself as the writer who can hit off a scene in a few lines just as a ready lecturer can hit off a problem in the few lines of a diagram on the blackboard.

The description of a specimen minute in the early amorous life of Kipps is a little gem carved in the shape of inanity. Kipps is sitting on a secluded seat half way down the front of the Leas :

There is a quite perceptible down on his upper lip, and his costume is just as tremendous a " mash " as lies within his means. His collar is so high that it scars his inaggressive jaw-bone, and his hat has a curly brim, his tie shows taste, his trousers are moderately brilliant, and his boots have light cloth uppers and button at the side. He jabs at the gravel before him with a cheap cane and glances sideways at Flo Bates, the young lady from the cash desk. She is wearing a brilliant blouse and a gaily trimmed hat. There is an air of fashion about her that might disappear under the analysis of a woman of the world, but which is quite sufficient to make Kipps very proud to be distinguished as her particular " feller," and to be allowed at temperate intervals to use her Christian name.

The conversation is light and gay in the modern style, and Flo keeps on smiling, good-temper being her special charm.

" You see, you don't mean what I mean," he is saying.

" Well, what *do* you mean ? "

" Not what you mean ! "

" Well, tell me."

" *Ah !* That's another story."

Pause. They look meaningly at each other.

" You are a one for being round about," says the lady.

" Well you're not so plain you know."

" Not plain ? "

" No."

" You don't mean to say that I'm round about ? "

" No. I mean to say—though——" Pause.

" Well ? "

" You're not a bit plain—you're " (his voice jumps up to a squeak) " pretty, see ? "

" Oh, get *out* ! " Her voice lifts also—with pleasure. She strikes him with her glove.

That is about thirty seconds of Kipps's private minute. No one can read of it without realising that those sharp, sure sentences were written by a man whose mind strips every scene down to its bare bones. No one, that is, who is in the least interested in the mechanics of authorship.

Mr. Wells's books, indeed, are full of vivid, urgent writing in which the idea moves forward with splendid insistency. Even in short passages such as this from *The War of the Worlds* we can feel the quick impulse of the energetic mind of a vigorous man :

It was sweeping round swiftly and steadily, this flaming death, this invisible, inevitable sword of heat. I perceived it coming towards me by the flashing bushes it touched, and was too astounded and stupefied to stir. I heard the crackle of fire in the sand-pits and the sudden squeal of a horse that was as suddenly stilled. Then it was as if an invisible yet intensely heated finger were drawn through the heather between me and the Martians, and all along a curving line beyond the sand-pits the dark ground smoked and crackled.

No two pieces of writing could be more unlike. But together they are very like Mr. Wells. For Mr. Wells lived two lives. One a poor shabby, miserable little life between the ages of thirteen and fifteen. And another from fifteen onwards, during which his busy brain has been buzzing all the time like a dynamo. During those two early years he served behind a counter in a draper's shop. And the manner of a shop-assistant bringing down box upon box of things to sell—even though they should happen to be theories of education and pacifist treatises and not cottons and tapes—has never entirely left him.

Neither has he altogether lost the manner he acquired at the Royal College of Science in the 'eighties. He has remained ever since the educated, almost over-educated, student in the vanguard of scientific progress ; the young man with an eye on creation.

His scientific romances of the kind of *The Time Machine* and *The War of the Worlds* are really fairy-tales designed to satisfy the modern credulity. They are the product of the alert, scholarship-winning brain of a B.Sc. Lond., and of the dreamy, roaming mind of a small draper's apprentice who would sneak off for a quiet thought or two ; a combination of a trained intelligence and a natural imagination.

If Mr. Wells had not written anything but these works we should still have reason to congratulate ourselves on the scholarship system. But it is those novels of the type of *Love and Mr. Lewisham, Kipps* and *Mr. Polly* which are our main concern. These works are romances of success ; pilgrimages from the Third-Class in life to the First. And it is the inevitable cosmic progress of nature towards perfection that Mr. Wells is showing us as it manifests itself in the social betterment of an awkward little tradesman.

It is such closely observed, and humorously imagined, and patiently recorded novels as these and *Ann Veronica* that are really self-supporting in the world of fiction. The

others of the kind of *The World of William Clissold* and
Meanwhile are the work of a man who is a journalist
before he is a novelist, a man whose thoughts present
themselves with the ephemeral emphasis of headlines.

If Mr. Wells had been just a little less perfect as a thinking machine he would have appeared a far larger figure
in fiction. Books have poured out from him by the bushel ;
and somewhere beneath that bushel his light of fiction
has become hidden.

* * *

It is a strange thing that if one were to attempt a portrait of Mr. Galsworthy the dramatist, one would have
to draw one man, and if one were to attempt the portrait
of Mr. Galsworthy the novelist, one would have to draw
a totally different man.

The first portrait would be that of a humanitarian who
is so humane that he is almost a humaniac ; a man with
a wet handkerchief on his blotting pad. The second would
be that of a country gentleman of culture ; a man with
a spaniel in the library. Of the two, the first is possibly
the more interesting figure, the man who takes the part
of the fox against the hounds, of the prisoner against the
gaoler, of the rabbit against the sportsman, and of the
prostitute against the policeman. It is the more interesting because it is the more startling.

At Mr. Galsworthy's cradle one might with no more
than averagely good luck have been able to take a shot at
the future and predict that this son of a barrister and a
company director would one day become an elegant,
respectable author. And if one remembers him as the
author only of *The Forsyte Saga* and *A Modern Comedy*, the
most magnificent social history of our time, one would
have been perfectly right.

But there is always the other Mr. Galsworthy, the gentleman gone rogue, and gone rogue in a gentlemanly angelic fashion. There is something at once savage and benign about this other Mr. Galsworthy. He is the sort of man who might walk out of Tattersall's Ring and give his tail-coat to a beggar. It is because he is this St. Francis with an Oxford accent that he is so puzzling to us. A creature has got only to be hurt or be hunted to have Mr. Galsworthy on its side for ever.

Actually this common sympathy for all things occasionally almost destroys his common sense for some things. Thus, one of his later plays, *Escape*, is not only mawkish but muddled. The play opens with one of those persuasive, eloquent, clergyman's-daughter type of prostitute who might be first cousin to Clare in *The Fugitive*, sitting on a seat in Hyde Park on the look-out for a customer. She sees a possible client, one of those easy, chatting, manicured Galsworthian males, and speaks to him. After a light exchange of persiflage about the oldest profession and the horrors of a life of vice, the impatient male manages to break away, and a plain-clothes man quite naturally arrests the woman for accosting. At once the elegant male returns, tells a thin story about an evening chat, advises the prostitute to run away, hits the detective on the jaw and kills him, and then stands up in the spotlight for us to admire him as the defender of the weak against the bully ; of Woman against her oppressor, Man ; of the victim of stupid legislation against persecuting Justice.

We are uncomfortably aware that it is less than half the truth that Mr. Galsworthy is showing us. The prostitute is a lurking spider, with envenomed blood waiting for the innocent male fly to destroy him. The plain-clothes man is there courageously performing his distasteful and apparently dangerous work of preserving the fly from the spider. He dies a martyr to service, and to a public school code of manners that cannot distinguish between a damsel in distress and a danger in the streets.

I am not pretending that all men who cross Hyde Park by night are innocent, or that all plain-clothes men are gentle philanthropic creatures supported through their doubts and difficulties by the beautiful thought of male chastity. But I am suggesting that it is at least as near the truth as Mr. Galsworthy's view.

That sort of hæmorrhage of the compassionate heart dries up outside the plays. The novels are sentimental as well as sensitive ; but they deal with hearts and not with causes. They never become propaganda in the cause of convincing God that he has been behaving like the very Devil. The only sacrifice on the altar of compassion in the whole extent of the Forsyte tapestry is Miss Collins's selling her sense of shame to save her unemployed husband and consenting to be painted in the nude.

Mr. Galsworthy as a writer of any sort was unfortunate in the accident of his birth. Harrow and New College are all wrong for a novelist. Hoxton Elementary School and the Free Library are immeasurably to be preferred. The shortcomings of understanding that resulted from Mr. Galsworthy's education are to be seen in the instant he leaves the silver spoon and clockwise port atmosphere of the Forsytes for the poor. Then he is like Thackeray imagining a new race with expressions like those of the figures on an illustrated charity appeal.

The Forsyte Saga is the book that we might have expected Mr. Galsworthy to write. It is the novel of Success that begins a generation after the Kipps period in the family has closed. It is the unique record of a world whose members are usually mute, the most accurate account in our national fiction of respectable English acquisitiveness.

Mr. Galsworthy's singular genius for capturing the forms and expressions of thought of a class that are loved by none so much as they love themselves—the upper middle class that moves in the limbo between tenant and title—has led to a great injustice having been paid to him. Mr. Galsworthy has been represented as a Deity in a college blazer telling the world that so long as it plays a straight bat, is courteous to women, and produces he-ancients of the calibre of Normal McKinnell all will be well.

In reality this is not a representation but a misrepresentation. The whole business of showing Mr. Galsworthy as an articulate prisoner in one little social cell has been absurdly overdone. A man has to be outside a thing before he can draw it. A complete prisoner, like a life-sentence man, or the Pope, would be a poor sort of person to draw an elevation of Wormwood Scrubs or the Vatican. And the Forsytes are the most perfect elevation in our literature of a family who are interesting not only because of what they are but because of what they happen to be. The inevitable accident of their birth is as fascinating and important as the avoidable accidents of their lives.

But *The Forsyte Saga* is a great deal more than an account of property and of the changes in the values than mankind has placed upon different kinds of it. Otherwise it would be no more interesting than an estate-agent's ledger. The characters that appear in the passing pageant of the Forsyte generations are really actors in a Morality play. And it is a new Morality that they represent. It is a Morality in which Divorce is a deliverance and not a damnation. Soames and Irene break apart not as two sinners in defiance of divine law but as an electric magnet and its keeper when the essential current is turned off. " The very simple truth that underlies the whole story," the author has uncompromisingly declared, "is that where sex attraction is utterly and definitely lacking in one partner to a union, no amount of pity, or reason, or duty, or what not, can overcome a repulsion implicit in Nature." That Soames remarries for the Forsytish reason that he wants an heir is really not so important as that he re-marries for the ordinary male reason that he meets an unusually pretty girl.

Mr. Galsworthy created Soames in the shape of a Mal-volio who is perpetually wondering why the world does not love him more than it does ; and he conceived Irene in the shape of Olivia equally puzzled as to why Soames should imagine that she loves him at all. There is no more hopeless tragedy in life than the breakdown of relation-ship and the break-up of a home when two mature, in-telligent people, both in the right and both fully aware of it, simply sicken of each other. And there is nothing harder to describe than the collapse of conjugality, without mak-ing one party appear a monster and the other a martyr.

The measure of Mr. Galsworthy's honesty of purpose and open-eyed sincerity of vision may be gauged from the way in which he exhibits Soames as being " unlovable without quite thick enough skin to be thoroughly uncon-scious of the fact," and not only within his rights but absolutely right in asking Irene for what she is not pre-pared to give ; and shows us also Irene " a concretion of disturbing Beauty impinging on a possessive world," out to save her soul by saving herself from Soames.

What has earned Mr. Galsworthy a reputation for sentiment as a novelist is his habit of looking at life as it recedes from him. He is like a lonely man on a crowded platform who watches a departing train. An uninvited,

SF

undismissible, irrational sadness invades the mind. There
are many passages in *The Forsyte Saga* written in the mood
that hangs over the lonely man before the porter comes
along to clear the platform :

> Opening the drawer he took from the sachet a
> handkerchief, and the framed photograph of Fleur.
> When he looked at it a little he slipped it down, and
> there was that other one—that old one of Irene. An
> owl hooted while he stood in the window gazing at it.
> The owl hooted, the red climbing roses seemed to
> deepen in colour, there came a scent of lime-blossom.
> God ! That had been a difficult thing. Passion—
> Memory ! Dust !

We seem almost to hear the melancholy train whistle. It
was the same even when Soames was merely burying the
dog. And it was the same, only better expressed, when
Soames sat on Highgate Hill :

> The waters of change were foaming in, carrying the
> promise of new forms only when their destructive flood
> should have passed its full. He sat there, subconscious
> of them, but with his thoughts resolutely set on the past
> —as a man might ride into a wild night with his face
> to the tail of his galloping horse. Athwart the Vic-
> torian dykes the waters were rolling on property,
> manners, and morals, on melody and the old forms of
> art—waters bringing to his mouth a salt taste as of
> blood, lapping to the foot of this Highgate Hill where
> Victorianism lay buried. And sitting there, high up on
> its most individual spot, Soames—like a figure of In-
> vestment—refused their restless sounds. Instinctively he
> would not fight them—there was in him too much

primeval wisdom, of Man the possessive animal. They
would quiet down when they had fulfilled their tidal
fever of dispossessing and destroying ; when the creations and the properties of others were sufficiently
broken and dejected—they would lapse and ebb, and
fresh forms would rise based on an instinct older than
the fever of change—the instinct of Home.

Mr. Galsworthy seems very like Soames in all that. He
is the same elderly Englishman, standing apart, sedate,
superior, a little supercilious. And just a little anxious
about himself.

THE NEW BATTLE OF THE BOOKS

When a survey of this kind reaches the present day the expression of the writer can usually be seen to change from that of a trained observer grandly watching a race from a distance to that of a nervous man on the course anxiously trying to spot the winner. Fiction becomes merely a list of names, all promising and all as well picked with a pin as with the mind.

It would be tempting, for instance, to write expansively of how Mr. Priestley has restored to the Novel the old elements of robust good-humour and concrete exactness of description, and has produced novels of a kind that are compared with Dickens, only because the eighteenth century which is their real origin has been forgotten ; of how Mr. Hugh Walpole has lately neglected the sensitive part of his brain that produced works like *Mr. Perrin and Mr. Traill*—a marvellously exact and subtle description of the wearing frictions that spring up when people are driven into as close company as monks—and has chosen to expend himself on the Herries series in which he is the biggest painter at the largest canvas with the wettest brush now working ; of Mr. Aldous Huxley whose *Point Counter Point* is what the French call "the voice of the modern consciousness," disillusioned, a little strident and educated to the teeth ; of Mr. Arlen, with all the brightness and some of the brains of Disraeli, casting his amused, Armenian eyes around the artificial English scene ; of Miss Delafield and Miss Rose Macaulay and Miss Margaret Kennedy and Miss Theodora Benson and the author of *Elizabeth*, women who can be relied upon to supply all the wit that can be needed to balance the heaviness of much modern male talent ; of the impudent genius of Mr. David Garnett and Mr. John Collier ; and of an endless succession of writers of distinguished talent. And though by that method the chapters would become as full and fat as a store's catalogue, by next year it would be as out of date as the store's catalogue of last year. To postpone the task for thirty years would be the only way of performing it in true perspective.

I propose, therefore, to leave the great men of the present, the Walpoles and Priestleys and the Mottrams, and describe one of the historic attacks on the continuity of English fiction, an attack that has begun a New Battle of the Books.

The offensive was launched in 1922 by Mr. James Joyce with *Ulysses* and has been supported in fierce little sallies, which the critics have tended to treat as Aunt-Sallies, with *Anna Livia Plurabelle* and *Haveth Childers Everywhere* which are portions of the author's " Work in Progress."

The extent of the influence of Mr. James Joyce is uncertain. Arnold Bennett, for example, praised him extravagantly but continued to write like Mr. Bennett and not like Mr. Joyce. Nevertheless there are hints and echoes and acknowledgments of Mr. Joyce in the work of a score of the younger writers who are uncertain of their aim but are determined that it shall be into the future.

Mr. Joyce is the best example of himself that can be found. His disciples are mostly timid with the timidity of half-conviction. This is not surprising, because Mr. Joyce is not only a courageous prophet but an outrageous punster ; and the reader never knows for certain whether he has missed the message or merely missed the joke.

What Mr. Joyce has been endeavouring to do is to

present the impressions of the outside world, not as they exist crystallised and mature, within the minds of his characters but as they enter the mind one by one. In this he is like a man at a beehive who is not interested in extracting the honey, but who sits contentedly plucking out the separate bees as they reach the end of their little tunnel. An unprejudiced observer may be forgiven for thinking that if he went farther he would fare better.

Ulysses proceeds in prose such as this :

> First night when I saw her at Mat Dillon's in Ter-enure. Yellow, black lace she wore. Musical chairs. We two the last. After her. Fate. Round and round slow. Quick round. We too. All looked. Halt. Down she sat. All ousted round. Lips laughing. Yellow knees.

Then there are passages in which the author sits down to enjoy himself with words ; passages in which the literary critic should give place to the musical critic. And quite nice music many of them would be too—to a man who did not know English. For example :

> He rests. He has travelled.
> With ?
> Sinbad the Sailor and Tinbad the Tailor and Jinbad the Jailer and Whinbad the Whaler and Ninbad the Nailer and Finbad the Failer and Binbad the Bailer and Pinbad the Pailer and Mindbad the Mailer and Hinbad the Hailer and Rinbad the Railer and Dinbad the Kailer and Vinbad the Quailer and Linbad the Yailer and Xinbad the Phthailer.

That is melodious enough ; a variation on a well-known theme. It is a victory for sound at the expense of sense. It

is to writing simply what humming is to conversation.
Indeed, the Duchess's advice in *Alice in Wonderland*, " Take
care of the sense and the sounds will take care of themselves " is more truly in line with the orthodox theory of
literature. And it is worthy of note that when the characters are drunk Mr. James Joyce's straying sentences are
most suitable for their purpose.

Ulysses would be a simpler piece of work if it were by a
man who were no more than a joker. But the author is
for ever obstinately giving us proofs that he is a scholar
also ; or at least a man who has gone into the library,
and the dictionary, at A and come out again at Z, having
remembered all the names he met with on the way. Thus
we come upon such passages as this :

> the natural grammatical transition by inversion in-
> volving no alteration of sense of an aorist preterite
> proposition (parsed as masculine subject, monosyllabic,
> onomatopœic transitive verb with direct feminine
> object) from the active voice into its correlative aorist
> preterite proposition (parsed as feminine subject,
> auxiliary verb and quasimono-syllabic onomatopœic
> past participle with complementary masculine agent)
> in the passive voice . . .

which leaves us wondering whether the mind that wrote
it is profound, funny or simply fuddled.

As we proceed we find ourselves following up long passages of archaic or technical prose, and identifying more
obscure references, Greek and Gaelic, topical and
obscene, than it seems fair of any writer to impose on his
readers. If it were not that Mr. Stuart Gilbert in his wonderfully patient *James Joyce's " Ulysses " : A Study* has
made an elaborate tracing-paper which, when laid over
the original, explains the allusions, many of them would

be lost to the reader who has not read where Mr. Joyce's spirit has listed.

Even more common than the classical references are the sexual references. And it is possible to have a great respect for the experimentalist with words who wrote *Ulysses* and still wonder whether the intellectual proportions of the novel are not a little gawkish, and whether Life really takes its business of reproduction so seriously that it can never forget about it.

The novel is comprised of descriptions of one long, lecherous day in a Dubliner's life with the heady drums of sex continuously sounding. It was for the frankness of the language of some of the scenes, notably the one set in the brothel, and of the long monologue of the nymphomaniac woman lying in bed that led to the banning of *Ulysses*. Actually there was not the slightest need for the censor to act. No one who could derive the slightest harm from *Ulysses* could ever have struggled through it as far as to arrive at the regions of danger.

It may be wondered how it is that Mr. Joyce has exercised any influence at all. And it may be due to the fact that he remains a fascinating figure no matter whether he is regarded as a valiant pioneer leaving his footprints startlingly distinct across the virgin snows of the mind— which is a perfectly just view—or merely as a man industriously and conscientiously commiting literary suicide. For Mr. James Joyce is either an Evangelist of a new literary faith or a man who has contrived on the strength of earlier works to be admitted to the home and has then committed *hara-kiri* on the best carpet.

In his earlier novel, *Portrait of the Artist as a Young Man*, Mr. Joyce revealed himself as a writer whose prose was as vivid as vermilion yet as plain as paint. And occasionally in *Ulysses* such an adjective as " crucified," when applied to a shirt hanging on a line, sets us wondering whether any writer has ever used isolated words with so much effect before.

In *Haveth Childers Everywhere*, however, one is set wondering whether any writer has ever used them to less :

> Amtsadam, sir, to you ! Eternest cittas, heil ! Here we are again. I am bubub brought up her under a camel act of dynasties long out of print, the first of Shitric Shinkanbeard (or is it Owllaugh MacAuscullpth the Thord ?), but, in pontofacts massimust, I am known throughout the world wherever my good Allengliches Angleslachen is spoken by Sall and Will from Augustanus to Ergastulus, as this is, whether in Farnum's rath or Condra's ridge or the meadows of Dalkin or Monkish tunshep, by saints and sinners eyeye alike as a cleanliving man and, as a matter of fict, by my half-wife, I think how our public at large appreciates it most highly from me that I am as cleanliving as could be and that my game was a fair average since I perpetually kept my ouija ouija wicket up.

In experiment Mr. Joyce has taught the lesson and set the fashion. Novels in which the only action is that which exists between mind and mind, and consciousness and consciousness, or takes place within the sphere of one consciousness, are now common. From Mr. Faulkner to Miss Sylva Norman the younger writers have shown that they have learnt the lesson and are in the fashion.

Mrs. Virginia Woolf, in *To the Lighthouse* and *Jacob's Room* and most remarkably in *The Waves*, has shown what an exquisitely graceful and orderly mind, educated in the tradition, can make of a disorderly modern method. In *Orlando*, a story in which neither Time nor Sex is as constant as it is in life, there is again to be seen that restless impatience with what have hitherto been regarded as the invariables, that is at the back of the modern mind.

That the novel at its most orthodox is still paying a handsome dividend of attention is indisputable. There is, however, an apparent discontent with orthodoxy. In reality this means very little more than that men have discovered the novel to be the medium in which any sort of thought can most easily be expressed. Thus so abstract and mystical a mind as that of Mr. Charles Williams, which in any other age would have turned, as Donne's turned, to poetry, brings its Platonics and symbols to fiction, and encases them in *The Place of the Lion* in the form of a " thriller " that is as formally correct as a sonnet, yet as exciting as its modern shape suggests.

One has only to remember *The Good Companions*, strong with the inherited strength of the huge family of picturesque, picaresque English novels that have gone before it, healthy, humorous and supremely honest about its intention of being purely a good story and not an essay in psychology, normal or otherwise and, say, the most recent of Mrs. Woolf, and Lawrence's *Lady Chatterley's Lover* and Mr. Tomlinson's *Gallion's Reach*, and Mr. Evelyn Waugh's *Vile Bodies* — to plot no more than a few points on the map of fiction of 1931 — to see what an area of the human mind the novel covers to-day ; and why as fast as definitions of the Novel are devised a new novel comes along to destroy it.

If one can make any generalisation about the modern novel it is that it is always strenuously endeavouring to do something else. The novel has become, like the sonnet, an exercise in ingenuity as well as a statement of life. Mr. Faulkner's *The Sound and the Fury*, for example, begins by being told by a congenital idiot, whose mental development is infantile, who has no sense of the passage of time and whose brain hands him out thoughts upside down and in the wrong order. For some reason—possibly a sense of fatigue, possibly a sense of failure—Mr. Faulkner, however, finally turns to a rational mind to complete the narration.

The human mind has lately been dissected in the laboratories of Vienna and the novelist has increasingly become the more or less popular exponent of the new theories. This, of course, does not mean that he is necessarily more wise or more penetrating than his predecessors. Wisdom and understanding can never be the product of a college course. It means merely that the modern novelist uses a new language to explain himself. And inasmuch as the new language is more exact and better suited to its purpose, his novel, if he is naturally a man of discernment, may excel in its revelation of the soul the novels of those writers who had to blunder blindly along with only the traditional vocabulary to help them.

But it is a mistake to imagine this or that novelist saying to himself : " I will be modern." Even if he does he is as likely to write like Mr. Evelyn Waugh as he is to write like Mr. James Joyce. And Mr. H. M. Tomlinson in writing *All Our Yesterdays*, which is a brilliant essay in atmospheres, is quite as much experimental as Conrad or as Mr. Faulkner, though his apparatus is not so pretentious as the latter's.

The present spate of experimental novels should not be crowned simply because they are experimental any more than they should be ridiculed simply because they look as funny as a foreigner. Experiment is primarily the affair of the experimentalist. And if he is honest his object is to write not differently but merely better.

The reader may be wise to suspend judgment until the first novelty of method has worn off before he attempts to say whether Mr. Bloom is finally as satisfying to the intelligence as Mr. Pickwick. And the writer should instinctively suspect a medium which is so easy that his mind can float and does not have to swim to keep in movement.

In short, the Golden Rule for readers would seem to be : " Beware of the contemporary writer : he is foolhardy," and for writers : " Beware of the contemporary reader : he is a fool."

If these Rules are observed, Literature a hundred years hence will be richer, even though we meanwhile may all have had to hang ourselves with vexation.

THE END

INDEX